PRAISE FOR *40 DAYS & 40 HIKES*

"Throughout *40 Days & 40 Hikes*, Ross wears her affection for the trail and the rich Niagara Escarpment ecosystem on her merino wool sleeve. . . . She tackles the Bruce Trail in a new way, so that readers don't have to."

— *Literary Review of Canada*

"Casual and experienced hikers alike will enjoy this unconventional memoir/travelogue/nature guide. Also ideal for readers who seek out opportunities to champion conservation and are curious about Canadian natural wonders, history and landmarks."

— *Library Journal*

"Nicola slows the pace down so we can re-live the best parts of the trail . . . If you want to expand your knowledge of the trail, this is a very interesting and enjoyable read."

— *E-Notes: Toronto Bruce Trail Club Newsletter*

"A great reminder of the many things that make our Bruce Trail so special. . . . Be ready to strap on your favourite pair of hikers and follow along on a trip that is filled with history, unique geological features and flora and fauna found along our beloved trail."

— Iroquoia Bruce Trail Club newsletter

"Nicola Ross is a captivating ambassador for the Bruce Trail, blending education and entertainment to showcase the trail's rich history and natural beauty. *40 Days & 40 Hikes* also doubles as a unique and clever guide for those eager to experience the trail for themselves."

— Nancy East, author of *Chasing the Smokies Moon: An Audacious 948-Mile Hike — Fueled by Love, Loss, Laughter and Lunacy*

40 Days
& 40 Hikes

40 Days
& 40 Hikes

LOVING THE BRUCE TRAIL
ONE LOOP AT A TIME

NICOLA ROSS

Published by ECW Press
665 Gerrard Street East
Toronto, Ontario, Canada M4M 1Y2
416-694-3348 / info@ecwpress.com

Editor for the press: Jen Knoch
Copy-editor: Lisa Frenette
Cover design: Jessica Albert
Interior images: Nicola Ross
Cover image: ELNEIT.COM

To the best of her abilities, the author has related
experiences, places, people and organizations from
her memories of them.

LIBRARY AND ARCHIVES CANADA
CATALOGUING IN PUBLICATION

Title: 40 days & 40 hikes : loving the Bruce Trail
one loop at a time / Nicola Ross.

Other titles: Forty days and forty hikes

Names: Ross, Nicola, 1957- author.

Description: Includes bibliographical references.

Identifiers: Canadiana (print) 20230587410 |
Canadiana (ebook) 20230587429

ISBN 978-1-77041-777-9 (softcover)
ISBN 978-1-77852-303-8 (EPUB)
ISBN 978-1-77852-304-5 (PDF)

Subjects: LCSH: Ross, Nicola, 1957-—Travel—
Ontario—Bruce Trail. | LCSH: Hiking—
Ontario—Bruce Trail. | LCSH: Bruce Trail
(Ont.)—Description and travel. | LCGFT:
Travel writing.

Classification: LCC FC3053.7 .H55 2024 | DDC
796.5109713/2—dc23

This book is funded in part by the Government of Canada. *Ce livre est financé en partie par le gouvernement du Canada.* We acknowledge the support of the Canada Council for the Arts. *Nous remercions le Conseil des arts du Canada de son soutien.* We acknowledge the funding support of the Ontario Arts Council (OAC), an agency of the Government of Ontario. We also acknowledge the support of the Government of Ontario through the Ontario Book Publishing Tax Credit, and through Ontario Creates.

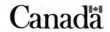

PRINTED AND BOUND IN CANADA   PRINTING: MARQUIS   5   4   3   2

For those who built, maintain,
love and hike the Bruce Trail.
Thank you.

LAND ACKNOWLEDGEMENT

I honour the lands of the Niagara Escarpment as the traditional territory of Indigenous Peoples, recognizing and thanking the Anishinaabek, Huron-Wendat, Tionontati, Neutral Nation, Haudenosaunee, Métis and all who have cared for these lands.

I am grateful to live, work and play here, and I acknowledge the need to reconcile broken covenants. I add my energy to the stewardship of the Niagara Escarpment through peace and friendship in the hope that our combined efforts will create a legacy of wild places.

CONTENTS

INTRODUCTION

Pati's eyes follow the direction of my arm as I point to a plume of smoke that's billowing high into the blue Mexican sky. Leaping to her feet, she gallops to her ancient, wood-panelled Suburban, yanks the door open and jumps in before I have a chance to move. She bellows: "My Sierra, my Sierra, it can't burn down." When I climb in the passenger side, she's groaning — a sound that emanates from somewhere deep in her belly. I wonder if this is how a mother responds upon learning of her child's serious injury. Pati wheels the truck around as though it's a getaway car. I crane my neck to look up at the catastrophe that has brought such angst to my friend.

"Has the fire spread?" she shrieks. "Can you see flames?"

I see nothing. I look again. Still nothing. "Pati," I say, "Pati, it's out, the fire's out. The Sierra. It's not burning."

≈

In bed that night, I replay the scene. Mexico's high hills, rising smoke, Pati's groans, the sweat-inducing fear of a forest fire. My mind slips to the Niagara Escarpment. It has been over 15 years since I've lived in Caledon, but I can see the Forks of the Credit as if I'd been there yesterday. From my imagined vantage point standing beside the Credit River, I observe the old ice cream store that was once a gas station. Above it soar sheer cliffs. Their grey limestone faces peek out from behind the trees of my youth: sugar maples, white cedars, birch, basswood. I see smoke, a steely grey column just like the one I saw with Pati that afternoon. It drifts skyward, slowly at first, then faster and thicker, darker. My heart races, and I feel cold sweat rise between my shoulder blades. "My Forks of the Credit," I think, "My Forks of the Credit, it can't burn down."

In that second, in that split second between wakefulness and sleep, it comes to me: I've been away too long. It's time to go home. Caledon, Belfountain, the Niagara Escarpment, the Forks of the Credit, the Devil's Pulpit — they beckon.

≈

Upon returning to where I spent the first 21 years of my life, it was hard for my siblings to grasp that I was no longer the university student who'd set out for Calgary in a 1972 Volkswagen Beetle. In the ensuing 17 years, I'd completed a degree in biology. I'd started and sold an environmental communications business. I'd married an Albertan cowboy with a Lanny McDonald moustache — and divorced him. I'd worked internationally as an environmental consultant. I was pushing 40.

Caledon's landscape, however, was another story. The lanky sugar maples, the spooky cedar forests, trilliums, trout lilies and Jack-in-the-pulpit, the Credit River, those Niagara Escarpment cliffs, they fit like a comfortable pair of faded jeans I'd recently discovered stuffed into the back of a closet.

Despite the call of the land, my career as an international environmental consultant flourished after I moved home. My dream of working around the globe with the World Bank, United Nations Development Programme and the Canadian International Development Agency was taking shape. I was on the fast track, in contact with climate change experts in Ottawa, Washington and developing nations. I'd proven I could handle myself in an international setting.

When I was invited to be the climate change expert on a three-person team hired by the World Bank/United Nations, I figured I'd arrived. Our job was to evaluate the success of an international funding agency's initial project phase. After time spent in New York and Washington interviewing project managers, I would head off to visit projects in Zimbabwe and the Philippines. It was a heady time. I'll never forget walking past the iconic flags that stand guard in front of the United Nations' headquarters in New York on my way inside. Similarly, I recall arriving in Zimbabwe's capital Harare and climbing into a tan-coloured Toyota Land Cruiser with the United Nations' logo on the doors.

In Zimbabwe, I was to look into an $8 million solar energy project. What had the money been spent on? Were the solar installations having an impact? Had the initiatives sparked a solar industry in this African nation? During my first two weeks in Zimbabwe, I was well looked after by my host, the United Nations Development Programme. I stayed in a good hotel, had useful meetings with the project's manager and staff members and had been escorted to interviews with two or three companies that, I was told, were importing and/or installing solar equipment. But my requests to visit an installation remained fruitless. Rather than take me to see a solar farm, my hosts accompanied me to Zimbabwe's tourist attractions. When I wouldn't let up on my demands, they finally relented. We drove to Bulawayo, Zimbabwe's second largest city, which was a six-hour drive away, and visited a project there.

I climbed into the Land Cruiser and, along with three staff members, we journeyed to Bulawayo. It took all day. The next morning, they picked me up at my hotel. Sometime later we pulled into Great Zimbabwe, the country's most popular tourist attraction. Despite my protests, I had to tour the site. A couple of hours later we were on the road again. Then we stopped for lunch. It was getting dark when we pulled up to a ramshackle building my hosts generously referred as a hotel. Accompanied by three tall strapping Zimbabweans, we walked over to what served as a reception desk. A young woman slouched in a chair. She didn't look up until the driver caught her attention. Glancing at the four of us, she asked, "How long do you want a room for? Will an hour do?" She proceeded to give us the rate in a monotone voice. Much to my relief, my colleagues were suitably embarrassed by this misunderstanding. They explained to the young woman that we were there to visit the bar. "Go ahead," she mumbled, vaguely waving us through.

The sun goes down quickly in Zimbabwe, and it was dark when we ducked our heads to enter the bar. Inside, it was brighter, but just barely. A single light bulb hung from a wire that dangled from the ceiling. In the dull glow, I could make out a roomful of men bent over bottles of beer. A radio blared static. This was the installation. The bar had a solar panel with enough juice to power a single light bulb and a radio so men could leave their families at home and get drunk.

On the long flight back to Toronto, I recalled a dinner party that I had attended when I'd been in Washington, DC. A colleague from Calgary had moved to DC where he was managing the environment division for a large international organization. He and his wife invited me for dinner along with several of his colleagues, all from distant nations. It was exciting to share a meal with such a diverse group. This was the world I wanted to be part of. In typical fashion, we talked about who we were, where we were from and the initiatives we were working on. Wine flowed and we all relaxed. As the main course dishes were being cleared, the discussion slipped from global concerns to office politics. The central topic for the rest of dinner was who had the best office and the newest computer. These highly paid foreign nationals were more interested in the perks of an international posting than in saving the planet. But I was young and ambitious. I shoved the experience to the back of my mind until, that is, I was on that Toronto-bound airplane.

The day after I arrived home from Zimbabwe offered up one of those September afternoons when Ontario is at its best. Not a cloud in the sky. No humidity. The crisp smell of fall approaching. I asked my partner to come sit outside with me for a bit; I wanted to tell him something. We sat on a grassy knoll overlooking a small pond next to a house we'd rented not far from Caledon. The water was smooth, still, quiet. It looked like I felt. After describing my shocking experience in Zimbabwe, and reminding him of that dinner party in Washington, I told him, "If I ever get on a plane again for an international project, it will be too soon." The shine had come off. I couldn't ignore the corruption, the greed. We talked about how beautiful it was where we were sitting, and I returned to a common theme: how much I loved Caledon.

We discussed our experience working with Pati in Mexico and how wonderful it was. Then I told him, "I'm going to do what Pati does. I'm going to start a non-profit to protect Caledon." I didn't want to charge around the world. Caledon is my place. It needs my help.

Inspired by Pati's Grupo Ecológico Sierra Gorda and dismayed by how far the Greater Toronto Area had slithered into Caledon's hills and valleys during my absence, the drive to take action came from deep inside. Maybe it's how a nun feels when called to serve. Our group had to convince urban politicians that meadows were not "vacant land waiting to be developed" and that subdivisions were not the route to prosperity.

In 1998, I started the Caledon Countryside Alliance, an environmental non-profit organization, to give nature a seat at the table. Our motto was CIAO: Countryside Is an Option. We battled urban sprawl and encouraged people to buy locally produced food. We rallied for a tree-cutting bylaw, a pesticide bylaw and no idling zones. We challenged Caledon to reduce its ecological footprint and lower its greenhouse gas emissions. We put together a gang of Weedgee Kidz who went door to door offering to pull dandelions and educate homeowners about pesticide-free lawns. The initiatives we pursued tended to be for something (e.g., pesticide-free lawns) rather than opposed to something (e.g., pesticide use).

For five exhausting but exhilarating years, I lead this group. With backing from our municipal government, engaged residents and supportive media, we had tremendous successes. I entered Caledon into a TV Ontario contest looking for the province's greenest town. I learned that we'd won a few days in advance of the official announcement that would be made live on TV. Keeping our victory a secret, then Caledon mayor Carol Seglins and I organized an event at a local restaurant that reminded me of a get-together to watch our team play the seventh game in the Stanley Cup playoffs. When TVO announced the result, a spontaneous cheer raised the roof beams. To celebrate, Mayor Seglins posted a sign at every road entering Caledon announcing our "greenest town" status. Caledon was a green dyke holding back an ocean of sprawl. Green was Caledon's colour — its identity and goal.

The alliance also led weekly hikes into Caledon's forests, along its rivers and across its meadows — often following the Bruce Trail (BT). We wanted our friends and neighbours to experience their home from the inside out. By smelling and hearing the forests in their backyard and becoming familiar with the trails, we hoped they'd fall in love with the landscape, its rivers and valleys, meadows, villages, birds, bees and, of course, its trees. And it worked. People who had lived in Caledon for years, sometimes decades, discovered a world of paths they never knew existed. We hiked into Caledon's embrace. Rather than count sheep at night, I traced the route of the Bruce Trail or the course of the Credit River as they passed through my precious home until I knew them by heart. I was humbled in 2004 when I was named Caledon's Environmentalist of the Year.

All the while I was writing for our amazing quarterly magazine, *In The Hills*, about threats to our piece of paradise. These were long, in-depth articles about complex topics. Under the tutelage of the magazine's publisher, I honed my skills, winning a coveted National Magazine Award for a story about reducing Caledon's ecological footprint. My pen became a tool in the battles we encountered. The organization was living up to its motto. It was making countryside an option. Our vacant land was increasingly valued for the environmental services it offered (clean water and air) and the recreational opportunities it provided.

Then I lost my way. Just like that. One day I was in the green trench, the next I was out of it. The well-marked trail I'd been following for five years was gone. Before me was a bewildering forest of trees.

I passed the Caledon Countryside Alliance on to a colleague. She changed the focus to local food — the issue of the day — making Caledon a leader on that front. When we came up against one another for a prize recognizing our civil contributions, she took home the honour. I was genuinely pleased for her, but it was a blow to realize local food was the alliance's mandate, not the broader shade of green I'd pursued.

The hikes continued, but the new hike leader changed them too. My goal had been to encourage as many people as possible to hit the trails with us on Sunday mornings. I called them "walks and talks," hoping they would stimulate discussion about important issues. I wanted as many people as possible to fall in love with the out-of-doors because I knew we protect what we love. I imagined a great big fat romance with Caledon. I'd wanted more times like that night when we won the greenest town award. I'd wanted lots of Stanley Cups! The new leader had a different idea. Rather than open the hikes up to anyone, she limited them to what became a small tight-knit group of friends.

Maybe I was having a mid-life crisis. Being menopausal was a contributing factor. I was flailing. After being so committed, so single-minded in my journey for years, I couldn't find solid ground. Not certain what to do next, I walked the Camino in Spain from Saint-Jean-Pied-de-Port to the cathedral where St. James's remains are buried in Santiago de Compostela. Then I walked on to Finisterre — the end of the world as Europeans once thought of the Atlantic Ocean. I don't believe I had an epiphany, and, while wonderful, my 34 days covering almost nine hundred kilometres did not settle me down.

Meanwhile, the signs that had so proudly announced Caledon's green, anti-sprawl approach faded; the lettering chipped away until their hopeful green message became illegible, and the signs were removed. Caledon maintained its reputation as a beautiful place and didn't entirely abandon its environmental programs, but green was no longer its battle cry. I teetered between wanting to beat the bastards who threatened Caledon and not caring. My partner and I separated. Winter's cold overcast leadened the sky. The frozen logs I stuffed into my fireplace sizzled unenthusiastically. I put on an extra sweater and got down on my hands and knees. Day in and day out, I painted the image of an intricate, multi-coloured carpet on the pine floor in my dining room. When that was done, I continued up the walls with green and yellow, checkerboard wainscotting. I painstakingly created arrow-straight lines between the squares, obsessing if the paint bubbled or the wrong colour seeped through the tape.

I felt helpless. Nothing I did or had done had made a difference. I was weepy and plagued by hot flashes. I woke up at night in hot sweats. Clearly all that estrogen I'd enjoyed for most of my life was drying up. Maybe it was depression. No one visited me that winter. The only time I went out was to teach a weekly journalism class at Humber College. I couldn't face another story about environmental woes. I admired the David Suzukis and the Pati Ruiz Corzos of the world who relentlessly beat the environmental drum, but I couldn't do it anymore. I had given up my green mantle. But I couldn't ignore the plight of the planet and just enjoy life.

It took a year or more for the clouds to lift. Not surprisingly, my "recovery" was helped along by a dashing man. Our six-month romance ended in Paris, but it reinvigorated me. I bounced back by becoming the editor of *Alternatives Journal*, a national environmental magazine at the University of Waterloo. This lasted for about six years. I was establishing a pattern of getting things started (or in the case of the magazine, re-started) and then moving on. Next, I talked myself into a job leading kayaking and canoe trips, teaching paddling skills and otherwise providing recreational opportunities for guests at The Lodge at Pine Cove on the French River in Northern Ontario. I'd settled into a wonderful relationship with Alex, the lodge's owner and innkeeper. The job was a summertime gig, involving lots of outdoor physical exercise. It was fun organizing things that people enjoyed rather than felt obligated to do, like read devastating news about the climate. Few lodge guests had experienced a river's early morning stillness or seen a moose in the wild. I began writing about Caledon for *In The Hills* again, now focusing on good things — sporty things such as skiing and skating, yoga, croquet, running, paddling, archery and, of course, hiking.

Then things got really interesting. Alex and I were having breakfast together when he announced, "Working here is just a stopgap. You should write another book. That's your calling." Then the bombshell. "For your birthday," he continued, "I'm going to help make that happen. For the next two years I'll cover your basic expenses so you can afford the time to write it."

I was stunned. What would I write about? The environment was too depressing. Sport? A novel? Years earlier the Boston Mills Press had published two of my books about local history. Maybe I should take another crack at that. I agonized over the possibilities, frustrating Alex and John Denison, my former publisher at the Boston Mills Press. Then John suggested I write a guidebook about the Bruce Trail's side trails. "Don't they all form loops with the main trail?" he asked. "Lots do," I replied, "but not all of them." John liked hikes that looped back to the start. I liked loops too. Pretty much everyone prefers a circle to walking in and out along the same trail. I knew lots of loop routes in Caledon and suspected there were many more. And while Caledon was hardly the Rocky Mountains, we had an existing network of trails, quiet back roads, the Niagara Escarpment, Oak Ridges Moraine and gorgeous villages. Caledon might not be the backcountry, but who finds a trailside café where you can stop for lunch, a beer or a latte while hiking in the Rocky Mountains? *Loops & Lattes*, I thought. This book would bridge my wish to live happily with my responsibility to Caledon.

When *Loops & Lattes: Caledon Hikes'* popularity far exceeded my expectations, I wrote a second guide. The books' clear instructions convinced thousands of people to get out onto local trails. People who had never signed a climate change petition or donated to an environmental cause began seeing themselves as stewards of the land. These hiking guides spoke to the converted and unconverted alike. Threats to Southern Ontario's countryside didn't go away, but more people were becoming engaged. And celebrating the good rather than railing against the bad allowed me to carry on.

Six years later, after completing my sixth guidebook, I didn't start a seventh. I'd crossed my threshold. It was time for a new adventure. I let myself dream. For as long as I could remember I'd wanted to hike the Bruce Trail from end to end. However, it's a day-use trail so it's not easy to do, especially if you want to walk it solo. I didn't relish carrying a heavy pack and having to sneak off the trail at night to find a hidden camping spot. Besides, wild camping was against the BT's rules. Hiking its nine hundred kilometres with a group of friends for a day here and there didn't appeal to me. I tried mapping a route that took advantage of accommodations along the way, but there just weren't enough places to stay to make it work. Trail angels who would give me a lift from my car to the trailhead were an option for some of the BT's nine sections but not all. Uber taxis? A good sport who'd follow along in their car or camper van?

Then one day I asked myself, what about those side trails? Several years earlier I'd been hired by *Bruce Trail Conservancy Magazine* to write about the southern Bruce Peninsula section of the trail. Staying at a great B&B in Colpoy's Bay north of Wiarton, I hiked for three consecutive days. I parked my car, walked about 10 kilometres along the main BT and then hiked back to my vehicle following side trails. At night, I had a comfortable bed and dinner. In the morning, I enjoyed a hot breakfast. The B&B even served lattes. In this way, it took me three days to make my way from Wiarton, up the spiral staircase, all the way to the end of the Snake Trail Boardwalk in Cape Croker Park. The BT may not offer overnight accommodations, but since its official opening in 1967, it has added an extraordinary 450 kilometres of side trails — many of which formed loops with the main BT.

Then it dawned on me: I could make my way from Queenston at the southern terminus to Tobermory at the northern in this loopy way. I would be self-sufficient, could sleep in a comfortable bed at night and start every hike with a latte. If I averaged just over 20 kilometres per hike, I could do a loopy end-to-end in about 40 days — 40 days for 40 hikes. It was a realistic goal. I'd walk at least 902 kilometres, the published length of the BT at the time, in 40 looping hikes. I would come to know the Niagara Escarpment better; I would be on a journey. I'd have fun and I'd write a book — this time a travelogue (not a hiking guide!) — about my experience. I hoped it might increase the number of people who love the Niagara Escarpment and are willing to protect it.

So here it is. My loopy love story about hiking the Bruce Trail. It's filled with stories: stories about a 91-year-old woman who swears that walking her dogs for four hours or more a day is her key to health, a 63-year-old unemployed etiquette teacher in a barrel and a 37-year-old mother of six who didn't hide behind a cow. It relates how Queen Victoria was key to making Canada the great nation it is and how First Nations were key to stopping US aggression in the Battle of 1812. It relays tales of the BT's intrepid founders and takes you to the Slough of Despond and through the bloodsucker infested Grimpen Mire. It investigates Wampum Belts and walking ferns. It weathers ticks, bears and derecho winds and introduces my wonderful sisters, family and friends — and devils, lots of devils.

The protagonist of all these stories is what singer/songwriter Sarah Harmer describes as "the backbone that runs across the muscles of the land," in her song "Escarpment Blues." It's the Niagara Escarpment, Gchi-Bimadinaa (The Great Cliff That Runs Along) to the Anishinaabe, and Kastenhraktátye (Along the Cliffs) to the Kanyen'kehà:ka, l'Escarpement du Niagara for francophones. This 1,609 kilometre long horseshoe-shaped scarp eroded from four-hundred-million-year-old limestone rocks dominates the landscape that has settled into my bones. The Niagara Escarpment rises in upper New York State, enters Canada at Niagara Falls and crosses Southern Ontario before forming the Bruce Peninsula, which splits Lake Huron from Georgian Bay. Then it returns to the United States running down the western shore of Lake Michigan until it peters out near Chicago. In Canada, the Niagara Escarpment is a UNESCO Biosphere Reserve; it's included in the Greater Golden Horseshoe Greenbelt and protected by the Niagara Escarpment Plan. But despite these layers of conservation, the Niagara Escarpment, this "ribbon of wilderness," is at risk in a growth-motivated economy. Concern about these threats inspired the BT's founding partners to create Canada's longest marked footpath. Knowing it more intimately inspired loopy me.

I hope my journey of adventure, love and observation inspires you to lace up your boots and take to the trails. Hike the entire BT or walk as far as your nearest stream. Gossip with friends, take along a sketchbook, bag that steep hill you've always wanted to climb. Breathe in the soft peaty smell after a rainfall, find your hidden patch of lady's slippers. Have lunch on a clifftop overlooking Georgian Bay. Chow down on hot, salty fish & chips. Enjoy the cool of a maple forest or warmth of a sunny meadow. Eat an apple from a tree. Listen as far away as you can. Laugh. And then stand up, stand up for the Niagara Escarpment and salute those who created and continue to maintain what founder Ray Lowes referred to as Ontario's geography of hope.

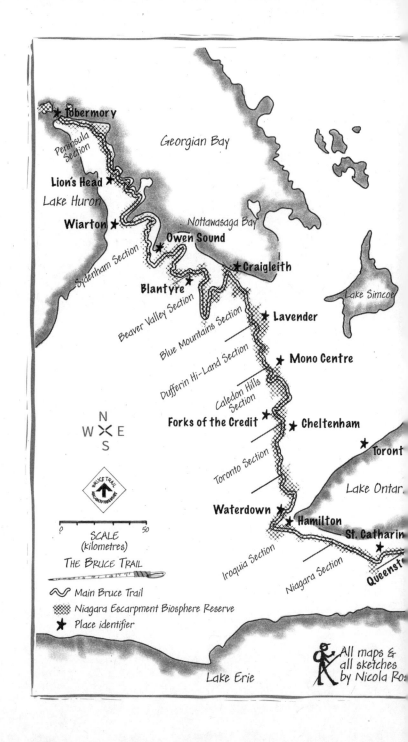

Georgian Bay

Tobermory

Peninsula
Section

Lion's Head

Lake Huron

Wiarton

Nottawasaga Bay

Owen Sound

Sydenham Section

Craigleith

Blantyre

Lake Simcoe

Beaver Valley Section

Blue Mountains Section

Lavender

Dufferin Hi-Land Section

Mono Centre

Caledon Hills
Section

N
W ⤬ E
S

Forks of the Credit

Cheltenham

Toront

Lake Ontar.

Toronto Section

Waterdown

Hamilton

St. Catharin

0   50

Iroquia Section

Niagara Section

Queenst

SCALE
(kilometres)

THE BRUCE TRAIL

〰 Main Bruce Trail

▨ Niagara Escarpment Biosphere Reserve

★ Place identifier

All maps &
all sketches
by Nicola Ro:

Lake Erie

The Bruce Trail

FIELD NOTES

TIME OF HIKES: between 7:30 a.m. Tuesday, May 3, 2022, and 5:23 p.m. October 7, 2022

WEATHER: a bit of everything, but mostly sunshine

TOTAL DISTANCE: 954.4 km

BT SECTIONS: Niagara, Iroquoia, Toronto, Caledon Hills, Dufferin Hi-Land, Blue Mountain, Beaver Valley, Sydenham, Peninsula

Niagara
Section

Day 1

QUEENSTON HEIGHTS / LAURA SECORD

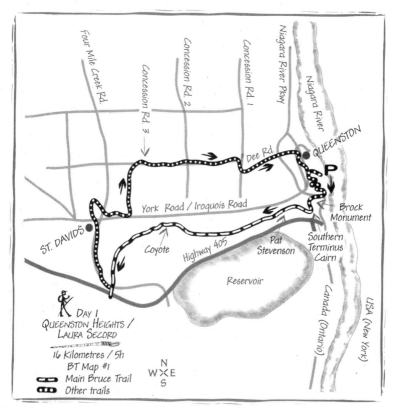

Day 1
Queenston Heights /
Laura Secord
16 Kilometres / 5h
BT Map #1
Main Bruce Trail
Other trails

N
W E
S

FIELD NOTES

START TIME: 7:30 a.m., Tuesday, May 3, 2022

TRAILHEAD WEATHER: cool, dull, threatening rain, though none came

DISTANCE: 16 km

ELAPSED TIME: 5h

BT SECTION: Niagara

BT MAP: #1

MAIN BT WALKED: 0 km to 5.3 km

ASCENT: 437 m / **DESCENT:** 408 m

SIDE/OTHER TRAILS: Sir Isaac Brock Side Trail, Laura Secord Legacy Trail

FLORA/FAUNA OF NOTE: American robins (*Turdus migratorius*), northern cardinals (*Cardinalis cardinalis*), downy woodpecker (*Dryobates pubescens*), hairy woodpecker (*Leuconotopicus villosus*), eastern wood-pewee (*Contopus virens*), eastern towhee (*Pipilo erythrophthalmus*), coyote (*Canis latrans*), blue beech (*Carpinus caroliniana*), horse chestnut (*Aesculus hippocastanum*)

In which I learn Niagara Falls is no match for an etiquette
teacher and her cat; Laura Secord didn't need a cow; Canadian
history isn't dull and nature could use
all the friends it can get.

Staring at green luminescent letters that read No Overnight Parking, I asked the machine in Queenston Heights Park, home to the Bruce Trail's southern terminus, "What do you mean no overnight parking? It's 7:30 in the morning and I'm here to begin my adventure."

When cursing wouldn't convince the machine that night didn't end at 10 a.m., I realized that hiking the Bruce Trail "my way" might be a dream — already a ticket dispenser was dictating my plans. I jumped back into my car and headed downhill toward the village of Queenston. Finding a more enlightened ticket dispenser, I parked my car and hoisted my daypack into place. With my GPS, notebook and pen in hand, my slightly altered journey had begun.

≈

The blue blazes of the Sir Isaac Brock Side Trail directed me onto an earthen path that zig-zagged up toward Queenston Heights Park to the official start of the BT. As I neared the top, I stopped at a clearing and looked down at the mighty Niagara River thinking, *Had I parked up above, I would have missed this view.* Linking Lake Erie to Lake Ontario and forming the border between Canada and the United States, its limestone-green clouded flow surges over Canada's Horseshoe Falls at 35 kilometres per hour making it North America's most powerful cataract and an irresistible draw for a 63-year-old unemployed dance and etiquette teacher named Annie Edson Taylor. In pursuit of fame and fortune, Taylor's gamble was to become the first person to plunge over Niagara Falls in a barrel. On October 24, 1901, with her orange cat clutched to her chest, this Michigander was sealed into a four-and-a-half-foot-long barrel made

Southern Terminus
of
The Bruce Trail

of one-and-a-half-inch-thick oak with the words Maid of the Mist hand-painted on the side. Her handlers pushed the barrel and its precious cargo into the Niagara River's surging current. It bobbed along, gradually gaining speed. Minutes later, it plunged over what amounted to a 14-storey-high building — a mere speck in the river's calamitous flow. Taylor and her cat, unlike four of the other 13 people who attempted this feat before it was outlawed, survived the ordeal. Accounts suggest that upon being released from her confine, she asked, "Have I gone over the falls?"

Over 12,000 post-glacial years, the relentless river has carved the 58 kilometre long Niagara Gorge at my feet. From my vantage point, I imagined some one thousand American militia scaling the steep cliffs to take British redcoats by surprise during the War of 1812. In the Battle of Queenston Heights, the invaders mortally wounded both Major General Sir Isaac Brock and his aide-de-camp, Lieutenant Colonel John Macdonell. The Americans would likely have been victorious that day had it not been for the Kanyen'kehà:ka chiefs Teyoninhokarawen (John Norton) and Ahyonwaeghs (John Brant) and about one hundred Six Nations warriors. Badly outnumbered, they held off the invaders long enough for British reinforcements to arrive and eventually win this pivotal battle.

Tulip-lined steps drew me away from the side trail into the park where a 4.8 metre tall Brock, one of the war's greatest heroes, poses atop an elegant Corinthian column. Equal in height to Niagara Falls, this limestone monument soars above the escarpment's edge, celebrating Canada's independence. Beneath it rest both Brock and Macdonell. Opened in 1853, the park's most notable landmark replaced a statue that was less imposing but had a compelling story.

The British and their Six Nations allies may have held off the Americans during the War of 1812, but that didn't mean everyone loved Mother England or that tensions between neighbours had eased. Few people, however, loathed the British with the intensity of American Benjamin Lett. Lett held Britain responsible for the death of his brother and assault of his sister and mother by Orangemen (members of the Orange Order, a Protestant political organization in Northern Ireland). When the British Canadian forces crushed William Mackenzie's rebellion of 1837, Lett couldn't let it go. For the next five years, he spearheaded murderous guerrilla attacks that almost caused a follow-up war with the United States. On April 17, 1840, in what is known as the Good Friday Terrorist Attack, Lett allegedly placed a keg of black powder inside Brock's original monument, laid a train and lit it. The resulting explosion cracked the column and catapulted Brock to the ground. Lett fled to the United States where, much to the chagrin of Upper Canada's government, the Americans gave him safe harbour.

〰

Moving on, I was drawn to a statue bearing a cameo embossed with the silhouette of a wrinkled, bonneted woman. I had a hard time reconciling this image with the slim young Laura Secord who adorns boxes of Canada's largest chain of chocolate stores. Secord was 37 when she made her 32 kilometre journey from Queenston to the British command post. Later in the day, I would follow a section of her historic route.

I crossed the park, finally arriving at the BT's southern terminus. It was a "big-gulp" moment. I was all alone with over nine hundred kilometres separating me from Tobermory. I should have been nervous. But I wasn't. I was excited. I couldn't wait to take my next step. I felt like a thoroughbred in the starting gate. I wanted to go. I took that big gulp and put one foot before the other. The BT's white blazes led me across manicured lawns to the Landscape of Nations Commemorative Memorial. It recognizes the role of First Nations in Canada's nation-building, featuring bronze sculptures of both Teyoninhokarawen (John Norton) and Ahyonwaeghs (John Brant).

None too soon, I entered the forest where the light softened and the pungent odour of damp soil filled the space between soaring hardwood trees. Time slowed, reminding me of my departure on Spain's Camino de Santiago almost two decades earlier. I recalled relishing the notion that for the next month, I had nothing to do but follow yellow arrows along that ancient pilgrimage. On the BT, white (main BT) and blue (side trails) blazes replaced those yellow arrows.

The forest was bursting like a riot of jacks from their boxes. At home in Caledon, the trilliums hadn't emerged yet, but here, some 150 kilometres farther south and over two hundred metres closer to sea level, our remarkable provincial flowers had popped through last year's leaf litter and unfurled into white harbingers of sunshine. Calls of courting birds punctuated the muted forest as I followed the well-worn main BT. I found my stride. This was going to be some adventure.

Blue jays, robins, cardinals, woodpeckers, pewees and towhees as well as those hard-to-identify warblers darted between trees. Their familiar calls ricocheted from one bird to the next as they wooed one another in their frantic need to reproduce. The forest was alive with avian sex. But birds weren't the only creatures on the prowl. Cracking branches to my left alerted me to a coyote. I stopped to watch the relative of both dogs and wolves amble by.

I came up behind a woman dressed in a pink fleece, comfortable trousers, sturdy shoes and a pale-blue cap. A pair of English retrievers accompanied her: 13-year-old golden Tory and seven-year-old black Juniper. "These dogs are my life," she volunteered. "I walk them for two hours twice a day and then I take them out for a walk around the block before bed." Patricia was slim, clearly fit, talkative — and 91. "My cardiologist asks me what my secret is. I tell him dogs." As I walked on, I felt the absence of Frida, my beautiful tiger-striped brindle who I rescued from a Mexican street. She was at home nursing a bad shoulder.

The trail dropped down the escarpment to the flatlands below, where I found signs for the Laura Secord Legacy Trail. Leaving the BT, I walked into St. Davids and then began my return trip to Queenston along a portion of Secord's journey in reverse. Following the historic Iroquois Trail (now York Road), I had an easier go of it than this mother of seven had more than two hundred years earlier. Secord avoided American troops not by pretending to milk her cow, as the legend goes, but by tramping cross-country for 32 kilometres through thick forest.

Secord was the daughter of Thomas Ingersoll, who loaned his name to the Ontario town. As the War of 1812 raged, American troops had taken Queenston, where Secord lived. When her husband James was wounded in the Battle of Queenston Heights, the young mother nursed him back to health in their home, where American soldiers had been billeted. No one is entirely sure how she learned of their plans to attack the British in Beaver Dams (now Thorold), but this information kicked off her Paul Revere–esque journey. Only Secord's warning was of the coming of the Americans, as the red-coated British were, of course, the "good guys."

That Secord made it to the British headquarters is not disputed. Whether she arrived in advance of the Battle of Beaver Dams, which was won mostly by Kanyen'kehà:ka warriors backed by a small contingent of British troops, remains a mystery. Regardless, Secord's daring war effort was unrecognized until 1860 when Albert Edward, the future King Edward VII, sent her £100 — the equivalent of about $25,000 Canadian dollars today — and she had become the wrinkled, bonneted woman I'd seen earlier.

In Queenston, the Laura Secord Homestead was closed, but I enjoyed strolling past this historic town's collection of beautiful homes. When I came upon a man topping the dandelions that decorated his lawn, I called out: "That's a losing battle." He agreed but couldn't bring himself to allow them to exist. He felt differently about the spectacularly tall chestnut that was the centrepiece of his backyard. I'd hoped this magnificent tree was an American chestnut that had survived the fungal blight, which all but wiped out the species. On closer inspection, it was the compound-leafed horse chestnut. Beautiful, but not a rare survivor. Bernd Heinrich, the author of a plethora of nature books including *Bumblebee Economics*, monitors almost 1,500 American chestnuts near his off-grid home in Maine. In his eighties, Heinrich expressed his views about nature in *Outside* magazine. "As social beings," he said, "we frame our worthiness in terms of becoming part of something we deem to be of value greater than ourselves, such as a sports team, a clan, a country. Why not Nature, to which we all belong?"

〜

Heinrich's sentiment registered for me as I neared the end of the first instalment of my 40-day-40-hike adventure. I thought of my journey in terms of loving the trail and the spine of land it followed. I hoped that by hiking the BT and putting pen to paper about it, as Heinrich has done so eloquently, I would become part of something greater than myself. I wasn't in this to break any records for speed or to cover every inch. I simply wanted to come to love the Niagara Escarpment and the BT more deeply with hopes that my enthusiasm would spread.

Norman Pearson, one of the BT's four founders, described what motivated him in his book *The Making of the Bruce Trail: 1954–2004.* "The appeal of the Bruce Trail," he wrote, "was that our people wanted to create something, to build something permanent for the ages, and to enhance the private properties and the various public lands we crossed." Yes, the BT's founders were searching for somewhere to walk, but that desire came from their keen need to conserve the Niagara Escarpment. Back in the mid-1950s, according to Pearson, a professional planner, Ontario had the "highest rate of urbanization in the world." Prophetically, he worried the province's farmland would be "swallowed up by urban sprawl and septic-tank suburbs." He might have added gravel pits and quarries to his list of concerns. The founders were all members of the Hamilton Naturalists' Club. The BT's original proponents were the Federation of Ontario Naturalists (now Ontario Nature) and the Conservation Council of Ontario. Over its 50-plus years, the BT's focus has drifted between hiking and conservation, recreation and environment. But there's no doubt, the BT's presence has played a key role in protecting nature. The trail has introduced hundreds of thousands of people to the wonders of the great outdoors, turning them into conservationists willing to protect what they love.

Day 2

WELLAND CANAL #3 /
WOODEND CONSERVATION AREA

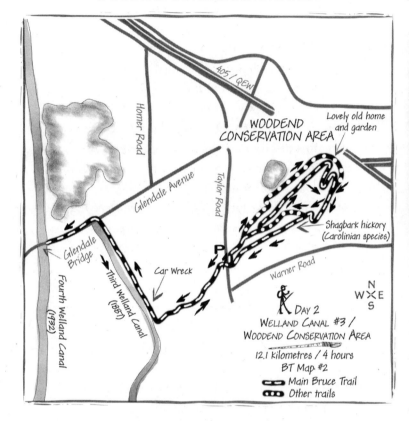

FIELD NOTES

START TIME: 10 a.m., Wednesday, May 4, 2022

TRAILHEAD WEATHER: soft, hazy overcast after 17 hours of rain

DISTANCE: 12.1 km

ELAPSED TIME: 4h

BT SECTION: Niagara

BT MAP: #2

MAIN BT WALKED: 13.5 km to 19.7 km

ASCENT: 439 m / **DESCENT:** 452 m

SIDE/OTHER TRAILS: Woodend Side Trail, Margaret Kalogeropoulos Side Trail

FLORA/FAUNA OF NOTE: forsythia (*Forsythia x intermedia*), shagbark hickory (*Carya ovata*)

In which I learn: "It's a river. It's the Welland Canal;
no, it's the third Welland Canal," before the killer
Deep Cut slashes the first gash through the backbone that
runs across the muscles of the land and muddy kids
remind me that I have laundry to do.

I sat out the rain until 10 a.m. and then set off with two destinations in mind. First, I wanted to walk to the Welland Canal, then I planned to explore the Woodend Conservation Area. I parked between the two and headed for the waterway. After 17 wet hours, I had to ford a stream, but that challenge was offset by the soft post-rain haziness that created a muted backdrop for the shrubbery's red-tipped buds. Each step along the squeegee trail displaced a whiff of spring. The trail skirted a golf course. The shorn grass moulded to the rolling hills and valleys making me feel as though I were crossing an English estate rather than hiking Ontario's BT.

After a kilometre, the trail made a sharp right-hand turn, and I walked alongside an arrow-straight waterway separated from the golf course by a line of trees. My reaction to it reminded me of the famous "It's a bird; it's a plane . . ." line from *Superman*: "It's a river. It's the Welland Canal; no, it's the third Welland Canal." Every 50 or 100 metres, five-metre-high walls of chiselled limestone reinforced the river's earthen banks, and the water cascaded down a concrete ramp through a restricted channel. They were remains of the third Welland Canal's 26 locks. Officially completed in 1887, it operated until the fourth, and current, canal took over in 1932. The third canal followed a slightly shorter route than the second Welland Canal (opened in 1845), which had detoured from its predecessor: Merritt's Ditch.

William Hamilton Merritt was a schemer. A captain in the War of 1812, he was captured in the Battle of Lundy's Lane and spent a year in prison. After the war, Merritt bought a sawmill near Twelve Mile Creek. When the river's temperamental flow made milling unprofitable, he didn't sell and move to a better location. No, Merritt convinced American financier John Yates to put up the money to build his ditch, otherwise known as the first Welland Canal.

In 1825, as Americans cheered the opening of the 454 kilometre Erie Canal, European immigrants began the arduous construction process. Using picks and shovels, they carved out Canada's more direct shipping route (44 kilometres long) for wages of about 50 cents per day and living conditions that were ripe with cholera and malaria. They used hand drills to bore into the rock, packed the holes with gunpowder and slowly blasted their way through the Niagara Escarpment's 400-million-year-old limestone.

The canal was meant to augment flow to Merritt's mills on Twelve Mile Creek with water from the Welland River, following a route that took advantage of existing waterways. Problem was, it had to dissect a ridge that ran between present-day Port Robinson and Allanburg. With nothing but those picks, shovels and pack animals, workers spent years gouging out what became known as the Deep Cut, a three-kilometre channel that was up to 20 metres deep. Its construction is estimated to have required those underpaid men and their long-suffering pack animals to remove enough material to fill three hundred Olympic-sized swimming pools. Then, on November 9, 1828, on the eve of completing the channel and after torrential rain, the Deep Cut collapsed, burying countless labourers under tonnes of earth, stone and rocks, their picks still raised above their heads, their horses' leads still in their hands.

The collapse not only contributed to a labour dispute, it prompted the canal's realignment to a route predicated on shipping rather than the transfer of water. When, on November 30, 1829, a pair of schooners left Port Dalhousie on Lake Ontario and two days later arrived in Buffalo on Lake Erie, what began as a way to improve his milling business turned into a bypass around Niagara Falls. It replaced the horses and wagons once used to transport goods around this formidable obstacle. Climbing the Niagara Escarpment's 99.5 metre height, it's a giant among the world's canals. (The Panama Canal uses 12 locks to raise ships a mere 26 metres over its 82 kilometre length, whereas the Suez Canal has no locks at all as it doesn't climb despite its 193.3 kilometre span.) Thanks to Merritt's audacity, his name dominates St. Catharines. I'd crossed Merritt Street several times; thought about hiking the 11 kilometre Merritt Side Trail; seen signs for Merritt House, which had been William Hamilton's home; and noted the community of Merritton.

Despite its follies, Merritt's Ditch eventually became part of Canada's mighty St. Lawrence Seaway. It linked the west to shipping ports in Montreal and beyond. When it opened in 1833, Confederation and the Trans Canada Railway were decades away. Like General Brock, Teyoninhokarawen (John Norton), Ahyonwaeghs (John Brant) and Laura Secord,

Merritt's actions were key to Canada's gestation. But they also cost countless labourers their lives and resulted in the first gash in the mighty Niagara Escarpment.

≋

Walking alongside this evidence of how long industrialization has been chipping away at Ontario's wilderness, I continued following the main BT's white blazes. After a kilometre, the trail turned sharply left, leaving the waterway and following a road that led to the "real" Welland Canal. I stopped to watch a massive ship pass by. It was destined to pass under Glendale Bridge (#5), a vertical lift bridge. It required much of the channel's 94.5 metre width, some 14 times that of its earliest predecessor and almost as wide as Niagara Falls is tall.

Glendale Bridge (#5) circa 1928

Afterwards, I turned around and retraced my route back to my car, where I entered the Woodend Conservation Area. A wide path pocked with potholes overflowing with muddy water led me into a rolling mature hardwood forest curiously devoid of undergrowth. Its nakedness gave the woods the raw feel of a recently sheared black sheep but made it ideal for seeing birds and a class of about 45 students. While I tiptoed around puddles, these teenagers were drawn to the muck like young piglets. At least half of them had muddy bottoms and several had painted their faces with the black goo. They gleefully slid down greasy hillsides happiest when their escapade ended in a wreck. I wondered if I'd ever walked in a forest with such reckless abandon. I'm happy when I'm walking, but their disregard for staying clean and dry and just rollicking was something else again. Youth. I guess that was when your mum did your laundry.

I passed by the elegant wooden house and outbuildings that continue to stand guard over Woodend's combination of hilly woods and flat farmland. I admired the forsythia, which had spread beyond the garden into a brilliantly yellow forest. But this was the Niagara Peninsula, so I couldn't escape history. Long before those yellow shrubs had been planted or the house had been built, both redcoats and their enemies, the American militia, used this lofty spot to observe the War of 1812's history-making battles of Queenston Heights, Beaver Dams and Lundy's Lane.

The fact that forsythia is an early bloomer likely accounts for it signifying anticipation. Farther north it doesn't grow with such vigour. The robust colour and profuse blooms of the patch on this observation point reminded me that I had a long way to walk and some climbing to do before I arrived in Tobermory. The Welland Canal is at an elevation of about 130 metres above sea level. When I would arrive nearer my home in Caledon, I'd be almost 400 metres above sea level. Well before touching the northern cairn in Tobermory (180 metres), I would ascend to the highest point on the BT (540 metres). Tucked in south of Lake Ontario and well below the 49th parallel that is normally thought of as the border between Canada and the United States, St. Catharines is Ontario's second warmest city (after Windsor) and Canada's sixth (the other four are in British Columbia). It brims with unique flora (Woodend has pawpaw trees) and overflows with colourful Canadian history.

Day 3

WELLAND CANALS #4 & #2 / BERT LOWE SIDE TRAIL

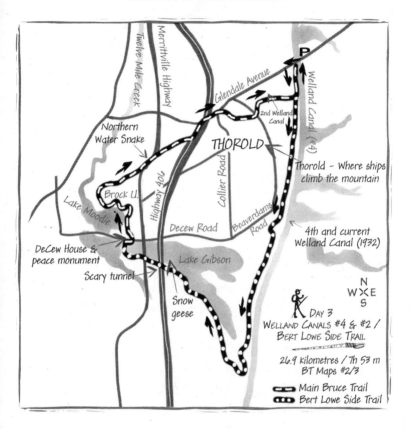

Twelve Mile Creek

Merrittville Highway

Glendale Avenue

P

Welland Canal (#4)

2nd Welland Canal

THOROLD

Thorold – Where ships climb the mountain

Northern Water Snake

Collier Road

Highway 406

Brock U.

Lake Moodie

Decew Road

Beaverdams Road

4th and current Welland Canal (1932)

DeCew House & peace monument

Lake Gibson

Scary tunnel

Snow geese

N
W ✕ E
S

DAY 3
WELLAND CANALS #4 & #2 /
BERT LOWE SIDE TRAIL

26.9 kilometres / 7h 53 m
BT Maps #2/3

Main Bruce Trail
Bert Lowe Side Trail

FIELD NOTES

START TIME: 7:30 a.m., Thursday, May 5, 2022

TRAILHEAD WEATHER: sunny, but cool

DISTANCE: 26.9 km

ELAPSED TIME: 7h 53m

BT SECTION: Niagara

BT MAP: #2/3

MAIN BT WALKED: 19.7 km to 31.2 km

ASCENT: 988 m / **DESCENT:** 996 m

SIDE TRAILS: Bert Lowe Side Trail

FLORA/FAUNA OF NOTE: trumpeter swans (*Cygnus buccinator*)

In which I run into John, Paul, George and Ringo
before I learn how Bert Lowe protected his daughter
and how Wampum and a cocoon help soothe relations
with First Nations people.

Finally, sunshine. Spring hadn't fully blossomed yet. While some ephemeral flowers, trees and shrubs had popped, others remained bronco-like just before the bucking chute opens; "Let me out," they seemed to be saying. Me too for that matter.

My hike began at the Glendale Bridge (#5). Built in 1928, this old timer is one of several vertical-lift bridges that span the Welland Canal. It's a utilitarian hunk of steel seemingly without embellishments unless you cross it on foot. Following the BT's white blazes along the bridge's pedestrian walkway, I noticed its railing was anything but utilitarian. Bridge #5's architect incorporated an ornate lattice design, a little flourish that gave the bridge an unexpected flair. On the far side, I turned left. Fifteen minutes later, I picked up the 12.3 kilometre Bert Lowe Side Trail (not to be confused with Ray Lowes, one of the BT's four founders) and followed it as this wide paved path paralleled the canal. Large ships replaced the trees that normally kept me company.

As I neared Thorold, I came upon a series of now dilapidated industrial buildings covered with murals that depict the area's history. Known as the Thorold wall murals, they are the creation of Shawn Reimer and a large group of volunteers who painted them in 2007–08. Sadly, they have been the target of graffiti bandits. Normally, I'm saddened by this sort of vandalism, but I chuckled in one case. With a few deft strokes, someone has turned the image of four men standing shoulder to shoulder dressed in period police uniforms into *Sgt. Pepper's* John, Paul, George and Ringo. It was Lennon's iconic eyeglasses that clued me in. As I admired this whimsy, a cyclist whizzed by. For the second time that morning, I was pleased to be on foot. Walking may be slow, but you get to smell the roses — and see the artwork.

I continued in the sunshine and arrived at Thorold, once known as Beaver Dams — the site of the eponymously named battle won by British and First Nation forces perhaps due in part to Laura Secord's heroic journey. The village's motto is: "Where ships climb the mountain," as Thorold is where the heavy lifting takes place. Locks four, five and six, collectively known as the Twin Flight Locks, are the largest locks in the world. Resembling a flight of giant stairs, they carry ships up 42.6 metres, almost double the rise of the Panama Canal's 12 locks.

The trail hugged the canal for another six kilometres. I took advantage of a bench that was protected from the stiff wind that had come up. It was sunny but chilly and my thermos of hot tea hit the spot. I was at the bottom of my day's triangular loop, which celebrated Bert Lowe — a key player in the birth of the BT. In the early 1960s, when the BT was little more than an exciting idea, Lowe was president of the Niagara Field Naturalists Club and had already blazed the

Escarpment Trail along the Niagara Peninsula and founded the Escarpment Trail Club. In other words, he was a perfect partner to help build the BT. According to David E. Tyson's book *Trail to the Bruce*, however, there was friction between Lowe and the enthusiastic BT builders. Tyson writes that Lowe was reluctant to commit to the larger initiative. He quotes a letter addressed to BT founder Philip Gosling suggesting Gosling would have to be patient if he was to win over Lowe. Though this avid hiker eventually folded his Escarpment Trail Club into the BT, he hesitated like a protective father unsure his future son-in-law is good enough for his beloved daughter. At the unveiling of the Bert Lowe Side Trail in 1968, another BT founder, Norman Pearson, recognized this hiking pioneer, noting the BT might never have happened if Lowe hadn't supported it.

Most people see the BT as I saw it as a teenager growing up in Caledon: a static path that just was (or is). In reality, trails have personalities — their unique characteristic inherited from their rich histories and the people who built, maintain, love and walk them. Trails change and mature over time. Bert Lowe and so many others are woven into the fibre of the path.

≈

I left the Welland Canal, entering land owned by Ontario Power Generation. The property consists of lakes, reservoirs and canals. Birdsong had replaced traffic hum and the path was gravel rather than asphalt. It was entirely pleasant — until, that is, I came to the long, dark tunnel under Highway 406. Walking through it — quickly — I better understood that encouraging expression: "There's light at the end of the tunnel."

Emerging from the underpass, I heard the raucous cries of a pair of the aptly named trumpeter swans. I watched as they performed perfect skid landings, the envy of any float-plane pilot, onto the smooth surface of Gibson Lake. Their black beaks are the easiest way to differentiate these beauties from the more common, similarly sized but non-native mute swans (orange beaks). Both are larger than the black-beaked tundras. Seeing me admire the birds, a local out walking his rottweiler explained, "The swans nest on the lake," before advising me to look up if I was interested in birds. "There are lots of bald eagles around." I didn't see any that day, but a few kilometres later, I watched a red-tailed hawk riding thermals with the graceful ease of a glider plane.

I left the Bert Lowe Side Trail at the DeCew House Heritage Park where I visited the First Nations Peace Monument, the work of Indigenous architect Douglas Cardinal. Best known for designing both the flowing Canadian Museum of History in Gatineau, Quebec, and the sculpted National Museum of the American Indian in Washington, DC, Cardinal's trademark is his use of nature in his design. Cardinal studied architecture in the 1950s at the University of British Columbia. There, his use of curving lines contributed to his being kicked out of the school and banned from applying to other Canadian universities. His ejection might have been the luckiest break in his life. Cardinal went on to study architecture at the University of Texas where he was influenced by Rudolf Steiner and the concept of anthropomorphism: the application of human traits and emotions to birds, animals, rocks, plants and maybe even trails.

The First Nations Peace Monument, more a living sculpture than a statue, celebrates the often-overlooked role of

First Nations in building Canada. Records estimate that some 10,000 Indigenous warriors from both sides of the border took part in the War of 1812. In its aftermath, both the British and Americans claimed victory. By many accounts, the losers were the Indigenous troops who received little of what they'd been promised when they agreed to fight. Yet history suggests fear of First Nations warriors paralyzed American soldiers and was key to the Yankee retreat across the Niagara River.

The monument's pair of bowed limestone benches form a semi-oval. Sitting within them I felt encased, protected inside an open-air cocoon. Simple patterns representing two important Wampum Belts are engraved into the backs of the benches. The William Claus Wampum Belt recognizes the re-establishment of peaceful relations between the British and First Nations following the War of 1812, whereas the Hiawatha Wampum Belt symbolizes the Haudenosaunee Great Law of Peace. Like all Wampum Belts, the ones reflected in the sculpture were made with tubular purple and white beads called Wampum that were crafted by coastal First Nations people from seashells. Wampum Belts were used for ornamental, ceremonial, commercial and, as in the case of the Hiawatha and William Claus Wampum Belts, for diplomatic purposes.

I was struck by Cardinal's use of the William Claus Wampum Belt. Appointed the deputy superintendent of Indian affairs in 1799 on the brink of war, William Claus sought support from First Nations leaders Thayendanegea (Joseph Brant, Ahyonwaeghs's [John Brant's] father) in Canada and Tecumseh in the United States. Accounts indicate Claus encouraged the Haudenosaunee to stand together in opposition to American aggressors. When war became a reality, however, the Haudenosaunee were split in their allegiance. Given the thought Cardinal puts into his artwork, I'm convinced he chose the William Claus Wampum Belt not only because it recognized the return of peace between the British and First Nations, but within the Haudenosaunee as well.

~~~

Leaden-grey clouds and a bitter wind had replaced the morning's sunshine. Reluctantly, I left my cozy cocoon. As I crossed the Brock University campus, I peeked inside the famed rowing centre, hoping to see the likes of Silken Laumann. Her bronze medal in the Olympic Games in Barcelona is one of the 45 Olympic rowing medals won by Canadians since 1904. I get shivers when I recall Laumann's heroic comeback after having her leg shattered in a boating collision just 10 weeks before she won bronze.

When I arrived back at the intersection of the main BT and the Bert Lowe Side Trail, a ship was chugging up the canal. *Ugh*, I thought. *If it gets the Glendale Bridge before I do, my hot shower could be a long time coming since I've parked my car on the far side.* After 26 kilometres, this seemed like cruel punishment. Noting the ship was travelling slowly, I thought: *Can I beat it to the bridge by booting it for that last kilometre?* It was worth a try. Off I went, arms pumping, hips swaying, water bottle sloshing. Huffing and puffing, I arrived at the bridge. The traffic light was green. "Yahoo," I roared as I looked over my right shoulder to see how tight the race had been. Expecting a close call, perhaps a photo finish, I was confused because the ship was nowhere in sight. "Hmm," I said as I squinted. And there it was, the tail end of a ship about a kilometre away. You guessed it — yup, that baby was heading in the opposite direction.

Day 4

DECEW HOUSE / SHORT HILLS PROVINCIAL PARK

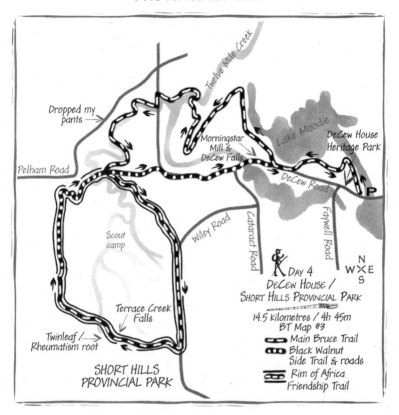

Twelve Mile Creek

Dropped my pants →

Pelham Road

Morningstar Mill & DeCew Falls

Lake Moodie

DeCew House Heritage Park

DeCew Road

P

Scout camp

Wiley Road

Cataract Road

Faywell Road

Day 4
DeCew House /
Short Hills Provincial Park

N
W ☓ E
S

14.5 kilometres / 4h 45m
BT Map #3

⬤⬤⬤ Main Bruce Trail
⬤⬤⬤ Black Walnut
Side Trail & roads
⬤⬤⬤ Rim of Africa
Friendship Trail

Terrace Creek Falls

Twinleaf / → Rheumatism root

SHORT HILLS PROVINCIAL PARK

FIELD NOTES

START TIME: 11:45 a.m., Friday, May 6, 2022

TRAILHEAD WEATHER: bitter, overcast, yucky

DISTANCE: 14.5 km

ELAPSED TIME: 4h 30m

BT SECTION: Niagara

MAIN BT WALKED: 31.2 km to 40.9 km

BT MAP: #3

ASCENT: 580 m / **DESCENT:** 576 m

SIDE TRAILS: Black Walnut Side Trail, Morningstar Side Trail

FLORA/FAUNA OF NOTE: shagbark hickory (*Carya ovata*), twinleaf root (*Jeffersonia diphylla*), skunk cabbage (*Symplocarpus foetidus*)

*In which tick tricks have me drop my drawers before
Laura Secord completes her journey and Canada's
fascinating past keeps me company.*

Parking at the DeCew House Heritage Park, I couldn't not
revisit the First Nations Peace Monument. Afterwards, I set
out under a heavy sky on the main BT toward Short Hills
Provincial Park. It was one of those raw days when vacuum-
ing seems more tempting than a hike.

A two-kilometre desolate stretch of exposed trail alongside Lake Moodie faded into the comfort of a maple forest. I
overlooked farmland as the trail skirted the escarpment's rim.
Finally, my blood was circulating. Passing the Morningstar
Side Trail and noting it led to Morningstar, I figured I'd
swing by on my return journey. The main BT led me down
the escarpment, across a road and into Short Hills Provincial
Park, where ominous signs warned that ticks were prevalent.
The number of ticks I'd encountered over the last few days
had been disconcerting, as I know several people who are
seriously ill with Lyme disease.

Twelve Mile Creek, the same one that ran through William Hamilton Merritt's land and was the route followed by the first two Welland Canals, gurgled along beside me. Rather than being 12 miles long, it drains into Lake Ontario 12 miles from the Niagara River. The convention extends to Fifteen Mile and Sixteen Mile ponds, Eighteen Mile Creek and the better known Twenty Mile Creek, which flows over Balls Falls.

Walking through the flat valley bottom was a surprise given the park's name is Short Hills. It was peaceful if muddy, and I was delighted to spy a shagbark hickory, a largely Carolinian species that is rare in Caledon. I'm not sure why I like these shaggy trees so much, but I'm always excited when I come across one. Even better would be to eat a shagbark hickory nut as they are not only edible, but unlike black walnuts, their thick husks break open voluntarily into four equal parts. The challenge is to beat the squirrels to them.

When I hike, I carry my phone/camera in my back pocket. I caught myself scratching a spot where the edge of my cell rubbed against the back of my thigh. When the irritation didn't go away, I recalled those warning signs. With a sick feeling, I thought *Tick*. My concern outweighed my worries about being caught with my pants down, so down they went. But no contortion allowed me to see the back of my thigh. Blindly, I wiped my hand over the irritated area and thought — imagined? — I'd felt a small insect. Wiping again, there was no

Blacklegged (deer) tick
(Ixodes scapularis)

tick, and I couldn't feel a bite, but there was blood — blood that soaked through my trousers, creating a loonie-sized stain.

The spit of blacklegged or deer ticks contains both an anaesthetic and an anticoagulant. The anaesthetic freezes the area around the bite, so you don't know this member of the arachnid family (along with spiders and scorpions) is burrowing into your skin. Proteins in their saliva then prevent your blood from coagulating, thereby ensuring an endless supply of their liquid lunch. Without your knowledge, these micro creatures deposit a cocktail of enzymes that dissolve your flesh, thereby creating a blood-filled micro-lake that they slurp from greedily. But tick tricks don't stop there.

Most of us curse the itchy swelling caused by a mosquito bite. It's the result of histamine, a compound your body releases for a variety of reasons, including an attack by an invader, such as a mosquito. The red itchiness caused by histamine might be unpleasant, but in addition to making us aware that we've been bitten, this natural immune response also rushes healing white blood cells to the site. Ticks, however, are onto histamine. In addition to freezing the area, dissolving a cavity of flesh and counteracting coagulation, tick spit contains molecules that denature histamine, thereby blocking the body's natural healing process. Hard as it is for someone who has never discovered a tick waving its spidery legs while dumpster diving into some unmentionable part of their body to believe (they like warm, dark, hidden crevices), these traits mean a tick, which can be as small as an itty-bitty poppy seed, can glug away on your blood for days without you noticing.

As I pulled up my pants, I didn't know all of this. Despite the warning signs at the park's entrance, the free flow of blood staining my pants and the irritation resulting from my phone rubbing my thigh, I did what so many sufferers of Lyme disease had done: I hoped for the best.

≈

When I came across signs for the Rim of Africa Friendship Trail, the first of nine friendship trails I would encounter along the BT (one in each of the BT's nine sections), I focused on it, putting the blood stain out of my mind. Friendship trails are a way for trail organizations around the world to raise awareness about their trail. In addition to the rugged 650 kilometre Rim of Africa Trail in South Africa, the BT has paired with trails in England, Wales, Costa Rica, Brazil, Lebanon, Korea, Australia and Greece.

The Rim of Africa is a rugged, backcountry 650 kilometre journey around South Africa's Cape Fold Mountains. Each year, the trail's organizers lead a group of 12 intrepid hikers chosen from among those who apply for a spot. You carry your own gear, including food, and you can do one or more of the nine individual traverses that make up the entire route.

≈

When I came to it, the Terrace Creek Falls was a surprise. Spring runoff surged over this pretty eight-metre-high cataract. The surrounding forest was Vancouver Island lush. While the leaves weren't fully fledged, the forest floor was a luxuriant sea of green. What I thought was wild ginger, were mounds of an unfamiliar plant. Instead of wild ginger's characteristic heart-shaped leaves, these beauties supported two leaves, one a mirror image of the other. It was *Jeffersonia diphylla*, more commonly known as twinleaf or rheumatism root, and not easy to find in Ontario. Diphylla means two-leafed and Jeffersonia refers to Thomas Jefferson because he grew it in his garden, and it blooms close to his birthday.

Leaving the valley bottom, I puffed up a steep incline. *Ah, I thought, so this is the short hill.* And indeed, it was. Short Hill Provincial Park is home to a number of these mini mountains, the result of Twelve Mile Creek carving through deep reserves of glacial debris.

As promised, I followed the seven hundred metre Morningstar Side Trail into Morningstar Mill, a property once operated by a family of the same name. Now owned by the City of St. Catharines, it's in remarkably good shape. Twelve Mile Creek cascades over 21 metre high DeCew Falls creating enough energy to turn Morningstar Mill's triplet of turbines. One operated a sawmill, one produced electricity and a third powered a grist mill (you can buy flour milled on site) that in turn ran a cider mill, a lathe and a shoddy mill (where fabric was made). How did these early settlers accomplish all this and have time to build the spiral staircase depicted in historic photographs on the site? Before it was torn down, the corkscrew contraption gave the family access to the creek in the deep ravine upstream of the falls.

I headed back toward my car thinking my surprises for the day were over. Before driving away, I visited what remains of DeCew House, once an elegant, two-story, circa-1812 stone home. After it burned down in 1950, its walls were capped at about waist height. When Captain John DeCew was captured in the War of 1812, the British used his home as their outpost. It was Laura's Secord's destination when she set off on her historic journey. Having just left Morningstar Mill, I recalled that the waterfall there was created by Twelve Mile Creek cascading over DeCew Falls. After the war, it was DeCew who built the original mill in what was then DeCew Town. But DeCew's empire building ended with Merritt's Ditch. When the canal that was to increase flow in Twelve Mile Creek morphed into a shipping channel, the new route all but cut off DeCew's water supply, putting him out of business. It wasn't until a new Welland Canal replaced Merritt's Ditch that DeCew Falls had enough flow for Wilson Morningstar to resurrect DeCew's milling business. Not only had I followed the BT alongside Twelve Mile Creek through Short Hills Provincial Park, I'd followed Canada's history as well.

Day 5

LOUTH CONSERVATION AREA / BALL'S FALLS

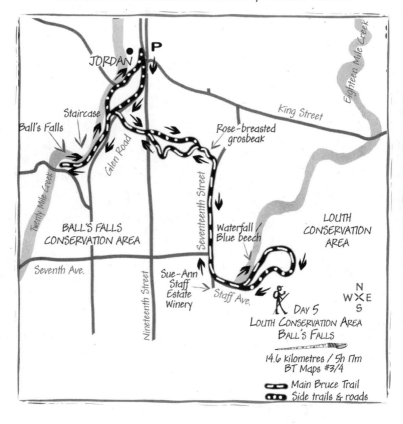

FIELD NOTES

START TIME: 7:55 a.m., Monday, May 9, 2022

TRAILHEAD WEATHER: spectacular

DISTANCE: 14.6 km

ELAPSED TIME: 5h 17m

BT SECTION: Niagara

BT MAP: #3/4

MAIN BT WALKED: 51.2 km to 57.9 km

ASCENT: 609 m / DESCENT: 634 m

SIDE TRAILS: Louth Side Trail, Staff Avenue Side Trail, Jim Rainforth Side Trail, Jordan Hollow Side Trail

FLORA/FAUNA OF NOTE: American robins (*Turdus migratorius*), blue jay (*Cyanocitta cristata*), American crows (*Corvus brachyrhynchos*), northern cardinals (*Cardinalis cardinalis*), downy woodpecker (*Dryobates pubescens*), blue beech (*Carpinus caroliniana*), bald eagle (*Haliaeetus leucocephalus*), rose-breasted grosbeak (*Pheucticus ludovicianus*)

In which I sweet-talk the starch out of a Prince of Wales Hotel matron before setting the CRA on a reluctant female vintner and charge up Ball's Falls' stairs high on negative ions and phytoncides.

Alex and I treated ourselves to a weekend stay in Jordan Station, where we dined royally at the Inn on Twenty, sampling local wines. Sunday was Mother's Day, so after watching a rowing regatta at Royal Henley Park in St. Catharines, we drove to Niagara-on-the-Lake hoping to have high tea.

Anyone familiar with Niagara-on-the-Lake would know that visiting this popular tourist destination on Mother's Day without a reservation for high tea at the regal Prince of Wales Hotel is, let's say, naïve. You pretty much need a reservation to park. Inside, the hotel buzzed. Every table in the dining room had at least one mother at it whose children had no doubt booked weeks in advance. And here we were short a mother and without a reservation. The host, her hair pulled back into a tight bun and wearing a starched white apron (or so it seemed), scowled as we approached. She inquired, "What name is your reservation under?" Sheepishly admitting we had no booking, we asked, "Would there be any chance that there might possibly be a small table for the two of us?" I think we shrunk down hoping to appear to take up less space. "Hmph," she replied, clucking as she scanned the overflowing dining room. And just then, a mother and daughter got up from a dear table tucked away on its own right beside a large window. At this, the starch left our host's apron and a whisp of hair came loose to caress her cheek. "Just let me clear that table," she purred (or so it seemed).

After enjoying English breakfast tea served in a proper teapot, hot scones with clotted cream flavoured with a hint of candied ginger and a three-tiered tray of petite sandwiches and delicate cakes that even impressed Devon-raised Alex, we decided to avoid the crowds in Niagara-on-the-Lake. Returning to Queenston, we admired the Mackenzie Printery & Newspaper Museum. For a short time, it was home to William Lyon Mackenzie and his newspaper, the *Colonial Advocate*. While in Queenston, Mackenzie wrote extensively about political and social reform in advance of his efforts to overthrow the Upper Canada government in 1837. Mackenzie is one of the more colourful characters in Canadian history, and his opposition to the British attracted Benjamin Lett — the same dissident who catapulted General Brock. Lett was among the rebels who took part in Mackenzie's failed rebellion, which culminated in a crushing defeat at the Battle of Montgomery's Tavern in Toronto. Was Lett stalking me?

≈

The next day, I waved goodbye to Alex and walked about three hundred metres to the trailhead to begin my figure-eight loop. It was the sort of morning I dream about: The sun was low on the horizon, its rays filtered through trees that promised leaves. The weekend's sunshine had given the trilliums a boost. The birds too. There were robins, of course, and blue jays and the odd crow. Cardinals seemed to be everywhere and the woodpeckers were adding their percussive pecks. I felt I could walk forever. Why can't we have 12 hours per day of morning light?

At the top of a rise, I looked back over row-upon-row of grapevines. Beyond them, Lake Ontario shimmered and I could just make out Toronto's CN Tower. The Twenty Valley is the heart of Ontario's wine country. It's home to now-familiar wineries: Angels Gate, Malivoire, Featherstone and Henry of Pelham. Alex and I had stopped by the Henry of Pelham vineyard where we learned that Baco Noir is to Ontario what Malbec is to Argentina. The grape's resistance to mildew makes it particularly well suited to the province's humid summers. Described as "meatier Pinot Noirs," Baco Noir wines are dark, full-bodied reds. Of all the wines produced on the Niagara Peninsula, Baco Noir is heralded as Ontario's own — yet it's not really. François Baco, the celebrated saviour of France's vineyards, bred the grape variety to resist phylloxera, an aphid that nearly wiped out France's vines in the early 1900s. Introduced to North America in the 1950s, it adapted well. Baco Noirs are produced elsewhere in Canada and the United States, but it's in Ontario that they flourish.

I turned onto Staff Avenue amid signs for the Sue-Ann Staff Estate Winery. Perched on a rise to my right was a well-cared-for farmhouse and outbuildings that had been in her family for two hundred years. Refreshingly, Sue-Ann's was a farm, not an architectural statement. As I came parallel with the house, a large dog began woofing. When a woman came out to quiet him, I couldn't resist. "Are you Sue-Ann?" She replied, "Are you from the CRA?" Before I responded, an OPP cruiser passed between us, so I retorted, "That's my backup." I asked her if many women-owned vineyards. "No," she said, "women are too smart." We waved goodbye and I was off.

I entered the Louth Conservation Area. The simple act of walking was chasing away those nagging worries like remembering to pay a bill or feeling guilty for forgetting a friend's birthday. I was free to listen and let my imagination roam. A hefty blue beech caught my attention. Also called a muscle tree because its trunk resembles a striated muscle, this beauty had a girth that was an order of magnitude grander than the forearm-sized specimens back home. Maxing out at about 10 metres in height, these famously hard trees are an understory species in a Carolinian forest. Canada's Carolinian zone extends south from a straight east/west line between Toronto and Lake Huron. Both the BT's Niagara and Iroquoia sections are included in this biologically super-charged part of the country, where trees such as pawpaw, blue ash, tulip and Kentucky coffee flourish. As Canadians, we tend to believe "beautiful" British Columbia is the queen of biodiversity given its mild climate, but this crown belongs to Ontario. The Carolinian zone makes up only 1 percent of Canada's land area but is home to more species of flora and fauna than any other ecosystem in the country.

I was walking through a Canadian outlier. The 49th parallel forms the border with the United States throughout Western Canada. Throughout the Maritimes, southern Quebec and, especially, Southern Ontario, the dividing line dips down by as much as six degrees. Vancouver sits on the 49th. If you follow a latitudinal line from Point Pelee, the southernmost point in Ontario, across the continent, it doesn't just arrive south of Vancouver, it doesn't even slice into Washington state or Oregon for that matter. Point Pelee is in line with Northern California.

Beyond the small grove of blue beeches, the unmistakable sound of a waterfall drew me in. Maybe a dozen feet tall, it featured a series of rocky ledges over which the water jumped and splashed. Droplets caught the morning sun and an odd ephemeral rainbow disappeared before I could catch it. I was all alone. Just the waterfall and my great big smile. I pondered why we like waterfalls so much. That they create negative ions is widely known. Maybe you recall the home negative-ion-generator craze? While these machines may not have lived up to advertisers' promises, waterfalls, according to scientists, do. The combination of light, air and water creates negative ions which, in turn, raise serotonin levels in your brain. Since serotonin controls your mood, it can make you happy. (It also regulates sleep and controls sexual desire.)

Eventually I had to head back. Following a series of side trails, I ambled along in no hurry. When I came across a log begging for my bottom, I sat down and did a little forest bathing. I was full of negative ions, why not add phytoncides (wood essential oils) released by trees. I suppose I didn't have to sit down to breathe in the compounds that studies have shown reduce stress and anxiety, but any excuse to stay longer in the forest was good with me. I'd done a forest bathing session with a certified professional for a story once, and I particularly enjoyed an exercise we did that day. Our leader had us listen farther and farther away. It's something we do naturally with our eyes. For instance, when I looked over the grapevines toward Toronto earlier, I'd squinted to make out the CN Tower. Now imagine doing that with your ears. You may hear a chickadee nearby, but farther in the distance is a robin, farther yet a woodpecker. See how you can stretch your hearing. As I strained to do so, an enormous bald eagle soared overhead and then chirping guided me to a gorgeous rose-breasted grosbeak.

Bald eagle
(*Haliaeetus leucocephalus*)

Returning to where I'd picked up the BT hours earlier, I continued west into the Ball's Falls Conservation Area. I'd seen the falls once before because my nephew was married there, but I'd never walked in along Twenty Mile Creek. The trail was level but seriously rocky. I had to keep my head down and come to a full stop or risk tripping when I wanted to admire the river as it pounded by, overflowing with spring runoff. After about a kilometre, I looked up at a long set of steep stairs. Fortunately, serotonin and phytoncides must have been coursing through my veins; I zipped up all 120 of those steps effortlessly — well almost effortlessly. I crossed behind a log house, a church and a big old barn where my nephew's wedding reception took place. I was once again drawn to the sound of falling water. The first time I saw the seven-storey Ball's Falls, I think *trickle* would have overstated its flow. This time, water coursed over the drop that, like the Punch Bowl near Hamilton and Niagara Falls, forms a horseshoe, a rainbow, a smile.

I wandered around, had lunch and then reluctantly turned back, making my way down those precipitous stairs and along the Jordan Hollow Side Trail. This was my last hike in the Niagara section. I'd covered roughly the same number of kilometres as the main trail, but in my peculiar way. I compared the experience of walking solo on five looping hikes versus the Niagara section end-to-end I'd done a few years earlier. I appreciate the drive to walk the BT end to end and to cover EFI — Every F-ing Inch. On the other hand, I recall little from that end-to-end trek. For instance, I don't remember the staircase and doubt I bothered to look at Ball's Falls.

There's an expression: Hike your own hike. Undertake your journey as it suits you. A BT enthusiast I know describes herself as a smell-the-roses hiker: if there's something to stop and see, she stops. Then there are hikers who "bag" peaks or strive for their personal best time. In 2022, Elias Kibreab covered the nine hundred kilometre BT in eight days, 16 hours and 55 minutes. That's an unimaginable one hundred kilometres per day. I guess he didn't admire Ball's Falls. Me? I abhor the idea of wearing a device that advises me of my speed and heartrate. I don't like kilometre markers on a trail and reluctantly carry my cellphone. I'm interested in flora and fauna and local history, but not with the diligence of a smell-the-roses hiker. I want to see and hear what the trail is telling me, but once I find my rhythm, I keep going. By hiking my own hike, I would retain many of the landmarks and memories, smells and sounds from this past week. Having had such an amazing day from my start in Jordan Station, I began thinking about the near trance-like effect the trail had on me as my "Jordan state of mind." I was coming to realize that this, this feeling of contentedness, was a large part of what made me jump out of bed early to get out hiking. Was "Jordan," I wondered, a place I could only reach while walking on my own?

Iroquoia Section

Day 6

DEVIL'S PUNCH BOWL / DOFASCO 2000 TRAIL

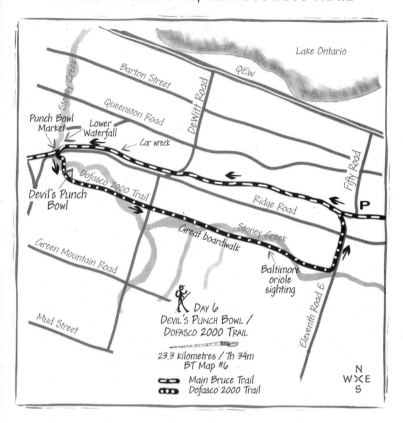

Lake Ontario

QEW

Barton Street

Queenston Road

Stoney Creek

DeWitt Road

Fifty Road

Punch Bowl Market

Lower Waterfall

Car wreck

Dofasco 2000 Trail

Devil's Punch Bowl

Ridge Road

Stoney Creek

Great boardwalk

Green Mountain Road

Baltimore oriole sighting

Mud Street

Eleventh Road E

P

DAY 6
DEVIL'S PUNCH BOWL /
DOFASCO 2000 TRAIL
23.3 kilometres / 7h 34m
BT Map #6

Main Bruce Trail
Dofasco 2000 Trail

N
W ✕ E
S

FIELD NOTES

START TIME: 7:35 a.m., Friday, May 13, 2022

TRAILHEAD WEATHER: gorgeous warm, sunny day

DISTANCE: 23.3 km

ELAPSED TIME: 7h 34m

BT SECTION: Iroquoia

BT MAP: #6

MAIN BT WALKED: 9.2 km to 19.8 km

ASCENT: 745 m / **DESCENT:** 772 m

SIDE TRAILS: Devil's Punch Bowl Side Trail, Dofasco 2000 Trail

FLORA/FAUNA OF NOTE: white trilliums (*Trillium grandiflorum*), white-tailed deer (*Odocoileus virginianus*), honey locust (*Gleditsia triacanthos*)

In which I salute those who braved the bullets, manure and slashed tires rained on them by a jittery, trigger-happy VIGILANTY COMMITTEE, before I slog up to a devil's brew where I find, instead, a delightful boardwalk.

I was up early having been awakened by one of my three housemates who were sharing the Airbnb I'd moved into for a few nights. It was an ordinary suburban house atop Hamilton's mountain. I felt as if I were back in university. On the good side, I chatted with the collection of people who were staying there. On the bad, there was an ever-present supply of someone else's dirty dishes.

After Niagara's flatlands, I was looking forward to cliffs, lookouts and even some climbing. Plus, I didn't know the Iroquoia section well. While *Hamilton & Area Hikes* is one of my Loops & Lattes guides, it was coauthored and co-hiked by my colleague Amy Darrell. Fiddling with a familiar phrase, I looked forward to putting a hike to a name.

The town of Grimsby is situated halfway between St. Catharines and Hamilton. It's where the Niagara region ends and the Hamilton region begins, as well as where the BT's Niagara section terminates and the Iroquoia section commences. From Grimsby, past Stoney Creek and into the Dundas Valley, the BT passes through a series of linear parks: Beamer Memorial, Woolverton, Winona, Vinemount, Devil's Punchbowl, Felker's Falls and more. Looking at the BT map, these parks appear as a narrow band of green that you might mistake for a river valley. Instead, the green demarcates the part of the Niagara Escarpment that is protected within Canada's first large-scale, environmental land-use plan: the Niagara Escarpment Plan.

In 1973, Ontario Premier Bill Davis's government passed the Niagara Escarpment Planning and Development Act. It grew from a groundbreaking report authored by Dr. Len Gertler who had been commissioned to write it by Premier Davis's predecessor John Robarts. The Act established the 17-member Niagara Escarpment Commission and charged it with developing a plan that would protect the 725 kilometre scarp of four-hundred-million-year-old limestone, sandstone, dolostone and shale that traverses the province from the tip of the Niagara Peninsula to the end of the Bruce. The major threat was environmentally inappropriate land use and "development." Premier Robarts was particularly concerned about the proliferation of aggregate pits and quarries, something that haunted my childhood and continues to trouble me today. From my family's old stone house and bank barn, our land dropped down into the forested West Credit River valley, the place we spent hours on hot summer afternoons swimming in the frigid creek. You can imagine my parents' alarm when our neighbour sold his adjacent family farm to a gravel company. This firm took possession of the property that abutted our swimming hole. It was just outside the planning area protected by the new Niagara Escarpment Plan.

It's unlikely the newly appointed Niagara Escarpment commissioners, which included BT founder Ray Lowes, fully grasped the vitriol that awaited them. In his report, Gertler had recommended the "Niagara Escarpment should be preserved, planned and developed as a simple park network." He set out an agenda for much of the Niagara Escarpment to be secured through easements or outright purchase. When word got out, rumours didn't need the internet to go viral. It was as if Laura Secord had galloped up the BT calling out, "The commissioners are coming. The Niagara Escarpment commissioners are coming." Landowners up and down the escarpment objected to government poking around their private property. The standing line was that commissioners would dictate that all barns be painted red. While today's environmental conflicts often play out in tweets and fake news, the battle over the Niagara Escarpment Plan happened at the community level. Opponents allegedly burned an effigy of Premier Davis; they stuffed proponents' cars with manure, slashed their tires, mailed shotgun shells to their homes. On one occasion, a commissioner claimed a knife-wielding landowner accosted him in a community hall washroom, an accusation easy to believe given the unsigned letter published in David E. Tyson's book about the BT. Addressed to Bruce Trail Members, it read: "We the land owners on the Niagara Escarpment have formed a VIGILANTY COMMITTEE from Tobermory to Niagara Falls. If someone of you get hurt don't say we have not warned you, a lot of Land Owners are very Jittery and some are Trigger Happy. So you better beware."

During the tumultuous 1970s, the BT became synonymous with the Niagara Escarpment Commission despite the Bruce Trail Association's efforts to distance itself. Landowners who had willingly shaken hands with Philip Gosling and others to allow the trail to cross their land revoked that privilege in their mistaken belief the BT was in cahoots with the commission. Lowes begged his fellow commissioners to stop denying development permission using the excuse that it was because the BT crossed their property. The association had to close trail after trail as much of the goodwill they'd built up over two decades evaporated. One good did come from the melee, however. René Brunelle, the then Minister of Lands and Forests, suggested that rather than rely on the government to acquire rights-of-way, the association should purchase them itself. It would take time for this to happen, meanwhile, the Bruce Trail Association took cover by identifying itself as a hiking group as opposed to a conservation organization.

Opposition didn't let up as community meeting after open house turned nasty. Those in favour of protecting the escarpment worried their support wouldn't counter the threats and intimidation. Proponents' worst fears seemed to come to pass when the majority of the 17 commissioners capitulated. In 1979, they voted to reduce the protected area of more than half a million hectares by two-thirds. Was this the beginning of the end? In 1984, Lowes resigned from the agency stating, "I'm protesting the failure of the NEC [Niagara Escarpment Commission] to carry out its mandate of protecting and preserving the escarpment." In the end, the commissioners prevailed. It took a dozen years; it wasn't perfect, and controversy about the bureaucratic agency continues. But in 1985, Ontario's Cabinet approved the Niagara Escarpment Plan. Canada had a precedent-setting, environmentally based land-use plan.

Further protection came in 1990, when the Niagara Escarpment planning area became a biosphere recognized by the United Nations Educational, Scientific and Cultural Organization (UNESCO). Encompassing nearly two hundred thousand hectares (the same area as is covered by the plan), it has the highest level of ecological diversity among Canada's 19 biospheres, including some three hundred species of birds, 55 mammals, 36 reptiles and amphibians, 90 fish and one hundred types of special-interest flora. Then in 2005, it received another layer of defence when it was folded into Ontario's Greater Golden Horseshoe Greenbelt.

History proves the BT requires every safeguard awarded the Niagara Escarpment. At a meeting in 1978, the Liberal MPP for Grey-Bruce, Eddie Sargent, said, "We could be the boom area of Canada if you people (the commissioners) would get the hell out of here and let us run our own show." Since that time, Southern Ontario has become the "boom area of Canada," despite the plan. Meanwhile, untold hectares of the Niagara Escarpment bordering those within the planning area — the lands that were once included — have been sold by those same let-us-run-our-own-show landowners to developers and aggregate operators. One of the latest is in my backyard.

Cataract is a hamlet within the Niagara Escarpment Plan's boundaries, but the land immediately to the north and west lies outside this protection. This is where Votorantim, a Brazilian giant that earned US$22.3 billion in 2021 revenues and boasts 34,000 employees worldwide, has amassed almost three hundred hectares of escarpment land where it wants to blast a seven-story-deep chasm to mine dolostone. It's a story that repeats itself along the length of Ontario's geography of hope.

The brave souls who saw the Niagara Escarpment protection through had foresight and perseverance. We need to thank them, but more importantly, we must keep their vision alive. In 1968, Lowes told an audience at the Niagara Escarpment Conference, "The simplicity of our request is astounding! We just want a strip of land that will be left alone." The battle between "development" and nature along the escarpment has intensified since the BT came into being more than 50 years ago. My childhood neighbour's century stone farmhouse still stands, but the fields where green timothy and alfalfa grew have been stripped of their topsoil and robbed of their aggregates. Someday, bulldozers will likely knock down the farmhouse too. Miners will strip away the last vestiges of grey gold deposited by glaciers twelve thousand years ago. Will the owners of my childhood home, Woodrising, be next to trade nature for cold cash just as all the landowners within Votorantim's three hundred hectares did? Despite the heroes — those landowners who have not sold out — nature is not safe when rich corporations tempt private landowners. Threats to the Niagara Escarpment put the BT at risk too. We all lose as development chips away at Ontario's ribbon of wilderness. The flora and fauna may have no way to fight back, but we have tools at hand — and foot. A good start is by walking — and loving — the BT.

≈

Despite my early morning start from the Winona Conservation Area and the filtering sunlight, I didn't have the same walk-forever feeling as when I'd left Jordan. The forest was still in a soft-green stage, the trilliums were showing off and I startled a white-tailed deer. But I couldn't ignore the industrial hum coming at me from Stoney Creek and the highway's drone. In stark contrast to just a few days earlier, I found myself tracking where I was in relation to the Devil's Punch Bowl, my turn-around point. The trail wasn't particularly hilly, but it was rocky and there were roots to contend with. Nothing out of the ordinary, but I couldn't shake my malaise.

White trillium
(Trillium grandiflorum)

Before noon, I arrived at the Devil's Punch Bowl Side Trail. Stopping to take my bearings, I looked up, way up at the cliffs — and climb — ahead. On top sat what I dubbed the "leaning cedar of Hamilton." I also spied the 10 metre tall metal cross erected in 1966 by Ontario Hydro. Fashioned from an old hydro pole, it's studded with 106 lightbulbs that light up the night sky.

Reluctantly, I slogged up the 1.2 kilometre climb. I put one leaden foot in front of another, stopping several times to catch my breath. What a difference from Monday's gallop up the staircase to Ball's Falls. Where were those negative ions when I needed them? When I "summitted," I delayed visiting the waterfall in favour of an early lunch at the Devil's Punch Bowl Market and Bakery (now sadly closed). I ploughed through a tasty Greek pasta salad, a bottle of iced tea and a delicious butter tart.

I made my way to the Punch Bowl where water crested Hamilton's third-highest, and arguably most impressive, cascade. (Tews Falls is the highest and the Lower Princess Falls is number two.) It plunged unimpeded for 37 metres, the equivalent of a 10-storey building. You don't need a lot of water to be impressed by this ribbon falls — a waterfall that is higher than it is wide. Estimated to have formed a million years ago, it's the result of melting ice and high water levels that carved out its unique punch bowl shape. No one seems to know for sure how it got its name, but I like the idea that it came from bootleggers who were doing devil's work by cooking up their moonshine in the woods nearby.

I walked to the base of the Devil's Punch Bowl cross. It soared overhead, forcing me to crane my neck to see to the top. Yet it was only a quarter as tall as the waterfall was high. I took advantage of the benches that surround the cross, before heading off on my 11.5 kilometre return trip along the Dofasco 2000 Trail. I let the sun warm me, hoping it would give reptilian me extra energy.

I hadn't expected much from the Dofasco 2000 Trail. What sounds more intriguing: a power-line-straight path named after a steel company or the Devil's Punch Bowl? Turns out, I couldn't have been more mistaken. The level trail alternates between wetlands and forests, and just when I thought it was becoming monotonous, the Hamilton Conservation Authority threw in a treat for the boardwalk-lover in me. Two kilometres of raised wooden platform through the Vinemont South Swamp. I love the word swamp. It conjures up rich earthy smells, slithering critters and moonshine. Could this be where those bootleggers brewed their devilish concoction? While swamp doesn't sound like a technical term, it's the name given to one of five types of wetlands. The other four are bog, fen, shallow open-water wetland (sometimes called a slough, another word I like) and marsh. The main difference between a swamp and a marsh is that swamps have trees while marshes have reeds, rushes and sedges.

The boardwalk ushered me through a landscape that is generally inaccessible without hip waders, a shellacking of bug spray and the risk of bloodsuckers. The afternoon sun had a summer-like intensity, so I ambled along in its warmth listening to the birds and frogs, eventually finding that space where I'd been on my previous hike. Regretfully, I arrived at the abrupt end to the Dofasco 2000 Trail at Eleventh Road — the link back to the BT and my car. Following it for a kilometre amid zooming cars wasn't ideal, but after more than seven hours and 23 kilometres, I was relaxed, pleasantly beat and able to shut out the din.

Day 7

FOUR FALLS / KING'S FOREST

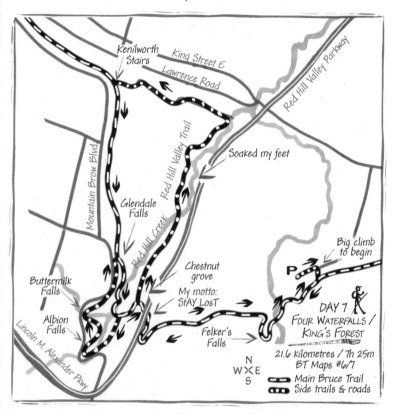

Kenilworth Stairs

King Street E

Lawrence Road

Red Hill Valley Parkway

Red Hill Valley Trail

Mountain Brow Blvd

Soaked my feet

Glendale Falls

Red Hill Creek

Big climb to begin

P

Chestnut grove

Buttermilk Falls

My motto: StAY LosT

DAY 7
FOUR WATERFALLS /
KING'S FOREST

Albion Falls

Felker's Falls

Lincoln M. Alexander Pkwy

21.6 kilometres / 7h 25m
BT Maps #6/7

N
W E
S

▬▬ Main Bruce Trail
▬▬ Side trails & roads

FIELD NOTES

START TIME: 7:25 a.m., Saturday, May 14, 2022

TRAILHEAD WEATHER: sunny and hot

DISTANCE: 21.6 km

ELAPSED TIME: 7h 25m

BT SECTION: Iroquoia

BT MAP: #6/7

MAIN BT WALKED: 22.0 km to 29.4 km

ASCENT: 903 m / **DESCENT:** 940 m

SIDE TRAILS: Veevers Park Side Trail, Red Hill Valley Trail, Kingsview Drive Side Trail, Kenilworth Drive Side Trail, Mountain Brow Side Trail

FLORA/FAUNA OF NOTE: mallards (*Anas platyrhynchos*), horse chestnuts (*Aesculus hippocastanum*)

In which I dispute Hamilton's world's-waterfall-capital claim before lamenting the loss of my motto: Stay Lost!, rail at a parkway and admire Fred Flintstone's handiwork.

There was no easing into today's hike. The trail went straight up the escarpment from Hamilton's Veevers Park. Once on top, however, I enjoyed the filtered sunshine in a wonderful forest on another spectacular morning. Yesterday's malaise seemed to be in abeyance.

My plan was to visit four waterfalls. Hamilton advertises itself as "the waterfall capital of the world." A bit cheeky don't you think? Maybe the steel capital, or home to the Tiger Cats, but waterfall capital? I don't think so. Then I checked it out. According to the Smithsonian in Washington, DC, Hamilton has 156 waterfalls within its limits, which is more than any other city in the world. Yesterday, I'd admired the Punch Bowl; today, I'd visit four more: Felker's, Glendale, Albion and Buttermilk. None of them are as tall as the Punch Bowl, but we're still talking five-storey-high waterfalls — ones that would break your bones if you were to accidentally go over.

I'd been to Felker's before, but as I stood admiring it this time, I thought, *I don't remember Felker's Falls being this spectacular.* It's a 22 metre high, terraced ribbon falls. Water slid over the edge, landing on one terrace before kissing the next rocky ledge below. Down and down to the deep shaded canyon. I realized that the other times I'd visited Felker's, I'd viewed it from across Davis Creek. This was undoubtedly Felker's better side.

Two kilometres later, I stopped by the modest 3.3 metre high Lower Glendale Falls at the Kingsview Drive Side Trail. Soon afterwards, the trail popped me out onto Old Mud Street, which was abandoned when they opened the hotly protested Red Hill Valley Parkway in 2007. First Nations and environmental groups lost their battle to keep the freeway out of the ecologically significant valley, despite it being within the Niagara Escarpment Plan area, part of the UNESCO Biosphere and within the Greenbelt. Not for the first time, nor the last, "development" trumped nature. I followed the old road down a slope under the parkway, passing between concrete pylons covered in layers of mindless graffiti. I was on the lookout for a more insightful message I'd seen years earlier. It read: "Stay lost," and it had become my motto. Sadly, it had been painted over by "Zoom" or "Bust" or some unremarkable scribble. On the other side of the underpass, a pair of mallards preened themselves in the sunshine, enjoying a small pond, seemingly unfazed by the traffic so close at hand. But I lamented the loss to nature and seethed at the choice of the name: Red Hill Valley *Parkway*. It reminded me of the ongoing battle at home over plans to build a superhighway, dubbed "the 413" that would cut across the bottom of Caledon.

Past the pond there was a small grove of horse chestnut trees, not to be confused with the American or sweet chestnuts I'd wished I'd seen in Queenston. Horse chestnuts have large leaves comprising five leaflets that fan out like the jolly green giant's hand. In spring, fantastic pink or white blossoms perch like miniature Christmas trees at the end of each branch. While both varieties bear nuts that are spit-polished brown after being removed from their outer spiny shells, American chestnuts have single leaves and long-legged blossoms. More importantly, American chestnuts are good to eat whereas horse chestnuts make you ill.

Carrying on, I left the BT, picking up the Red Hill Valley Trail. Crossing over Red Hill Creek several times, I walked through a marsh (not to be confused with a swamp) pleased to see efforts to rehabilitate the valley, both by planting native species and releasing Atlantic salmon into the creek. It was hot, but pleasant despite the not-so-distant freeway, so I stopped at the edge of the stream, pulled off my sandals and soaked my feet in the cool water. I resisted the temptation to have a nap.

To link back to the BT, I walked along a labyrinth of suburban streets in an East End neighbourhood called Rosedale until I came to the Kenilworth Drive Side Trail. It climbs part way up the Kenilworth Stairs, one of five city-built escarpment staircases in Hamilton. (There are two other more rustic sets of stairs.) The Kenilworth Stairs are solidly built, have two lanes, 387 stairs and a difficulty rating of three to four out of five, making them a moderately difficult climb according to Greg Lenko, a Hamilton-based fitness coach. The toughest are the Wentworth Stairs (498 stairs with a rating of five), and the least challenging, but hardly easy, James Street Stairs (227 stairs with a rating of one to two). Hamiltonians clearly take their escarpment staircases seriously.

The BT crosses the Kenilworth Stairs midway up, so I turned left to follow its white blazes and begin my return journey, secretly relieved for this excuse to cut my climb short. The BT traversed the escarpment through a mature forest that passed by one of the more rustic escarpment stairs. It looked as though Fred Flintstone had had a hand in building them. I bypassed the first turn-off to the Mountain Brow Side Trail, then picked up the second to follow the 2.8 kilometre loop that offers views of both Albion and Buttermilk falls. Until I viewed Felker's that morning, I'd thought Albion Falls was my favourite. Seeing Albion again, I realized it was a toss-up between the two. At 19 metres, Albion Falls isn't as high as Felker's (22 metres), but it's a classic cascading falls, meaning it's about as wide as it is high, and drops more regularly than a terraced falls. It seemed meatier, more powerful.

Then it was around the waterfall's bowl and into a parking area where I stopped at the viewing platform for one more look. Three young female bylaw officers came by wearing smart matching uniforms. Their job was to keep order in the park. "It's mostly education," one told me. "People don't know the rules. When I tell them they can't have a barbeque on the trail, they claim they didn't know it wasn't allowed." Mostly, the officers deal with people who climb the fence to get a closer look at the waterfalls. "Do many people do that?" I asked. "Yesterday, we had six, but the record is 12 in one day," she explained. We chatted a bit longer and then the quietest of the officers complimented me on my hiking attire. "So well prepared," she said. "Do you like wearing uniforms?" I asked. "Oh yes," they chimed in unison, throwing their shoulders back and posing like models on a runway.

Farther along, I saw Buttermilk Falls, the fourth of the day. It's hard to get a good look at this 23 metre high terraced ribbon falls that apparently came by its name because the land around it was once a farm. From here, I climbed back down into the valley where I followed the main BT back to my car. Enroute, I enjoyed a second look at both Glendale and Felker's, making it a six-pack waterfall day.

Day 8

DUNDAS VALLEY / JORDAN STATE OF MIND

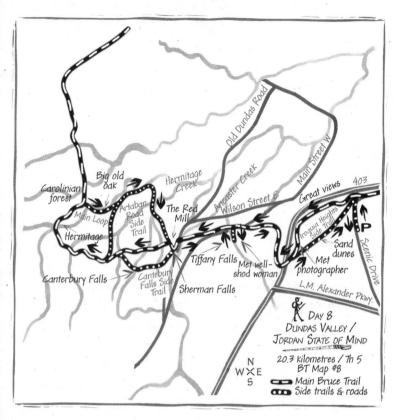

Carolinian forest

Big old oak

Hermitage Creek

Old Dundas Road

Ancaster Creek

Main Street W

Great views

403

Main Loop

Artaban Road Side Trail

The Red Mill

Wilson Street E

Iroquoia Heights Side Trail

Scenic Drive

P

Sand dunes

Met photographer

Hermitage

Canterbury Falls

Canterbury Falls Side Trail

Tiffany Falls

Met well-shod woman

Sherman Falls

L.M. Alexander Pkwy

Day 8
Dundas Valley /
Jordan State of Mind

20.3 kilometres / 7h 5
BT Map #8

Main Bruce Trail
Side trails & roads

N W E S

FIELD NOTES

START TIME: 7:30 a.m., Sunday, May 15, 2022

TRAILHEAD WEATHER: sunny and really hot

DISTANCE: 20.3 km

ELAPSED TIME: 7h 5m

BT SECTION: Iroquoia

BT MAP: #8

MAIN BT WALKED: 40.5 km to 51.5 km

ASCENT: 886 m / **DESCENT:** 907 m

SIDE TRAILS: Tiffany Falls Side Trail, Main Loop, Artaban Road Side Trail, Iroquoia Heights Side Trail

FLORA/FAUNA OF NOTE: white oak (*Quercus alba* L.)

*In which good footwear trumps short shorts at
Tiffany Falls before Sherman is Sherman-like,
Canterbury is un–Canterbury-like, a white oak
survives and Frank Sinatra croons a tune.*

Sunday morning on another gorgeous sunny day. What else
would I want to be doing? And where else would I want to
start the day's hike but by walking through a mature maple and
oak forest with the early-hour sunshine playing hide and seek
in the trees? The trail followed the edge of a near-cliff overlooking Hamilton — and, sadly, Highway 403. But somehow
the noise didn't get under my skin as it had earlier in the week.

Unseasonably high temperatures (30+ degrees Celsius)
had brought spring to an abrupt end. The most stubborn
buds had burst into leaves like popcorn on a hot burner.
The birds had either found their mates or become exhausted
trying, and the trilliums were drooping, seemingly in need
of a tall glass of cold water. I, on the other hand, whose definition of a perfect day is one where the butter has already
melted in the butter dish by 7 a.m., was in my element. All
that warmth had thawed the last throes of winter in the
deepest crevasses in my bones. I felt lithe, agile.

The trail left the forest and passed through an open meadow where I came across an older man carrying a camera. His giant lens gave him away as a birder. "Have you had any luck?" I asked, nodding at his camera. Delighted by my question, he had me look through his viewfinder. I made out a bald eagle flying overhead, its curved talons wrapped around a small animal, likely a rabbit. Since I was carrying a notebook, he wondered if I was a birder too. "No," I said. "I'm just taking notes for a writing project." Pondering my reply, he told me, "My wife died four years ago. This is my new reality." I wasn't too sure how to respond, so I gave him my condolences and went on my way, hoping he was finding solace in the early morning sunshine.

≈

I took the overpass over Highway 403 and shortly afterwards picked up the Tiffany Falls Side Trail. As I was now in the lee of the escarpment, the sun was only catching the tops of the trees. Down below where I walked, it was gloomy and dank. I crossed a wooden pedestrian bridge where the conservation authority had stapled black plastic mesh to the wooden railings. A sign read, "For your safety: Remain on gravel path and viewing platform." Had I not been chatting with those bylaw officers, I would have thought these precautions were overkill; now I wasn't so sure.

Later, someone told me a young woman had fallen off the bridge and died, hence the mesh. It turned out my informant had the story muddled. What happened was that in 2015, a 23-year-old nurse had been crushed while viewing Tiffany Falls when a large branch from an old oak tree suddenly let go. A tragedy for sure and one that left her father searching for answers. I can't imagine what he went through, and I understand why the conservation authority cut down the oak tree despite its innocence, but it's unreasonable, in fact impossible, to remove all risks. And who would want to live in such a world anyway? A year before this tragic accident, a young boy was similarly killed while on a school trip in Hamilton's Royal Botanical Gardens. The ensuing coroner's inquest made 18 recommendations, including that the Royal Botanical Gardens hire an arborist to monitor its 27 kilometres of trails — *on a daily basis*. Concerns about liability and the extreme steps taken to avoid litigation are destroying much of our enjoyment of the natural world in Canada. I'm not sure how we can change this trend and require people to take responsibility for themselves. If a tree falls on me as I walk along the BT, that's bad luck, not someone's fault.

My irritation was short-lived for there before me was Tiffany Falls. Twenty-two metres high and only six metres wide, this elegant ribbon falls was named after Oliver Tiffany, a much-loved Ancaster doctor who had a rural practice for 40 years before dying in 1835.

Returning to the main BT, I met two young women, one was dressed in a bikini top, denim short shorts and sturdy boots. You know, a typical BT hiker. I told her that I was going to say something that would make her smile. "Because I hike a lot," I said, "people often ask me what to wear when out on the trails." Despite my assurance, I could see her bristle. I continued. "While I wouldn't recommend a bikini top and short shorts, what's critical is what people put on their feet. And you," I pointed out, "are wearing excellent footwear. Congratulations." Her bristles turned to feathers, and this tough young woman gave me an enormous smile. I didn't have the heart to warn her of ticks, Lyme disease and poison ivy. One step at a time.

Next up was a waterfall I'd wanted to visit for some time. For the cover of each of my hiking guides, I commission a painting by a local artist. *Sherman Falls*, painted by Robert Ross (no relation), adorns the front of *Hamilton & Area Hikes*. In having one of Ross's paintings, I'm in illustrious company. King Charles has one, as does Bill Clinton. At 17 metres, Sherman Falls is not as high as some others, but at eight metres across, it seemed massive. It was named after the Sherman brothers who started Dofasco, one of Hamilton's pair of competing steel producers.

Next up was Canterbury Falls. As I admired it, I thought anywhere else in Southern Ontario it would be a showstopper. At nine metres in height, it lacks the overwhelming splendour of its British namesake, Canterbury Cathedral, but I liked its modesty. I wondered what possessed the reputedly dour Anglican Church, which owned the surrounding land, to name it after a UNESCO World Heritage Site, ranking up there with the Taj Mahal, the Giza pyramids and Chichén Itzá.

Past Canterbury Falls, the rocks changed to the moss-covered ones I like so much. They tumbled one over another creating rocky mounds, reminding me of the terrain at home in the Forks of the Credit — and making me homesick. I was only on day eight of my BT journey, not a quarter of the way to Tobermory. For the most part, I like walking solo, but there are times when it's lonely, especially given my dog, Frida, was still absent. My solitude made me wonder: *Where is everyone?* It was 10 a.m. on a gorgeous day in May. If nature had a personality, surely they would want people to admire their mastery of trees and flowers and mossy rocks — and not just gawk at waterfalls. While solitude was great, I recognized the trail needed more traffic. I knew the more people who hiked it and fell in love with it, the more likely we could hold off inappropriate development.

Continuing past Tiffany Falls with love on my mind, I recalled singer/songwriter Sarah Harmer's prophetic words in the foreword to my *Halton Hikes* guide. She wrote, "Forests, grasslands and waterways aren't always as protected as we might think. Get out there and fall in love with the landscapes. They may need you to step up for them one day." Raised on the Niagara Escarpment near Mount Nemo, Harmer, like me, has her childhood home buried deeply in her DNA. In 2006, along with her band, Harmer embarked on a "I Love the Escarpment" tour. They walked the BT, and along the way, they put on concerts to raise awareness and encourage people to protect Southern Ontario's backbone. I attended their show, which rocked, knocking the dust out of the walls of the Mono Cliffs Inn in Mono Centre. Harmer's resulting music DVD, *Escarpment Blues*, won a JUNO in 2007. Her battle against aggregate mining continues through the Reform Gravel Mining Coalition and CORE: Conserving our Rural Ecosystems.

Continuing through the Dundas Valley Conservation Area, I came to the ruins of what had been Ancaster's most prestigious estate: The Hermitage. Born in Scotland, George Gordon Browne Leith and his family created this working farm, comprising an enormous stone house and a multitude of outbuildings, including a laundry room, nursery, carriage house, barns and more. Built in the late 1850s, it met the fate so common in earlier times: fire destroyed it in 1934. Sulphur Creek runs through the estate. Just off the trail there's a stone fountain where rotten-egg-smelling water gushes through a valve. A plaque explains there was once a hotel and spa nearby. People seeking the therapeutic properties of the spring's mineral water came to bathe in and even drink it. The well-documented anti-bacterial and anti-fungal properties of mineral water high in sulphur attract those seeking its therapeutic benefits. Yet, on its website, the conservation authority refers to the stream's healing properties in the past tense: "... once thought to have curative properties ..." I wondered, *When did Sulphur Creek's therapeutic properties go away, and where did they escape to?*

Leaving the main BT, I followed the Main Loop. It crossed Sulphur Creek, leading me out of the valley past an enormous white oak that I'd been looking forward to revisiting. I'd passed by it about four years earlier during a spongy moth (gypsy moth) outbreak. Back then, this enormous 150-year-old landmark had been stripped of its leaves. Unfamiliar with spongy moths, I thought the old timer was dead. Sometime later, we experienced a similar outbreak in Caledon. Though most trees survive an infestation, I was relieved to see for myself that this beauty had made it. I gave her a pat and carried on.

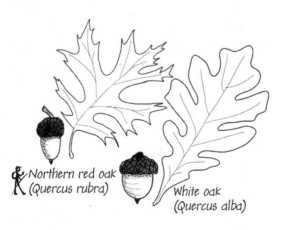

Northern red oak (Quercus rubra)

White oak (Quercus alba)

The Artaban Road Side Trail took me back to the main BT where I stopped to rest on a shaded bench. Three consecutive days of 20-plus-kilometre hikes had worked their magic. Thinking back to my glorious walk from Jordan Station to Ball's Falls, I recalled that song. You know the one. I could hear Sinatra crooning it:

. . . I'm just wandering through the Escarpment's pines.
I'm in a, I'm in a, I'm in a Jor-dan state of mind.

Day 9

BORER'S FALLS / ROCK CHAPEL / ROYAL BOTANICAL GARDENS

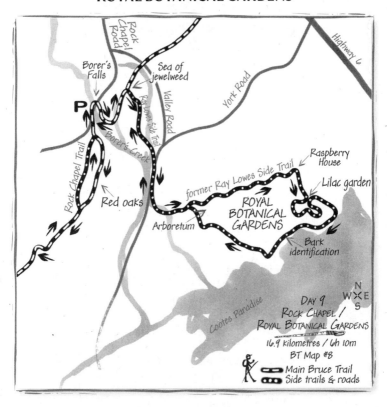

FIELD NOTES

START TIME: 8:30 a.m., Monday, May 16, 2022

TRAILHEAD WEATHER: car-stopping rain then misty

DISTANCE: 16.9 km

ELAPSED TIME: 6h 10m

BT SECTION: Iroquoia

BT MAP: #8

MAIN BT WALKED: 59.8 km to 63.8 km

ASCENT: 655 m / **DESCENT:** 667 m

SIDE TRAILS: Ray Lowes Side Trail, Rock Chapel Trail

FLORA/FAUNA OF NOTE: lilacs (*Syringa*), jewelweed (*Impatiens capensis*), snakebranch Norway spruce (*Picea abies* f. *virgata*), dawn redwood (*Metasequoia glyptostroboides*), bald cypress (*Taxodium distichum*), magnolias (*Magnolia acuminata*), black cherry (*Prunus serotina*), white birch (*Betula papyrifera*), shagbark hickory (*Carya ovata*), black locust (*Robinia pseudoacacia*), white oak (*Quercus alba* L.), red oak (*Quercus rubra*), apples (*Malus pumila*), pears (*Pyrus communis*)

*In which philandering oxygen molecules hook up
like hippies at Woodstock and muddy-tasting river fish
come clean before Ray Lowes lends Nike its slogan and
sweet-smelling singles outdo the doubles.*

The forecast was for a full day of rain, so I contemplated staying put and catching up on my notes. But hiking in the wet stuff is okay if it's not torrential. And after days of hot sunshine, the change would be welcome. Then I looked out the window. The sky was the angry shade of purple that spelled downpour. Perhaps foolishly, off I drove to the Rock Chapel parking lot anyway. As I pulled in, the heavens let loose. Fork lightning split the bruised horizon. It rained so hard I may well have been parked under Sherman Falls.

After 20 minutes, the deluge abated, so I got out of my car and was greeted not by rain but by the metallic smell of ozone that accompanies an electrical storm. When lightning flashes, it splits atmospheric molecules, releasing free radicals that, like hippies at Woodstock, hook up with other friendly molecules. Sometimes they form threesomes, becoming ozone (O_3 vs. more stable oxygen, O_2). In other instances, these free radicals attach to coquettish pollutants, thereby neutralizing them like a good marriage sometimes tames a philandering mate. In this way, scientists believe lightning removes up to 10 percent of the atmosphere's contaminants.

The main BT passes through Rock Chapel, which comprises the upper section of the Royal Botanical Gardens. Below my perch atop a dramatic cliff, McMaster University came into and out of view as a veil of mist drifted down the valley that separated us. I noticed another distinct post-rain odour: the earthy one that is produced by soil bacteria called streptomyces. Rain pushes a chemical called geosmin into the air and voilà, it smells like spring. Much as I love its scent, a whiff of geosmin is a canary in a coal mine for fruit flies. These insects avoid over-ripe fruit if they detect geosmin since it indicates the presence of pathogens that can harm them. It's also the compound that makes river fish taste "muddy," grapes seem to be "off" and water in need of filtering. Humans sense geosmin in concentrations that defy belief: we are put off if there are 50 drops in an Olympic-sized swimming pool.

The trail was muddy and puddled. The cloudy red water that rushed alongside me in Borer's Creek gave away the presence of Queenston shale, the brick-red layer that underlies the Niagara Escarpment. I live near the Cheltenham Badlands where over-grazing eroded the land into red whalebacks striped with bands of greenish shale. As kids, we called them the clay banks, and it turns out that in geological lingo, we were right. Clay is the most plentiful compound found in shale, a common type of rock that splits into thin layers — a property known as fissility.

Given we were near Hamilton, there was — predictably — a waterfall. Borer's Falls is a 10 m high plunging or curtain waterfall, one that falls unimpeded for a time. Borer's Falls gushed with the morning's precipitation. I took a picture of it framed by a pair of lilac bushes — one purple, the other white. I liked the contrast between the sweet blooms and the creek's bullish flow. Then it was down the cliff face through dense forest. I scrambled over greasy rocks, thankful I had a hiking pole. Near the base of the escarpment, I waded into a sea of verdant jewelweed. It looked as though someone had doctored it as a photographer might tint a photograph. Could its vividness be due to nitrogen released by the lightning? It seems not. Instead, high concentrations of chlorophyll, a green pigment essential to photosynthesis, is responsible — chlorophyll in diffuse morning light: a photographer's dream.

I picked up the Ray Lowes Side Trail and walked into the Royal Botanical Gardens' arboretum and Rasberry House (built in 1860 by William Rasberry), the BT's headquarters from 1983 until the organization outgrew the space and moved to Dundas some 30 years later. Lowes, it seems, inspired Nike. His favourite line ended with "Let's do it," and began, more often than not, with: "To hell with the feasibility study . . ." Of the team of four original BT founders, Lowes was the visionary. Norman Pearson, the planner, wrote in his book that Lowes dreamed of a walking trail extending the length of Ontario from the Niagara Peninsula to Tobermory on the Bruce Peninsula. John Muir (1838–1914), father of the Sierra Club, inspired Lowes. While living in Ontario, this pioneering naturalist explored the Niagara Escarpment. Muir's legacy is tainted by his derogatory comments about Black and Indigenous people. But, according to biographer Donald Worster, who wrote *A Passion for Nature: The Life of John Muir*, he made strides on his mission of "saving the American soul from total surrender to materialism." Meanwhile Lowes's gift was his doggedness. He couldn't let go of his dream. According to trail historian David E. Tyson,

Lowes wrote to Walter Tovell, the then president of the Federation of Ontario Naturalists, "There comes a time when an idea just about buzzes around in one's head so persistently that it must be let out — maybe its time has come — in any case my head can no longer contain it and so, for better or for worse, I am passing it along to you."

Three years later, in 1963, when the Bruce Trail Association (now Conservancy) was incorporated, Lowes was its secretary, a role he held for 10 years until he was named the foundation's honorary president. Considered the Father of the Bruce Trail, Lowes referred to the trail as his "geography of hope for Ontario." In a 1965 article in *Maclean's* magazine, Lowes told journalist Fred Bodsworth, "I got tired of walking into 'no trespassing' signs whenever I tried to hike in the country." Bodsworth embraced the dream. In the same article, he wrote, "There is a sense of freedom, in this age of 'no trespassing' signs and superhighways, in just walking a trail that one knows stretches on and on." Lowes may have been a dreamer, but even he would be impressed by how much hope his trail engenders in the BT's 1,500 volunteers and almost 13,000 members. The organization received over $15 million in donations in 2021–22. Over 80 percent of these funds were used to acquire land, conserve it and to maintain the trail.

Down I slipped and slithered, walking pole firmly in hand, then along York Road, under the railway bridge and back into the 980 hectare Royal Botanical Gardens. It comprises five cultivated gardens, has 27 kilometres of trails, 50 species at risk, over 2,500 plant types and some 231,000 individual plants — but who's counting? Sadly, the section of the Ray Lowes Side Trail that connects York Road to Rasberry House has been closed since I walked it. It's lamentable the Royal Botanical Gardens had to take this step to prevent visitors from using the BT to avoid paying an entrance fee. It's sadly ironic that "No Trespassing" signs would soon be erected on the trail named after the man who was inspired to create the BT especially because of these signs.

Despite the forecast, the day was soft and mostly dry. Everything looked freshly washed. I wandered through some of the 136 species of conifers. In addition to Ontario's 12 native species, I spied a snakebranch Norway spruce, a dawn redwood and a bald cypress, among dozens of others. I stopped for a short break on a picnic table by Rasberry House, hoping there might be a café where I could get a cup of coffee. No luck. When Charley, one of the arborists happened by, he recommended I visit the lilac garden.

Common lilac
(Syringa vulgaris)

What a display. The Royal Botanical Gardens, famous for their collection of nine hundred lilac bushes, offers guided walks in May when Ontario's most iconic, though non-native, Syringas are blooming. One wasn't scheduled, so I wandered about on my own, seeking the knowledge of two plant interpreters who were on site. The lilac garden is organized in a series of "rooms," each featuring variously coloured cultivars

— from white, through mauve to deep purple — with either single or double blooms. While the gardens have nine hundred lilac plants, they *only* have six hundred different cultivars of the two thousand that exist worldwide. This makes their collection the most varied, though not the largest, in the world. Another contribution is the McMaster centennial — a white, double-flowered French hybrid (*Syringa vulgaris*) bred on-site and released in 1987 to commemorate the university's one hundredth anniversary.

After wandering through the lilacs regularly putting nose to bloom (the single blooms have more fragrance than the doubles), I visited the magnolias. They were past their prime but, if possible, were even more sensational than the lilacs. The difference between the magnolias I'd seen all through the Niagara Peninsula and the ones back home reminded me of the Christmas trees I'd grown up with versus Charlie Brown's. The trail hugged Hamilton Harbour before it narrowed into western Lake Ontario's only remaining marsh. Known as Cootes Paradise, it was named after a British naval officer, Captain Thomas Coote who hunted and fished there in the 1780s. I came across a unique self-guided tour. It involved identifying trees by their bark. I knew a few of them: black cherry, white birch and shagbark hickory. But the bark of honey locust and white oak were unfamiliar.

I looped back to York Road and retraced my way up the escarpment, admiring the now clear view of McMaster University across the broad valley. Not ready to end my hike, I followed the BT for another two kilometres through a forest dominated by white and red oaks. Then I looped back along the Rock Chapel Trail through an orchard of apple and pear trees, pleased I'd not let the threat of rain keep me inside organizing my notes.

Day 10

SMOKEY HOLLOW / WATERDOWN

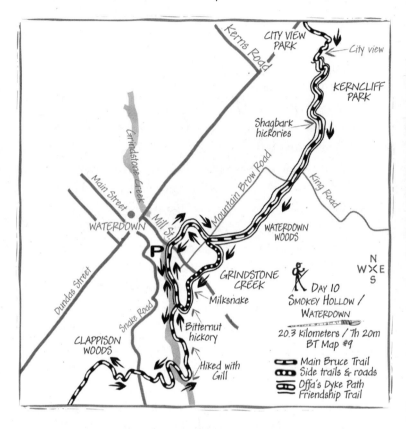

City view

CITY VIEW PARK

KERNCLIFF PARK

Kerns Road

Shagbark hickories

Grindstone Creek

Main Street

Mill St.

WATERDOWN

Mountain Brow Road

King Road

WATERDOWN WOODS

Dundas Street

P

GRINDSTONE CREEK

Milksnake

Snake Road

Bitternut hickory

CLAPPISON WOODS

Hiked with Gill

N W×E S

Day 10 Smokey Hollow / Waterdown
20.3 kilometers / 7h 20m
BT Map #9

Main Bruce Trail
Side trails & roads
Offa's Dyke Path
Friendship Trail

FIELD NOTES

START TIME: 8:30 a.m., Tuesday, May 17, 2022

TRAILHEAD WEATHER: sunny, cool

DISTANCE: 20.3 km

ELAPSED TIME: 7h 20m

BT SECTION: Iroquoia

BT MAP: #9

MAIN BT WALKED: 67.5 km to 76.5 km

ASCENT: 987 m / **DESCENT:** 999 m

SIDE TRAILS: McNally Side Trail, Norman Pearson Side Trail

FLORA/FAUNA OF NOTE: wood anemone (*Anemone quinquefolia*), wild geranium (*Geranium maculatum*), wild roses (*Rosa acicularis*), bitternut hickory (*Carya cordiformis*), eastern milksnake (*Lampropeltis triangulum*), rose-breasted grosbeak (*Pheucticus ludovicianus*)

In which a jovial BT work party rescues the damsels before we remember the problem with in-and-out hikes lurks in our genes, and I recognize the BT founders' complementary skills.

For the first time on this journey, I had company. It rumpled my routine. I'm used to getting up when I wake up, having coffee and heading off to the trailhead at whatever time that may be. This morning, I'd arranged to meet Gill Stead at the trailhead at 8:30 a.m. Gill has designed all my hiking guides. She's a talented artist and a good friend. Predictably, I was raring to go by 7 a.m. To fill in the time, I did what I never do pre-hike: I checked my emails. I don't like doing this since I never know what I might find: a notice from the tax man, an unexpected bill. I hadn't totally avoided the world while on my loopy BT hike, but I put it off until evening. There weren't any disturbing messages, but reading them put me into a work mode, nonetheless. When I hit the road, I'd left ample time to get to our meeting spot, but then my GPS took me to the wrong place. Then I missed a turn. Then, as I pulled into the parking lot in Smokey Hollow with Gill behind me, a man blocked our way, informing us the parking lot was reserved for a BT work party. He explained they were replacing some steps and suggested we hike elsewhere. This was not how I'd envisioned the day. Would I find "Jordan"?

Fortunately, we sorted it out. The work party was a jovial gang, delighted to assist two maidens through the construction zone. We set off with their encouragement, "Have a great hike," they chimed. I don't remember much about the first kilometre. I know Grindstone Creek roared downstream alongside us dropping from rocky ledge to rocky ledge. And I know we visited a waterfall. But between emails, my GPS, the construction and trying to keep up to Gill who was walking at a blazing pace, I don't recall many details. Fortunately, the oaks and maples; the wild geraniums and wood anemones; and, perhaps, Grindstone Creek's negative ions and Gill's banter did the trick. My head drifted out of the cyber-cloud and back to Earth.

Like so many Southern Ontario towns, Smokey Hollow was a hive of industrial activity in the 1800s. A larger, more robust Grindstone Creek provided power for "saw, grist and flour mills, a woollen mill, brass foundry, tanneries, rake, snaith, cradle, and basket factories," according to the Flamborough Archives and Historical Society. A "snaith," since you asked, is the handle of a scythe. The name Smokey Hollow came from all the smoke that emanated from all that industry, none of which remains today.

In typical BT fashion, rocks and roots littered the path as we climbed up and down, into and out of creek bottoms. The sun filtered through the trees and, thankfully, Gill eased her pace. We chatted, easy in our friendship. We'd seen each other through divorces and difficult relationships, moves and, of course, the long grinding process of putting together six hiking guides. It was fun·walking with company, especially someone I was comfortable with. When we ran into a group of women on a BT-organized hike led by a garrulous leader, we advised them of the construction ahead.

I'd set up the hike so that we'd follow the main BT for about five kilometres to the Rockcliffe Side Trail in Clappison Woods and then turn back, following the same route as we'd just walked. Most of the trail was new to both of us, so I hoped this would outweigh our seemingly deep-seated dislike of in-and-out routes. When it came time to turn back, Gill said, "I'm sure not looking forward to climbing back up those hills." *Ah*, I thought, *the dark side of an in-and-out hike.* But as is often the case — though not always — both climbs had only grown in Gill's, and my, imaginations.

We zoomed back, not sure what we'd find when we returned to the construction zone. But we needn't have been concerned; the crew was ready for us. Ever chivalrous, they not only helped us through, they'd left a passageway knowing we'd be returning. In no time, we were heading to the Copper Kettle Café in Waterdown for lunch — and a latte, of course.

Gill had to get home, so she dropped me in Kerncliff Park where the Offa's Dyke Path Bruce Trail Friendship Trail begins. The 285 kilometre Offa's Dyke Path follows an earthen bank that separates England from Wales in the same way Hadrian's Wall separates England from Scotland. The Welsh have their own Devil's Pulpit, and like its mate in the Forks of the Credit, it's a narrow pillar of limestone. Unlike Caledon's Devil's Pulpit, which derived its name from an Indigenous story of unrequited love, Offa's Dyke's version involves the devil who used the pulpit to tempt monks to abandon their Christian ways.

Its sister trail skirted the edge of a steep scarp. In the distance, the Burlington Skyway — the long, wind-ridden pair of bridges that carry vehicles across the tip of Lake Ontario from Burlington toward Niagara Falls — reminded me that "civilization" wasn't far away. I took a photo of an enormous five-trunked red oak that would take at least three people joining hands to reach around, before I arrived at the McNally Side Trail and then the Norman Pearson Side Trail.

In reading his book, I had been impressed by Pearson's keen awareness of the need to protect the Niagara Escarpment and his belief that a trail would help accomplish it. His certainty stemmed from his upbringing in England, where trails, he explained, "are very ancient rights, and jealously guarded." Pearson, who helped build the Pennine Way down the spine of his homeland, was a brilliant strategist. Based on the tone of his book, he was also an enthusiastic supporter, a positive guy and the planner needed to convert Lowes's "To hell with the feasibility study" approach into a campaign that could be implemented by doers like Philip Gosling. Pearson writes, "The model was the Appalachian Trail . . . We noted it took 15 years to create the Appalachian Trail, but we wanted to do this in less than seven years, for Canada's Centennial in 1967."

The Norman Pearson Side Trail follows a ridgetop before exiting onto a pretty back street in Waterdown. Here I took a photo of some street-side humour. A dog lover had erected a sign on a telephone pole. At the top there was an image of a dog centred in a green circle. Below, it read Dog Water. Below that was an arrow pointing to the ground where there normally would be a bowl of water. The funny part was that someone had placed a strip of pink tape diagonally across the sign and had written on it, "Closed for the season." I chuckled. The road disappeared into the forest where I came across wild geraniums in full bloom and a riot of roses that weren't showing off yet. The Norman Pearson Side Trail ended at the main BT, which I followed to the McNally Side Trail to complete the friendship trail. As I ambled out of Smokey Hollow through an open field, I came across a lovely Eastern milksnake lazily sunning itself. It didn't bother to move when I approached so I had a good look. Though not uncommon, they are a species "of concern." Urbanization, that bane in Pearson's side, is the primary reason for their declining numbers.

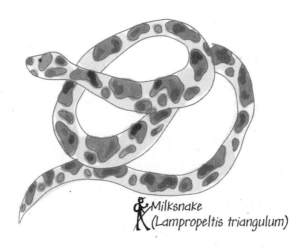

Milksnake
(Lampropeltis triangulum)

Farther along the trail, I spied a bitternut hickory, a BT heritage tree. While not unheard of farther north, it would become increasingly less likely that I would see one. Unlike shagbark hickories, its bark is unremarkable. Its nuts, however, live up to their bitter name as even squirrels only eat them when there are no other options.

Day 11

CRAWFORD LAKE TO RATTLESNAKE POINT

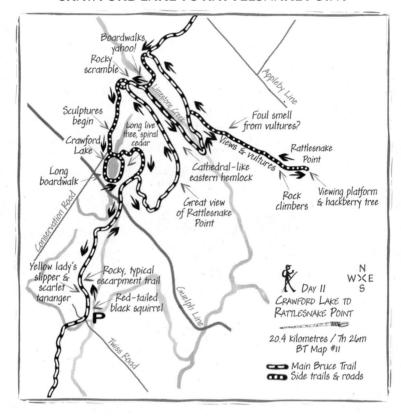

Boardwalks, yahoo!

Rocky scramble

Sculptures begin

Long live thee, spiral cedar

Crawford Lake

Long boardwalk

Limestone Creek

Foul smell from vultures?

Views & vultures

Rattlesnake Point

Cathedral-like eastern hemlock

Great view of Rattlesnake Point

Rock climbers

Viewing platform & hackberry tree

Appleby Line

Conservation Road

Yellow lady's slipper & scarlet tanager

Rocky, typical escarpment trail

Red-tailed black squirrel

Guelph Line

P

Twiss Road

N W E S

Day 11
Crawford Lake to
Rattlesnake Point

20.4 kilometres / 7h 26m
BT Map #11

⬤▬⬤ Main Bruce Trail
⬤▬⬤ Side trails & roads

FIELD NOTES

START TIME: 8:30 a.m., Friday, May 20, 2022

TRAILHEAD WEATHER: mist gave way to sunshine and wind

DISTANCE: 20.4 km

ELAPSED TIME: 7h 26m

BT SECTION: Iroquoia

BT MAP: #11

MAIN BT WALKED: 102.6 km to 111.9 km

ASCENT: 743 m / **DESCENT:** 732 m

SIDE TRAILS: Rattlesnake Point Side Trail, Leech Porter Side Trail, Canyon Bypass Side Trail, Crawford Lake Side Trail, Crawford Lake Trail, Hide and Seek Trail

FLORA/FAUNA OF NOTE: red-tailed black squirrel (*Sciurus carolinensis*), yellow lady's slipper (*Cypripedium parviflorum* var. *pubescens*), scarlet tanager (*Piranga olivacea*), eastern hemlocks (*Tsuga canadensis*), ancient cedars (*Thuja occidentalis* L.), common hackberry (*Celtis occidentalis*), marsh marigolds (*Caltha palustris*)

In which I learn silver foxes are melanistic red foxes,
panthers are melanistic leopards and black squirrels with
red tails are melanistic/erythristic grey ones before I look
out over a misfit river in a re-emergent valley and wave
farewell to my corkscrew comrade.

I'd walked most of this route when writing my *Halton
Hikes* guide six years earlier. I'd loved it then, especially the
Nassagaweya Canyon and the wood carvings of endangered
species around Crawford Lake, so I was looking forward to a
return visit. I picked up the main BT at Twiss Road, clamber-
ing over large slippery rocks along a cavern-like trail. The sun
hadn't penetrated yet, so it was dark, almost spooky. Luckily,
the rocks gave way to a wide trail through a mixed hardwood
forest before the boogeyman got me.

All concerns about monsters disappeared, however, when
I spotted my first yellow lady's slipper of the season. It's one
of four species of orchids that I've knowingly seen in Ontario
(yellow, pink, showy and broad-leaved helleborine), though
the province has 62 of Canada's 74 species of native orchids.
Who knows how many I've spied with no idea they were
orchids? In my defence, some have minute blooms that only
appear orchid-like under near microscopic scrutiny (e.g., the

Yellow lady's slipper
(*Cypripedium parviflorum*)

broad-leaved helleborine). I still recall the first time I saw a yellow lady's slipper. It was in the Forks of the Credit, and I couldn't believe my eyes. Its bulbous blooms seem too exotic to grow in staid Ontario.

Then a black squirrel with a red tail caught my eye. I knew black squirrels are the same species as grey ones. Their colouration is due to melanism, which creates black pigment. Similarly, silver foxes are melanistic red foxes, and black panthers are melanistic leopards. Some biologists label red-tailed black squirrels melanistic/erythristic grey squirrels. Melanistic, because of their black bodies, and erythristic, as it's a genetic mutation that results in their red tails. What a morning, because just then a male scarlet tanager flitted by. Their song is familiar, but seeing one is a treat because the bright-red males and olive-coloured females are shy.

From the Crawford Lake Conservation Area, I looked across the Nassagaweya Canyon toward the distant hump-back of Rattlesnake Point. In between, an uninterrupted expanse of maples, beeches, basswoods and a dozen other hardwood trees formed a riotous forest rich in texture and shades of green. Ontario's tulip trees, sassafras, sycamores and other Carolinian species were waning. Throughout my twenties and thirties, I lived in Calgary. While there, I covered Western Canada's battles over old-growth forests, such as BC's Carmanah Valley and Clayoquot Sound. I've visited the enormous Sitka spruce and Douglas firs that were central to those desperate fights. Yet it wasn't until I read about plans to clearcut a hardwood forest in Eastern Canada that my heart stopped. I realized that as much as those giants in the west impressed me, it was the trees I was looking at in the Nassagaweya Canyon that penetrated at my soul. They drew me back to Caledon.

In his discussion with *Outside* magazine, biologist, writer and ultramarathoner Bernd Heinrich says, "My new race in the last passage of my life is to learn to love more deeply." I wondered if in the more than two decades since I'd returned to Caledon, I'd loved the Niagara Escarpment enough.

The view was remarkable because for the first time since I'd left Queenston, it was unobstructed by buildings, highways or bridges. There weren't even any barns or farm fields. Just nature. I related to Bodworth's words in that *Maclean's* article about the freedom of walking along a trail that stretches on and on.

The path into the Nassagaweya Canyon bears the warning: Difficult Terrain Ahead. The route is so tricky the BT has added a bypass that descends more gradually into the valley. Nonetheless, I decided to risk life and limb. With an Indiana Jones swagger, I negotiated my day's second encounter with slick boulders. Two hundred metres later, I brushed imaginary sweat from my forehead muttering sarcastically, "Phew, I survived." Joking aside, I favour easier passages that avoid the escarpment's relentless rocks. Heaven knows I'll need them myself soon enough, but the ominous warning had the feel of a liability-conscious conservation authority. It seemed like overkill, but then I once again remembered the experience of those uniformed officers in the Albion Falls parking lot.

The canyon was as peaceful and beautiful as I recalled. Sunrays sparkled as they backlit towering lacey eastern hemlocks. The height of these trees relative to the narrowness of the canyon gave it a cathedral-like feeling, as though I was walking down an aisle toward "I do." Stopping to compare notes with a purposeful young woman walking toward me carrying hiking poles and a heavy backpack, I asked, "Where are you headed?" Rather than Queenston as I'd expected, she replied, "Everest Base Camp." Colleen was training for this arduous trek that she was doing in September. Impressed (though not tempted), I wished her luck. (Colleen made it, by the way.)

Too soon, I crossed Limestone Creek and began the gradual ascent. I recalled a wonderful walk along the clifftops following the Rattlesnake Point Side Trail, and the hike this time didn't disappoint. The day was now bright and sunny with puffy cumulous clouds. These clouds need heat to form, so they herald summer's arrival. A fresh wind kept the bugs away, and the temperature was perfect. I stopped at several of the lookouts — Buffalo Crag, Nelson, Pinnacle — to admire the view back across the canyon and asked myself: Is there anywhere else I'd rather be?

I stopped to chat with three rock climbers, all women about my age. They offered to give me a lesson, but it didn't seem like the opportune time to start a rock-climbing career. One of them explained how things have changed since they first began. "We used to tie off to anything, mostly the cedar trees," she said. When they learned their anchors were among the oldest trees in Ontario (over four hundred years old), they stopped the practice. Wisely, climbing associations and conservation organizations have since installed permanent metal rings.

Rattlesnake Point isn't only important to climbers, it's a provincially significant Life Science Area of Natural and Scientific Interest (part of Ontario's system of important natural areas). It lies within the Milton Outlier — a portion of the Niagara Escarpment separated from the main formation by the Nassagaweya Canyon. A pre-glacial river carved a deeper, broader canyon, which filled with ice during the last ice age. As the ice melted, the Nassagaweya Canyon meltwater channel deposited millions of tonnes of sand and gravel throughout the region. Hence the mad drive to mine this grey gold from the precious, and sometimes disturbingly thin, strip of nature I was following.

From atop Rattlesnake Point, I descended the cliff via a set of metal stairs. Part way down, I was delighted by a common hackberry tree. If exposed to the elements, its soft wood almost immediately rots, accounting for its nicknames: sugarberry and beaverwood. I climbed back up the stairs and retraced my route along the clifftops on the main BT. From earlier experience, I knew it was more picturesque than the forested options. Turkey vultures lazily riding the thermals generated by the midday sun hitting the cliff face entertained me when I stopped for lunch at a magnificent lookout. Destination Ontario states that while Rattlesnake Point is a popular hangout for vultures, it has no rattlesnakes — which is true. But it wasn't always the case. Timber rattlesnakes were once common throughout Southern Ontario. So common that on December 18, 1795, Lady Simcoe (wife of Lieutenant Governor John Graves Simcoe) wrote in her diary, "Mr. Jones, the surveyor, says seven hundred rattle-snakes were killed near Burlington Bay this summer." Now extirpated (locally extinct), they leave the massasauga as the province's only rattler. Drop for drop, the massasauga's venom is more toxic, but massasaugas usually don't release as much toxin as the timber whose Latin name is *Crotalus horridus*.

I made my way back into the canyon via the Leech Porter Side Trail. The thick carpet of needles that had built up below the reforested pines smelled like autumn. Along the canyon floor, I followed a boardwalk bordered by marsh marigolds, another sign of spring. The cumulous clouds I'd seen from the cliffs might indicate summer, and it smelled like autumn midway down, but in the valley, spring ruled. I climbed out of the canyon choosing the Canyon Bypass Side Trail this time and picked up the Crawford Lake Side Trail, anticipating its series of entertaining sights.

Bypassing the visitors' centre with its reconstructed long-houses, I detoured along the Hide and Seek Trail to admire its amazing wooden carvings. Four accomplished wood carvers sculpted these larger-than-life tributes to endangered species, including, among others, a Jefferson salamander, a monarch butterfly and, my favourite, a wolf. With Crawford Lake stretching out before me, I was reminded that it's a rare "meromictic" lake, one so deep that the surface water layer doesn't mix with the bottom water layer. The result is that whatever settled in those sediments is still there, including pollen dating from the 1300s. Evidence of fifteenth-century longhouses alerted researchers that this area was once home to a large Iroquoian population.

I was tired from what had already been a long walk so I contemplated bypassing the Crawford Lake Trail. Then I spied the boardwalk. I don't know what it is about boardwalks, but

I'm drawn to them. *I'll just walk a little way along it*, I thought. Just to where it ends. Little did I know that it goes all the way around the lake, so you can guess what I did. But my love of boardwalks was rewarded. About 250 metres in, I came across the twisted, three-trunked cedar tree that I'd admired when I wrote *Halton Hikes*. Sadly, two of its thigh-thick trunks were no longer standing, and the one that remained was distressed. I saluted this corkscrewed tree as I would a dear friend, fearful I'd not see it again.

Some people find my anthropomorphizing trees odd, but Bernd Heinrich wouldn't. In his book *The Trees in My Forest*, he writes about the similarities between humans and trees: "Trees take in nutrients and respond to their environment. They grow, have sex, reproduce, and senesce. They have predators and protect themselves against them. They succumb to viral, fungal, and bacterial diseases, but they also have defenses. They contend with intense competition from their own kind and others. Although rooted in place, they move, respond to stimuli, and have elaborate mechanisms of dispersing and invading new territory."

Given the healthy forests I'd been walking through, it appeared trees managed an enviable balance between protecting themselves and caring for others.

≋

This was my last hike in the Iroquoia section. Two down, seven to go. I'd covered over two hundred kilometres in 11 hikes, averaging about 19 kilometres per hike. At this rate, I couldn't cover the entire BT in 40 loops. To do that, I had to walk over 24 kilometres per hike from now on. Rather than being spooked by that realization, I liked the challenge.

Jordan kicked in quickly each morning, and I was getting hiking "tough," as they say. Bring on a 30 kilometre hike. The trail was my drug.

Toronto Section

Day 12

HILTON FALLS / DUFFERIN GAP

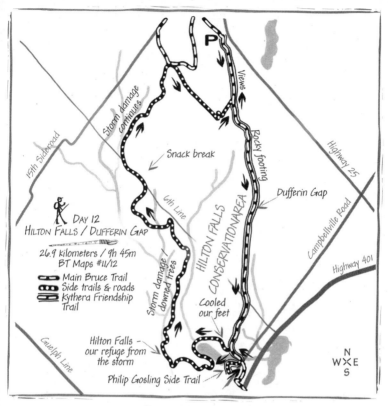

Day 12
HILTON FALLS / DUFFERIN GAP

26.9 kilometers / 9h 45m
BT Maps #11/12

Main Bruce Trail
Side trails & roads
Kythera Friendship
Trail

Storm damage
continues

15th Sideroad

Snack break

6th Line

P

Views

Rocky footing

Dufferin Gap

HILTON FALLS CONSERVATION AREA

Highway 25

Campbellville Road

Highway 401

Storm damage /
downed trees

Cooled
our feet

Hilton Falls –
our refuge from
the storm

Guelph Line

Philip Gosling Side Trail

N
W E
S

FIELD NOTES

START TIME: 8 a.m., Saturday, May 21, 2022

TRAILHEAD WEATHER: sunshine, thunder, hard rain and Canada's first derecho windstorm

DISTANCE: 26.9 km

ELAPSED TIME: 9h 45m

BT SECTION: Toronto

BT MAP: #11/12

MAIN BT WALKED: 1.0 km to 8.9 km

ASCENT: 869 m / **DESCENT:** 890 m

SIDE TRAILS: Philip Gosling Side Trail, Hilton Falls Side Trail

FLORA/FAUNA OF NOTE: common milkweed (*Asclepias syriaca*), red-winged blackbird (*Agelaius phoeniceus*), mute swan (*Cygnus olor*), eastern red-spotted newt (*Notophthalmus viridescens*), female rose-breasted grosbeak (*Pheucticus ludovicianus*), sulphur butterflies (*Colias philodice*)

In which dynamite blows a hole through the
Niagara Escarpment before we find the only cover
within a 10-kilometre radius and survive a derecho,
though 11 others weren't so lucky.

I called my friend Susan:

"I'm going for a walk on Saturday, wanna come?"

"How far?"

"'bout 25 k."

"How long will it take?"

"Maybe eight hours."

Fortunately, Susan Gesner is up for that kind of adventure. We often hike together, and it's always fun. We walk at a similar pace and she's well prepared, though she teases me about walking with my head down.

I picked her up at 7 a.m., and an hour later, we were at the trailhead. I worried that the parking on St. Helena Road would be full, but we were ahead of the crowd. With little ado — no BT construction crews — we followed the Kythera Hiking Friendship Trail, the third of nine BT friendship trails. Kythera Hiking is a series of 11 routes ranging from 2.7 to 16 kilometres on a Greek island named Kythera. Located just south of Crete, it's surrounded by the Mediterranean Sea. When thinking about hiking destinations, Greece hadn't come to mind — until now. The hikes have themes, such as Pirate Invasion and Architectural Tour. Photos depict rocky landscapes, azure skies, sparkling beaches and ancient buildings. I particularly liked Kythera's version of "Take only memories, leave only footprints." The Greeks added, "Ants and other insects have not yet discovered how to consume plastic. Take all rubbish with you."

We ambled down the trail chatting. Sometimes I feel guilty about getting lost in conversation when hiking and failing to observe what's around me, but I didn't worry about that today. After so many solo kilometres, I indulged myself. But a potential Gary Larson *Far Side* comic did come to mind. It would depict a couple of hikers, clad in I Love Nature T-shirts. Alongside the trail, an amazing array of rare plants and animals are waving their branches or paws desperate to catch the hikers' attention. But alas, the pair are so busy gabbing they pay no heed.

Before I knew it, we were at the Dufferin Gap. Other times I've approached it, I've been sadly aware of this travesty from a kilometre or more away. Being Saturday, the warning reverberations of gravel trucks, rock crushers and other evidence of a massive aggregate operation were absent. "Oh," I said, looking up, "Here we are." Susan had never visited the Dufferin Gap, nor did she know its history. Built in 1991, the Dufferin bridge spans a 40-metre "gap" in the Niagara Escarpment. Blasted out in 1962 so trucks allegedly had a quicker route from the quarry to Highway 401, this insult to the escarpment sparked a public outcry. In the late 1980s it was declared a UNESCO Biosphere. I'd always understood the Dufferin Gap to be the only break in the escarpment. Having recently walked past Thorold's Twin Flight locks, however, I realized that while ships might climb the mountain, the Welland Canal went through it.

We picked up the seven hundred metre Philip Gosling Side Trail. It passed through a regenerating meadow under enormous hydro towers where someone hoped to attract monarch butterflies by planting common milkweed and other native plants. It reminded me of a remarkable book I'd just finished. Called *Bicycling with Butterflies*, it chronicles the 16,000-kilometre cycling journey of Sara Dykman. On a bike she describes as "a cross between a salvage yard and a garage sale" (her rear panniers were cat litter boxes), she followed the migration of monarch butterflies from their overwintering home in central Mexico, through the US and into Canada. Then she turned around and followed their great, great, great grandchildren back to the El Rosario Preserve. The book described a great adventure, one with a purpose I could relate to. Dykman wanted to know more about monarchs, aware that her story would help protect these miracles of nature. Could I do the same for the Niagara Escarpment?

Red eft / juvenile eastern newt
(*Notophthalmus viridescens*)

I've met Philip Gosling several times and could imagine him having undertaken a Dykman-like expedition in his youth. It surprised me that this unremarkable path that led to a parking lot bore his name. Then I discovered that the intersection of Gosling's namesake trail and the main BT celebrates the spot where he and his crew painted the BT's first blaze in July 1962. Among the four founders, it was Gosling who travelled the length of the Niagara Escarpment coordinating teams of volunteers who built and blazed the trail. While in his thirties, Gosling took a year's leave from his real estate career and headed out on a life-changing adventure. David E. Tyson describes this Member of the Order of Canada as a "man of action," someone who is intolerant of lengthy debates about "what side of a large rock the trail should go on." Gosling was the perfect complement to Lowes's dreamy stick-with-it-ness and Pearson's strategic planning. No wonder the BT was completed so quickly.

Returning to the main BT under blue skies, we ambled along the 9.2 kilometre Hilton Falls Side Trail with its shimmering reservoir to our left. The temperature was skyrocketing and so was the humidity. When we spied a small stream, we stripped off our shoes and socks, and let the fast-flowing water cool our feet. Bliss. Back on the trail, we entered a cedar forest; gradually the light grew dim. While cedar forests can be gloomy places, this was different. Looking behind us, we discovered the sun had been replaced by a bank of ominous purple clouds, not unlike the ones I'd seen in Rock Chapel about a week ago. We were going to get wet.

The trail continued through the cedars over rocky terrain where there had once been a bustling town, built on the power of Sixteen Mile Creek. I tried to picture stores and hotels, horses and carts, people going about their business. We admired a large pothole, about two metres in diameter. It was formed when running water caused stones and other debris to swirl around and around inside a depression in the rock until it had created a cylindrical hole. Another natural wonder.

We clambered down the stairs to look at Hilton Falls, joining a family with a chubby golden retriever. He was splayed out in the cool stream, maximizing his body surface to water ratio. As we climbed back up, the air prickled with energy. Hoping we could finish our lunch before the downpour, we sat on a bench bordering a fire pit. But when great plops of rain threatened to mush our sandwiches, we knew we were in for it. The falling air pressure, the plummeting temperature, the metallic smell spelled deluge. Luckily, right behind us was a woodpile protected under a rustic tarpaulin lean-to. It must have been the only shelter within 10 kilometres. Hauling on our rain jackets, we ducked inside and sat down on damp wood amid spiders and earwigs. Instantly, the plops graduated into a monsoon. What light we had disappeared, thunder barrelled down the river valley and we did our best to avoid sitting under leaks in the tarpaulin. We bunched closer together when two more hikers joined us. The tempest raged. We joked with the newcomers, but this storm wasn't a laughing matter. We couldn't see much, but we heard the cracks of thunder intensify as the front closed in. Rivulets of water streamed under the sodden logs beneath us. The gloom intensified.

Then it was over — fast and furious. The rain let up as though someone had turned off a tap. The atmospheric pressure had bottomed out; the temperature had plunged. "The worst of the storm has likely passed," Susan deduced. Leaving our raincoats on to protect us from dripping trees and the cold, we ventured back onto the trail. Negotiating large puddles, we followed the trail as it wound through a scrub forest of immature trees. Minutes later, there was a gust of wind, then another, stronger this time. The trees swayed, their branches straining like laundry on a prairie clothesline. Spooked by the intensity of these outbursts, we instinctively took cover behind the largest of entirely inadequate trees. We hoped the trunks would give us some protection if branches or, worse yet, an entire tree came down. It was that kind of wind — the kind that makes you afraid to be outside in a forest. The kind of wind never experienced by those who believed trimming could prevent trees in the Royal Botanical Gardens from being blown down. As we waited, motionless, we heard a crack, followed by smashing foliage to our left. We couldn't see through the dense brush, but we both knew it was what we feared most: a falling tree. What to do? The wind whipped and whirled. The trees shook, shedding moisture like a dog shakes itself free of pond water. There was nowhere to go. No protection. No well-placed lean-to. We had no choice but to wait it out hoping that luck continued to be with us. Our saving grace was that we were in a scrub forest of apple and hawthorns rather than among basketball-player maples that are more vulnerable to the ill effects of wind. Nonetheless, we were paralyzed as the gale slammed into us.

Then, suddenly, the wind stopped. Silence prevailed. We looked at each other. Is it over? Or is this the eye of a tornado? The quiet before the tempest? Adrenalin coursed through my veins. "What the f--- was that?" I asked Susan. She responded, "I don't f---ing know." Should we continue? Should we head back? Should we wait?

Wary of what Mother Nature had in store for us next, we took a few hesitant steps along the trail, looking to each other for assurance that this was the right thing to do. The sky was leaden. It was still, muted, eerie. The atmosphere was thick. It pressed in on us. The Hilton Falls Side Trail snaked through forests, across meadows and onto an earthen dyke overlooking a mist-shrouded wetland. It was dead calm. Red-winged blackbirds chattered nervously and a pair of swans floated idly on the still water.

Walking on through a mature forest, our way was blocked by an uprooted maple. Pondering how to get around it, Susan said, "It looks like that tree just came down." And sure enough, its leaves hadn't begun to droop. Two minutes later, an enormous oak obstructed the path, and then another. In a short stretch, six mammoths had succumbed to the tempest. Bad as it had seemed as we waited out the driving rain and then the blustery wind, we had clearly been spared the worst of it. An hour later, as we neared my car, the clouds disappeared and sunshine streamed through the trees. The morning's humidity had vanished. It was impossible to imagine ourselves huddled with the firewood, spiders and earwigs under that leaking tarpaulin or crouched with our arms protecting our heads behind a whip of a young apple tree.

Driving home we listened to reports about the storm. Indeed, we had been lucky, very lucky. Described as a historic, high-impact derecho, it packed winds of up to 190 kilometres per hour along a one thousand kilometre path. Three cities in Southern Ontario declared states of emergency and, I learned later, insured damage resulting from nature's fury was estimated at $875 million, making it Canada's sixth costliest natural disaster ever. More disturbing yet: while we were tucked in behind those inadequate saplings, 11 people died — almost all of them victims of falling trees.

Day 13

LIMEHOUSE TO SPEYSIDE

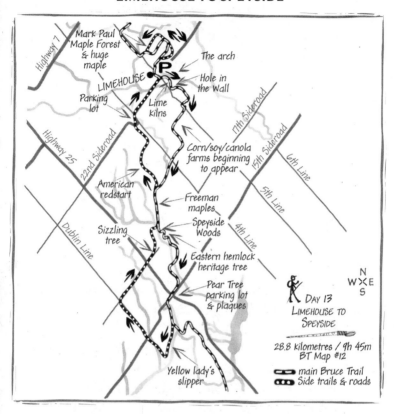

Mark Paul Maple Forest & huge maple

Highway 7

The arch

P

LIMEHOUSE

Hole in the Wall

Parking lot

Lime kilns

17th Sideroad

15th Sideroad

6th Line

Corn/soy/canola farms beginning to appear

5th Line

Highway 25

22nd Sideroad

American redstart

Freeman maples

Speyside Woods

4th Line

Sizzling tree

Dublin Line

Eastern hemlock heritage tree

Pear Tree parking lot & plaques

N
W · E
S

Day 13
LIMEHOUSE TO
SPEYSIDE

Yellow lady's slipper

28.8 kilometres / 9h 45m
BT Map #12

main Bruce Trail
Side trails & roads

FIELD NOTES

START TIME: 7:15 a.m., Monday, May 23, 2022

TRAILHEAD WEATHER: sunny and cool, turning to high overcast

DISTANCE: 28.8 km

ELAPSED TIME: 9h 45m

BT SECTION: Toronto

BT MAP: #12

MAIN BT WALKED: 10.6 km to 24.0 km

ASCENT: 1052 m / **DESCENT:** 1040 m

SIDE TRAILS: Al Shaw Side Trail, Vanderleck Side Trail, Canada Goose Side Trail, Ridge Side Trail, Todd Bardes Meadowland Side Trail

FLORA/FAUNA OF NOTE: northern cardinal (*Cardinalis cardinalis*), Freeman maple (*Acer x freemanii*), eastern hemlock (*Tsuga canadensis*), mayapples (*Podophyllum peltatum*), American redstart (*Setophaga ruticilla*), ruffed grouse (*Bonasa umbellus*), ruby-throated hummingbird (*Archilochus colubris*), yellow birch (*Betula alleghaniensis*), Canada geese (*Branta canadensis*), bobolink (*Dolichonyx oryzivorus*), black-legged tick (*Ixodes scapularis*)

*In which I struggled with corsets and crinolines
before griping about hedgerows, admiring an American
redstart, revisiting Queen Victoria's maple and falling
for meadow-loving Todd Bardes.*

It was Victoria Day, a holiday that heralds the beginning of barbecuing season. The celebration derives its name from Queen Victoria (born May 24, 1819), who reigned from 1837 to 1901. We equate her name with corsets, crinolines and expanding the British Empire. She famously stated that women's rights were a "mad, wicked folly." Yet Canada has been celebrating Victoria Day since before confederation because Alexandrina (her actual name) favoured unifying Canada's provinces into an independent nation. While James Bruce (after whom the Bruce Peninsula was named) was governor general, Queen Victoria sat the throne.

Despite the early hour, I had company in the Limehouse Conservation Area. I marvelled at a stylish couple — him in a white sports jacket, open-collared shirt, black dress pants and spit-polished shoes. She in a cardinal-red dress with spaghetti straps and black slingbacks. It was six degrees. A photographer clicked away as his chilly subjects posed before dramatic limestone rocks. As I looked on, a bishop-red northern cardinal flew by, perhaps investigating the presence of a rival. The trail passed a lime kiln, powder house, the keystone bridge and, most fun of all, the keyhole. I was ahead of the kids who would undoubtedly be out later in the day slipping through this narrow passage, climbing up strategically placed ladders and leaping across gaping fractures in the limestone. When asked to recommend good hikes for kids, this one is high on my list.

Once past the conservation area's popular sights, I was alone with the birds, squirrels and trees. It was a beautiful morning, and I relished the quick transition into a rural landscape. Hike by hike, I was leaving the more urban sections of the BT behind. The path dissected a tangle of hawthorns that separated farm fields. It was Canada's less dense version of a solid British laid hedge. While hedgerows provide great habitat for wildlife, I find walking in them can be frustrating. Beyond the hawthorns and apple trees stretched rolling hills, open fields and sunshine. Inside, all I could see were my feet, and even they were hard to make out in the dim light. Let me out, I wanted to cry. From the hedgerow, it was back into the forest, where I came across a sign announcing it was a swamp nursery — home to wetland-loving plants including Freeman maples: naturally occurring hybrids of silver and sugar varieties. In the fall, if you find a maple leaf that has turned half yellow and half red, look around for a Freeman. Ten of the world's one hundred species of maple are native to Canada: sugar, black, silver, bigleaf, red, mountain, striped, Douglas, vine and Manitoba. Freeman isn't included because it's a hybrid.

I had a long day ahead, so I kept up the pace, but uprooted trees, victims of the storm Susan and I had survived, slowed me down. (In total that day, I encountered over 30 blow-downs, many of them huge maples and oaks.) Meteorologists described the derecho (which means straight ahead in Spanish, as opposed to "derecha," which means right) as a long-lasting, far-reaching violent storm seldom experienced in Southern Ontario. Scientists say we can expect to have more of them as our climate warms. Leaving the nursery swamp, I entered Speyside Woods where a sign explained it was a successional forest, making me think of a classroom of teenagers on their way to becoming adults. Shade-loving eastern hemlocks, a species favoured by deer and by me, dominated. Despite the forest's youthful billing, some of them were huge, including one with a double trunk selected by the BT as a heritage tree, according to a trailside sign. Canadian hemlocks, as they are sometimes called, have no relation to the poisonous herb made famous by Socrates who ended his life by ingesting it. When ground, Canadian hemlock needles apparently smell like their noxious namesake.

Eastern hemlock
(Tsuga canadensis)

The trail was rocky and uneven. Good for strengthening the supporting muscles in my ankles — good for spraining them too. I walk in Keen sandals because I have a condition known as Morton's neuroma, and Keens don't irritate the affected nerves in my feet. Most of the time, my Keens are perfect, but on this terrain or in muddy conditions, they aren't ideal. I was happy to reach Speyside, where I stopped in the BT's Pear Tree parking lot to give my hardworking feet a break and have a bite to eat.

The parking lot features a loose arrangement of large rocks, each bearing plaques that recognize BT donors. While I was sitting among them munching away, a pair of hikers arrived. They looked confused, so I offered assistance. Of course, we fell into conversation, so I told them a story about the plaques related to me by a BT volunteer. About a year earlier, the BT discovered that most of the plaques had been chiselled off the rocks. They never found the pranksters, but the BT figured the thieves would have had a well-deserved surprise when they went to a scrap-metal dealer and discovered their bounty were "bronze" plaques in name only. Ice broken, the couple asked me what the trail was like while holding up my *Halton Hikes* guide. I suggested that if they followed the guidebook's directions, they'd never get lost.

Just past Speyside, I turned back, following the Al Shaw Side Trail to the Vanderleck Side Trail. Birds kept me company and I continued to encounter fallen trees. The side trail led me onto a long stretch of dirt road. As I walked, lost in my thoughts, I was distracted by a sizzling sound. I looked up at a roadside tree and sure enough a powerline, no doubt dislodged by the storm, rested on its uppermost branches. Sparks had scorched the tree and continued to crackle. I called Halton Hills Hydro to alert them to what looked like a power outage and fire in the making.

Later, I was rewarded for my good deed. As I climbed over another downed tree, I looked up and not five feet away was a flashy American redstart, its black colouring patched with orange and red giving away its boyhood. Males have both yellow and red carotenoids, which mix, giving this

warbler its orange blotches. Females look completely different with white breasts and yellow patches as they have no
red carotenoids. I also heard a ruffed grouse imitating a lawn
mower and a hummingbird zipped by. Finally, I arrived at
the Canada Goose Side Trail, which took me to Limehouse.

Back in this pretty village, I resisted calling it quits.
Memories of a tree spurred me on. Some years ago, when
I was walking nearby, I'd come across an enormous sugar
maple. I wanted a second visit. I continued along the main
BT, making it up a steep climb made steeper by my tired
legs. On top was a row of old-growth maples and oaks. The
tree I was looking for was not among them, but they were so
spectacular I cheered up. Stopping for a chat with Dorothy
and her husband, Garret, I learned these keen hikers had just
returned from walking England's 293 kilometre Coast-to-
Coast Walk. They'd stayed at inns along the way, which made
it sound like my kind of trip. Garret introduced me to Cindy,
their four-legged companion who had walked the BT from
end to end four times.

When I finally arrived at "my" tree, I was delighted to see
that unlike the poor, old, corkscrewed cedar near Crawford
Lake, it was hale and hearty. Since I'd last visited, the BT
had erected an information sign. Clearly, I wasn't the tree's
only admirer. I learned that this elder was "born" at about the
same time as Queen Victoria.

Turning back, I branched off onto the Ridge Side Trail
and then the Todd Bardes Meadowland Side Trail. What a
relief. I felt as though I had a kindred spirit in Bardes. He
must have loved meadows as much as I do. Sadly, this former
president of the Bruce Trail Conservancy died while snor-
kelling in Costa Rica. He was only 68. I passed an official
Monarch Waystation, a "resting place" along the Monarch's

highway between Mexico and Canada, where there are plants to attract these regal butterflies and other pollinators. There were bird boxes as well as chairs and benches. I thought I spotted a bobolink "bobbing" along in its characteristic flight pattern and promised that one day I'd visit this fine memorial trail early in the morning.

Day 14

SCOTSDALE FARM / SILVER CREEK / DUFF'S PIT

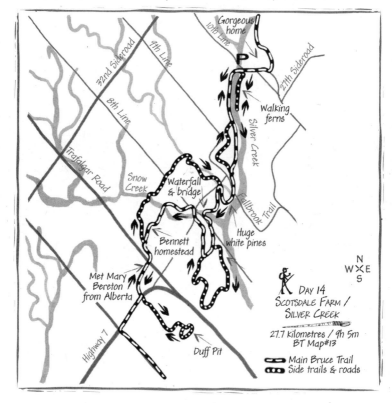

FIELD NOTES

START TIME: 7:30 a.m., Thursday, May 26, 2022

TRAILHEAD WEATHER: overcast, humid, turning to sunshine

DISTANCE: 27.7 km

ELAPSED TIME: 9h 5m

BT SECTION: Toronto

BT MAP: #13

MAIN BT WALKED: 28.4 km to 38.7 km

ASCENT: 1011 m / **DESCENT:** 988 m

SIDE TRAILS: Great Esker Side Trail, Duff Pit Side Trail, Bennett Heritage Trail, Roberts Side Trail, Walking Fern Side Trail

FLORA/FAUNA OF NOTE: mute swan (*Cygnus olor*), Jack-in-the-pulpit (*Arisaema triphyllum*), purple and white violets (*Viola*), eastern white pines (*Pinus strobus*), hop-hornbeam (*Ostrya virginiana*), shagbark hickory (*Carya ovata*), blue beech (*Carpinus caroliniana*), groundhog (*Marmota monax*), marsh marigolds (*Caltha palustris*), red-winged blackbirds (*Agelaius phoeniceus*), larch (*Larix laricina*), basswood (*Tilia americana*), eastern chipmunk (*Tamias striatus*), walking ferns (*Asplenium rhizophyllum*)

In which wrestling an eight-legged, disease-bearing pest from behind my knee proves you have to be there, before Mary sings the BT's praises and I'm too quick to curse a poor walking fern.

My previous hike, my 13th, lived up to its billing. I arrived home after that lovely walk along Todd Bardes Meadowland Side Trail and had a hot shower. As I towelled off, I felt something suspicious behind my right knee. Taking a look, I made out the waving legs of a tick solidly embedded in my flesh. Worse, there was the telltale bullseye rash, a single pinkish circle about the size of a loonie, fading to white and then an angry red dot and those flailing legs. Using tweezers, I tried to gently remove the tick without twisting it so its head didn't pull off and without squeezing it so it didn't panic and release more spit. I'm not sure who came up with those instructions, but they have never performed this procedure on a live tick on the backside of one's own leg. I can now confirm that a tick could be slurping away for a long time without you knowing it. I only discovered the beast because my hand brushed over its exposed legs. But hiding their presence isn't the last tick trick. They also inject a cement-like compound that adheres them to you so they can glug away without risk of being knocked from their perch.

swrp!!

A lyme-carrying tick behind my knee.

Squeezing and not twisting, I wrestled that sucker, or most of it, free. I figured I'd mauled it beyond recognition, but those bu--ers are tough. As the rash suggested, it was a dreaded deer or black-legged tick — the type that can carry Lyme disease. I dropped it into jar, noting that it wasn't fully engorged, but it was a lot bigger than a poppy seed, the size of the males in spring. I cleaned the bite with rubbing alcohol and cursed my luck.

Not everyone gets a rash, but if you do, it's a symptom that takes about three days to appear. Could that tick have been burrowing into my leg for three days? Doctors recommend taking a single dose of antibiotics within two days of the bite. So, fingers crossed, I took the drug and by the next morning a sample of my blood was on its way to the Peel Board of Health for testing. In the meantime, I was to monitor myself for symptoms (a rash, flu, sore muscles) and wait. If the test came back positive or I had symptoms then I'd take a two- or three-week round of antibiotics. With Lyme disease, the earlier you treat it, the less damage it does.

When I hit the trail again, I tucked my pants into my socks and sprayed my ankles and waist with bug repellant containing DEET. These measures were no guarantee I wouldn't be bitten again, but they would help. The Ontario government reports a dramatic increase in the human cases of Lyme disease and while you can get your dog vaccinated, currently there is no inoculation for humans. (In 2023, Health Canada registered a botanical repellant called Tick Attack that is reported to be very effective and is available online. Efforts are underway to develop a vaccine or other method of tick protection for humans.)

$$\approx$$

I parked on the 10th Line of Halton in the valley bottom near a magnificent stone house — one we admired as a family when I was a kid. I was in home territory. The mansion is surrounded by large ponds each connected by waterworks. I remember it having swans — and so it did today. A lone mute cobb cruised by, protective of his mate, the pen, who was likely tending her eggs or young cygnets. What a magical sight on a misty morning.

I followed the main BT into the Silver Creek Conservation Area, where the slippery rocky terrain I'd been encountering since entering the Toronto section of the BT continued. After the night's precipitation and with the trees fully leafed out, the forest was fecund, jungle-like. Branches, heavy with moisture, leaned into the trail. Soon, I was writing around the wet splotches on my notepad. There wasn't a ripple of wind, just stillness and birdsong. Bloodroot and trilliums were past their best-before date, replaced by Jack-in-the-pulpit. Yellow, white and purple violets overflowed the cracks and crannies of the limestone outcroppings. Victoria Day may have passed, but spring's ephemeral flowers weren't done yet.

I followed the trail down to Silver Creek past wide-girthed white pines, Ontario's provincial tree, and turned left onto the Great Esker Side Trail. The last time I'd walked it was about 20 years ago when I was leading the Caledon Countryside Alliance's Sunday morning hikes. It reminded me of how successful they'd been at engaging people in protecting nature. I never would have guessed that of all the initiatives we undertook, these hikes had been the most effective. In hindsight, it's no wonder my Loops & Lattes hiking guides had a similar effect.

On either side of the Great Esker Side Trail, the land fell away, making it seem as if I were walking atop an old railway bed. This was the esker, a long winding ridge of layered sand and gravel. I came across both hop-hornbeams and hornbeams, two species that are easy to identify because of their unique, though entirely different, bark, but that are sometimes confused with one another. Hop-hornbeams have a "shreddy" bark consisting of narrow strips of loose material that curl away from the trunk. Their dense wood is very hard, accounting for it being commonly referred to as ironwood. The trunk of a hornbeam (also called blue beech as I mentioned when I was hiking in the Louth Conservation Area in Niagara) is sinewy, resembling a flexed muscle. Its bark is smooth and sleek. Like hop-hornbeams, hornbeams are hard, accounting for their also being referred to as ironwood. Hence the confusion.

When I began hearing the dull roar of busy Highway 7, I wanted to ignore it. I wanted to be in that Jordan state of mind. I wanted to adhere to the Mexican approach: if I didn't like the sound of the highway then don't listen to it. I tried putting the highway's drone out of my mind, hopeful it would fade like the itch of a mosquito bite left unscratched. When a groundhog scurried by, it broke my reverie. It seemed I had returned to Jordan. I couldn't recall what had occupied my grey matter as I walked along, but it wasn't worrisome details about unpaid bills or forgotten birthdays. Is this meditation, I wondered, *Was I in the moment? Had I conquered my monkey mind?* I'm not sure, but I sure liked it. *Ah*, I thought, *that trail drug again.*

I picked up the Duff Pit Side Trail, following it past evidence of quarries as well as through a lovely forest that skirted a large pond. After stopping for lunch, I began retracing my way back toward Scotsdale Farm. Owned by Ontario Heritage Trust, it's become a rural Hollywood, as portions of big-name films have been shot there. I recall arriving to hike and finding the entrance had been turned into an American prison complete with razor wire and large signs announcing it was Property of the United States Government. Films shot at Scotsdale include *The Recruit*, starring Al Pacino and Colin Farrell and *Rabbit Hole* starring Keifer Sutherland as well as the adaptation of Margaret Atwood's *The Handmaid's Tale*.

Coming around a corner, I ran into a fellow hiker. Mary was carrying a good-sized pack and had a map in hand. From Grand Cache, Alberta, she had left Tobermory on May 1 and hoped to arrive in Queenston by about June 6. "You're going in the wrong direction, aren't you?" I asked. It turned out I wasn't the first person to suggest walking from the cold north in May to the hot south in June was backwards, and to wonder why she'd go from the wilds of the Bruce to the suburbs of the Niagara. Mary agreed she'd miscalculated. "I train in the Willmore Wilderness Park," she told me, "but I prefer the Bruce Trail because I don't have to worry about grizzly bears or flash floods." Later that summer, Mary hiked PEI's Island Walk, and in Newfoundland she completed the T'Railway,

East Coast Trail and a route through Gros Morne National Park. I learned later that the BT won out. Mary said, "My favourite hike was the BT. The ECT was dramatic, but the BT seemed remote . . . and it also had variety. I never knew what each day would be like."

Walking on, I imagined the trail through Mary's eyes. She would be unfamiliar with the sugar maples, basswoods, hop-hornbeams, hopbeams, shagbark hickories and others. The trilliums, trout lilies, Jack-in-the-pulpit and yellow lady's slippers would be alien. Luxuriant green foliage versus spare lodgepole pines, white-tailed versus mule deer, red versus ground squirrels and, of course black versus grizzly bears.

I finished my day with the Walking Fern Side Trail, a 1.7 kilometre return trip. I couldn't give up the chance to see another walking fern. I'd travelled this short trail before and recalled it ended at a rich marsh. The trail was rough. Sharp, slippery rocks tested my balance and pierced my sandalled feet. Maybe it was the 27 kilometres I'd already covered, but it sure felt like the most difficult trail I'd come across so far. To make matters worse, mosquitos swarmed as I arrived at the marsh, which was all dried up (probably the work of beavers) and smelled of rotting vegetation. More disappointing, I hadn't seen a single walking fern on my trip in. *Grrrr.* Determined to save the day, I walked more slowly on my way out. Surely, I could find one walking fern on the Walking Fern Side Trail.

Though they look decidedly un-fern-like, walking ferns are easy to identify once you've seen one. Typically, ferns consist of a frond, comprising a stem and a blade. The blade has many pinnae: small leaves that radiate from the rachis, which is what the stem is called once it has pinnae radiating from it. Each pinnae comprises many pinnules. Now forget that. Although most of the Niagara Escarpment's 50 species of ferns have that general makeup, walking ferns (and Hart's-tongue ferns) look entirely different. Walking ferns have long triangular individual leaves. Their name comes from the fact they tip root. When the end of one long leaf touches the ground, it roots and forms a new plant. In this way, it "walks." If you see a walking fern (generally there is a grouping of them) along the BT, you know you are on the north face of the Niagara Escarpment.

Fortunately, nature saved the day on my return journey. I struck the walking fern jackpot. It was the best display of these rare plants that I'd ever encountered.

Day 15

TERRA COTTA / CHELTENHAM BADLANDS

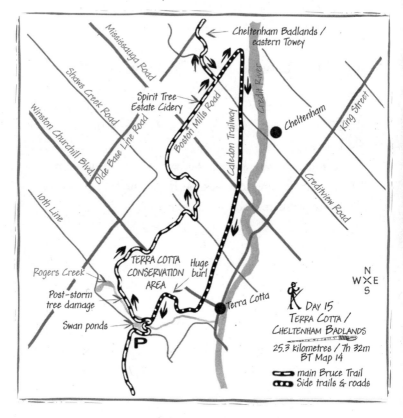

FIELD NOTES

START TIME: 7:40 a.m., Friday, May 27, 2022

TRAILHEAD WEATHER: overcast, humid, threatening rain

DISTANCE: 25.3 km

ELAPSED TIME: 7h 32m

BT SECTION: Toronto/Caledon Hills

BT MAP: #14

MAIN BT WALKED: 38.7 km to 50.3 km / 0 km to 1.4 km

ASCENT: 817 m / **DESCENT:** 831 m

SIDE TRAILS: Caledon Trailway, Badlands Trail, Terra Cotta Side Trail

FLORA/FAUNA OF NOTE: common duckweed (*Lemna minuta*), American bullfrog (*Lithobates catesbeianus*), red squirrel (*Tamiasciurus hudsonicus*)

*In which I imagine my mum as a head of state and owe
Alex a case of oatcakes before visiting one of Ontario's most
popular sights and pondering: Do I love it enough?*

The Caledon Hills section of the BT doesn't line up with municipal boundaries. While still within the Toronto section of the BT, I entered the municipality called the Town of Caledon when I crossed Winston Churchill Boulevard or, as I prefer to call it, the 6th Line. A boulevard is a wide street generally lined with trees. University Avenue in Toronto qualifies, but not the 6th Line, which happens to be the road I grew up on. Until midway through university, I lived in the same stone house at the end of a long driveway with two older sisters, an older brother and a younger sister. I attended the same public school (Belfountain) for eight years and then Mayfield Secondary for five. The perfection of our upbringing cracked as time wore on. Dad had a stroke when I was 14 and suffered from dementia and loss of vision. He died too early: when I was 21. And my mum's beauty and refined upbringing didn't translate into her being a nurturer. In fact, it's amazing we grew up at all given her parenting style, which my sibs and I jokingly refer to as benign neglect. When Mum died at 94, my brother wrote her obituary: "She was a nut — but in a good way. Her brand of looniness was inspirational, a lesson to all. If only she had been named head of state, she would have united the country through laughter and disbelief." He continued, "She could skate and sing. She could play tennis and ride a horse. She could play bridge. She could perform almost any melody on the piano, as long as it was Beethoven's 'Für Elise' or 'Smoke Gets in Your Eyes.'" Kooky? Yes. But she loved us unconditionally and kept us united. I know she admired — and probably related to — my adventurous spirit. I can't think of a time when she dampened my parade. If she'd been born at a different time and hadn't had five children, I could imagine she'd have escaped on her version of my loopy BT hike.

≋

Starting again from the swan house, I climbed into the Terra Cotta Conservation Area via a bridge over Rogers Creek, a tributary to the Credit River. It was a mirror image of yesterday: the humidity so high it was practically dripping moisture. Having lived in Calgary for all those years, I knew that for Mary this would feel more like the tropics than Canada.

The main BT passes through the Terra Cotta Conservation Area, but it skirts the parts we visited when we'd badgered Mum enough that she took us there. Not only was the water warmer than the Credit River, but there was a sandy beach and, the pièce de résistance, a concession stand. It took a lot of whining, but she'd eventually give in and buy us a treat: sweet tarts or a candy necklace. Gloriously pure sugar dyed with some cancer-causing chemical no doubt. We loved it.

That swimming area is now a wetland. Unless you had visited it in the 1960s, it's hard to imagine the colourful buoys that separated the shallow from the deep end. It's a healthier environment now, home to turtles and birds and muskrats. But it sure was a fun spot when we were innocent kids.

Terra cotta means baked earth. The term brings to mind flowerpots stacked in garden sheds. Where I walked today, burnt-red Queenston shale is more dominant than anywhere else along the BT. Queenston shale is always present as it's the principal bedrock below the Niagara Escarpment, but around Terra Cotta and the Cheltenham Badlands, Queenston shale struts its stuff. Just past the bridge over Rogers Creek, I came across a red hillside eroded into a mini badland. The trail was slick, the result of clay comprising flat minerals that slip past each other and clog the treads of hikers' boots (and sandals).

As I passed a small pond, it was as if the 10 lords were leaping. Leopard frogs and green frogs and maybe even bullfrogs made great plopping sounds as they hopped into the clear water. Clear now, but I knew this pond would soon be cloaked in radiant-green common duckweed. Despite its name, this floating water plant is part of a healthy ecosystem. Frogs, for instance, rely on it. Amphibians are carnivorous and even tadpoles can't digest plant material such as duckweed. But the bacteria that break down duckweed are an

American bullfrog
(Lithobates catesbeianus)

important part of a tadpole's diet, and without tadpoles there wouldn't be any frogs.

My first exposure to bullfrogs was at my partner's lodge on the French River. One night, I couldn't get to sleep because of the deep guttural sounds emanating from the cove below our bedroom. In the morning, I asked Alex, "What was that noise coming from the cove last night? Moose?" That might sound dumb, but believe me, I'm not the first person to ask this question. I'm not even the first biologist to ask it, so I didn't believe Alex when he said, "No, not moose. Those were bullfrogs." I looked at him trying to decide if he was pulling my leg. This, I had a hard time believing. Bullfrogs might be the largest frog in North America — an adult can weigh up to 750 grams — but no way a frog made those sounds. I refused to believe him. Then we looked it up. Put it this way, I bought Alex a case of his beloved oatcakes.

Buried in the conservation area's forest, I came across the first of what turned out to be dozens of downed trees. Not little trees, but huge oaks and maples with multiple trunks, yanked out by their roots. Lines of them. It looked as though a tornado, rather than that derecho, had smashed through the forest. It was some storm.

I'd been noting the changing vegetation as I walked north. There were only vestiges of Carolinian tree species and the grape vines I was seeing were the wild ones. There were more red squirrels and fewer bushy-tailed eastern grey (and black) ones, and I was now more likely to hear cows mooing than a freeway droning.

When I came to the Spirit Tree Estate Cidery, it was lunchtime, so I treated myself to a rest and some great food. Walking curbs my appetite, which isn't always a good thing as my occasional grumpiness on the trail is usually due to low blood sugar. For fun, I used an online calculator to estimate how many calories I burn while out on the trail. Given my height and weight, and the size of my daypack, it told me I burn three thousand calories on an eight-hour hike. No wonder I was losing weight.

Back on the BT, I turned into the scrubby forest behind the Cheltenham Badlands. The sun had burned off the mist, and thankfully, the trail was dry. Queenston shale becomes a slippery mess when it's wet. One rainy day when I was walking this trail, I came across women pushing strollers, grandfathers leaning on canes and kids in flipflops who couldn't climb the gentlest incline. It reminded me of cars on a Vancouver street after a snowfall. As I'd done that day, I left the main BT and followed the short Badlands Trail to the platform that looks over this much-loved example of erosion. It's a provincial Area of Natural and Scientific Interest and one of Southern Ontario's most visited sites. It's hard to explain the attraction; there are more dramatic landscapes, but there's magic at play here. Before the badlands were fenced off, I walked through the red hills, jumping from one whaleback ridge to the next. I could feel their buzzing energy.

The road past these clay banks is hilly, though it used to be much hillier. We'd bug Dad: "Drive faster, faster." Our Buick station wagon would seem to fly off the hilltops and we'd leave our stomachs on the floorboards. It was also the setting for one of my mum's misadventures. One winter day before the road was paved, she was driving to pick me up at what's now the Caledon Country Club. Three-quarters of the way up the steepest hill, the tires on her car began spinning. Short of the top, they stopped altogether and her stationwagon began sliding backwards. It wasn't just icy; it was very icy. The road must have tilted toward the ditch since that was where she was heading — in reverse. Rather than risk going over the embankment, my mum opened the door and managed to get out. The car be damned. And damned it was. A total wreck. In hindsight, it was a smart move. I think my dad even admitted it, but this exploit is up there among our family's anecdotal mum stories.

I turned back from the lookout. Leaving the BT, I picked up the Caledon Trailway, following it until it linked into the BT's Terra Cotta Side Trail. From here it was a straightforward walk to my car. At the swan pond, I stopped to admire the cobb as it preened, seemingly unaware of my presence — or so I thought. Slowly at first, it swam toward me, then it sped up. Its intent was obvious, and it wasn't friendly. I backed off not wanting to upset him, aware they can be aggressive, especially when cygnets are involved. I thought about the deep-seated parental instinct, recalling several occasions when my mum was equally as protective. How she ignored her own wellbeing to ensure we were safe. I wondered if it's possible to love anything else with the intensity of the bond between a parent and their offspring. Bernd Heinrich said he wanted to love more deeply. Did I love the Niagara Escarpment enough? What did that feel like? Did it resemble my colleague Pati's panic when she thought her Sierra was on fire? To what lengths would I go to protect the Forks of the Credit?

Caledon Hills Section

Day 16

FORKS OF THE CREDIT / BELFOUNTAIN PARK

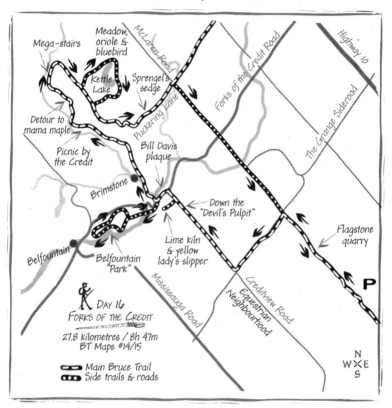

Mega-stairs

Meadow, oriole & bluebird

McLaren Road

Forks of the Credit Road

Highway 10

Kettle Lake

Sprengel's sedge

The Grange Sideroad

Puckering Lane

Detour to mama maple

Picnic by the Credit

Bill Davis plaque

Brimstone

Down the "Devil's Pulpit"

Flagstone quarry

Belfountain

Belfountain "Park"

Lime kiln & yellow lady's slipper

P

Mississauga Road

Crediview Road

Equestrian Neighbourhood

Day 16
Forks of the Credit
27.8 kilometres / 8h 47m
BT Maps #14/15

N
W E
S

◆━◆ Main Bruce Trail
•━• Side trails & roads

FIELD NOTES

START TIME: 7:20 a.m., Monday, May 30, 2022

TRAILHEAD WEATHER: overcast, warm, threatening rain, turned to sun

DISTANCE: 27.8 km

ELAPSED TIME: 8h 47m

BT SECTION: Caledon Hills

BT MAP: #14/15

MAIN BT WALKED: 2.8 km to 14.6 km

ASCENT: 1214 m / **DESCENT:** 1234 m

SIDE TRAILS: The Ring Kiln Side Trail, Trimble Side Trail, Crow's Nest Side Trail ("my" side trail), Mill Pond Side Trail, Meadow Trail, McLaren Road Side Trail

FLORA/FAUNA OF NOTE: maidenhair spleenwort (*Asplenium trichomanes*), walking ferns (*Asplenium rhizophyllum*), shagbark hickory (*Carya ovata*), goldenrod (*Solidago canadensis* L.), common milkweed (*Asclepias syriaca*), lilacs (*Syringa*), Baltimore oriole (*Icterus galbula*), horsetails (*Equisetum*), Sprengel's sedge (*Carex sprengelii*)

*In which I'm unapologetic for wallowing in childhood
memories before being interrupted by an officious
"You are trespassing," a goat and her runner are
remembered and I relive my life as a wiener.*

When I set out from Queenston 15 loop hikes ago, my
ultimate destination was Tobermory. But my first goal was to
get "home." Today I arrived. I walked on paths embedded in
my genes and alongside rivers that course through my veins.
If I have trouble falling asleep, rather than count sheep, I
trace the route of the Credit River and the layout of the local
BT in my mind's eye.

I parked at the dead end of Chinguacousy Road, not far
from the Cheltenham Badlands, and took off on the main
BT as it climbed to "the quarry" through a dense forest.
There was scant sun beneath the thick canopy, and I had
to watch my footing along the rocky trail. Bedrock surfaces
through here, a fact taken advantage of by the owners of a
flagstone quarry that has been around longer than the BT.
When I was a kid, if the owners caught us riding our horses
along the quarry road, they'd accuse us of trespassing and
chase us away.

Following this childhood-memory-filled road, I passed by bayou-like swamps and between mosquito-rich ponds. The mud was seriously black, pungent and earthy; it would suck you under if you strayed too close. After passing the quarry entrance, the main BT climbed "the mountain" and entered Caledon's Equestrian Neighbourhood. As I walked along the familiar dirt road, I could feel the rhythmic sway of sitting in a saddle. Several years ago, Alex and I bought four horses in Argentina. For two months, we explored Patagonia, camping out by night and sauntering along back roads and well-worn paths by day. If I smell a horse, I'm back in Patagonia or the barn at Woodrising.

Turning right onto Creditview Road, the main BT takes advantage of the road allowance to get down to the Forks of the Credit. It's amazing how much of the trail follows these remnants of public land, and it's a good thing too. If the BT didn't follow them, I'm not sure cash-strapped municipalities could resist selling these parcels of land to adjoining land-owners who'd erect the No Trespassing signs that motivated Lowes. Without abandoned railway lines, utility rights-of-way and unopened road allowances, there wouldn't be a BT.

The trail dipped and dodged through maples and beeches and ironwoods alongside a two-metre-high wire fence posted with the dreaded signs. Behind it are some of Caledon's most stunning views, now "owned" by a prominent Canadian. As much as I dislike that fence, at least the prominent Canadian and the one before him kept this large block of land intact. It's part of an expanse of green, some of it privately owned and some of it public, that accounts for Caledon's reputation as a natural landscape.

I weaved through rocks as I approached what people refer to as the Devil's Pulpit — a protuberance in the cliff face that gave rise to this moniker. I looked out over the Credit River valley, a green expanse that stretches as far as I could see. Though I didn't want to, I looked for the only house that interrupts the forest. This multi-million-dollar mansion is simultaneously a familiar landmark and a blight. I hope that one day, trees will obscure it. I began my descent via irregularly spaced stone steps that hug the wall of the escarpment. A handy rope that loops from metal rings drilled into the limestone acts as a makeshift railing. By providing a landing from which the stairs descend diagonally down the cliff face, the Devil's Pulpit was the BT's final link.

The BT was to have been blazed and ready to hike from Queenston to Tobermory by Canada's centennial: July 1, 1967. Less than a month earlier, however, when the Honourable René Brunelle, Ontario's Minister of Lands and Forests, officially opened the trail, Ray Lowes's dream was incomplete. There was a gap from the Grange Side Road to the Forks of the Credit — the exact route I was walking. It was Philip Gosling who came to the rescue. On a hunch, he bushwhacked in a straight line along what he hoped was the unopened road allowance. When he emerged on Chisholm Street in the Forks of the Credit, he knew his instinct had been right. Not only did the BT not require permission from the senator who owned the surrounding land, but as luck would have it, the right-of-way lined up with the Devil's Pulpit, providing a way to negotiate the Forks of the Credit's formidable cliffs. By month's end, the route bore the BT's white blazes; the ribbon joined Niagara to Tobermory.

Down I went over slippery rocks decorated with maidenhair spleenwort and through towering cedars. *How many times have I walked this route?* I wondered. I chuckled recalling a photo I took of my mum on this trail. She's wearing

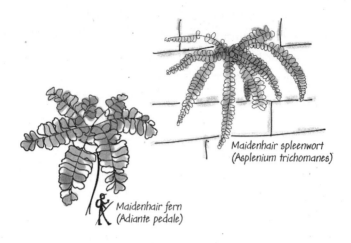

Maidenhair spleenwort
(Asplenium trichomanes)

Maidenhair fern
(Adiante pedale)

a navy-blue sweatshirt. Emblazoned in large white letters across her chest are the words Sixty and Sexy. I'm now older than she'd been when I took that shot. How was that possible? I was reassured when I spied a healthy cluster of walking ferns on the rock where I expected to see them. Cold air escaping from deep crevices made me shiver. I detoured down the tricky in-and-out side trail to the ruins of the Hoffman Ring lime kiln. Long before the BT added this side trail, I came looking for the lime kiln Indiana Jones–style. When the ruins loomed before me, I thought I'd been transported into a Mayan jungle. I wasn't prepared for their size, or how, over a century, the once dome-shaped structure had become shrouded in cedars. Part of me was sad when the BT opened the side trail and exposed my secret.

It was a scramble back up to the main BT and then down over the railway tracks first operated by the Credit Valley Railway. Service between Toronto and Orangeville began in 1879. My mum used to flag the train from the station once located at the end of the long trestle bridge. Currently, the tracks are being pulled up as the railway line enters a new chapter as a hiking trail. Below the tracks, the path reaches Chisholm Street, as did Gosling all those years ago. In 1967, as he bushwhacked the route, he would have passed by the one-room red-brick schoolhouse, SS#19, where my sister and brother attended class under the tutelage of Mrs. Longstreet. It closed in 1963, and students were transferred to the new Belfountain Public School. I followed the BT along the Forks of the Credit Road, picking up the Trimble Side Trail at Dominion Street. From there, I couldn't just smell home, I could taste it.

The Trimble brothers, Roy and John, inherited their father's blacksmith shop in Belfountain, turning it into a garage. From the building that now hosts a café, several stores and, for a time, a yoga studio, they sold gas and cared for locals' cars, including my parents'. The brothers often told us stories about life back then. John's wife, Berniece, captured the area's history in a book entitled *Belfountain: Caves, Castles and Quarries in the Caledon Hills*. Roy Trimble was a fine paddler who guided the Group of Seven members who painted in the Forks of the Credit. Belfountain was a popular spot even then, and the Trimbles knew the area better than most. When I hiked into the real Devil's Pulpit, we found John Trimble's name carved into the limestone.

The trail left the road beside a bridge where the West Credit tumbled over rocks and I entered the Willoughby Property. Owned by Ontario Heritage Trust, it's a 40 hectare parcel of land with wonderful views and evidence of quarrying that is now mostly hidden — unless you know where to look. I decided I'd try visiting the Belfountain Conservation Area. It had been closed for a couple of years for renovations, and I wanted to have a peek as it was scheduled to reopen in about a week's time. In the early 1900s, it was the summer home of C.W. Mack, famous for inventing the rubber stamp. He must have had a sense of humour as he turned his property, called *Lukenuf*, into an amusement park complete with a "Niagara Falls," a swinging bridge, bell-topped fountain (think Belfountain), Yellowstone cave and other features intended to entertain his guests. Rumour has it, Mack threw some wild parties.

The Trimble Trail was plastered with signs warning the park was closed, but with Ray Lowes's "just do it," attitude, I walked on. If I ran into problems, I'd improvise — or plead. A pair of uniformed young men met me as I entered. I sweet-talked them into allowing me to take a quick look around. Wow, it was a big change. The pond was now a narrow, manicured stream bordered by a boardwalk; the cement pool where I swam as a kid was a lily pond; "Niagara Falls" was a metre lower. It was unfair to condemn the changes as I was only there for a few minutes, but the place felt done up like the perms my mum used to get. It was obvious that a lot of effort had gone into the renovations though. The new stonework was real rather than textured cement, and I could see that with time, it would evolve into a natural setting. The transition of my childhood swimming spot in Terra Cotta into a wetland took years.

The young men shooed me out, looking nervously over their shoulders. But they were too late. From behind, I could hear a voice: "Excuse me. Excuse me." I decided to ignore her, but she called again, this time on the uncomfortable side of shrill, "EXCUSE ME." When she caught up, also clad in a uniform, she puffed up her chest before demanding, "What are you doing?" I contemplated glancing down at my hiking attire and giving her a look that said what part of hiking don't you get but resisted. Then I considered confessing to being an eco-spy sent by the Town of Caledon. But she didn't wait for my explanation. "The park is closed. You are trespassing. Blah, blah, blah." I explained since the park was about to open, I thought I'd sneak a preview. But she was not to be dissuaded of the seriousness of my crime. So, I changed tack. "You've done such a great job of the park," I told her. "I grew up here. I used to swim in the pool you've cleverly turned into a lily pond. Wow, what a great job you've done." My captor had no interest in my compliments, nor did she have a modicum of curiosity about how *her* park appeared to a member of the public. In her defence, she's probably had to deal with too many people who climb fences to get up close to waterfalls. But really, uniform or no uniform, what could she do? I wished her a good day, turned around and as I ambled unhurriedly away, I gave her a big old country wave.

When I came to "my" trail, as I'm the BT captain (a.k.a. caretaker) for the kilometre-long Crow's Nest Side Trail, I turned left and followed it in a counterclockwise direction. If I'd walked down the Devil's Pulpit's cliffs a hundred times, I'd walked this route a thousand. When I returned to the Trimble Side Trail, I retraced my way back to Dominion Street where I picked up the main BT. The "forks of the credit" converge just upstream from the Dominion Street bridge. A prized fly-fishing stream, the Credit River meanders through villages, towns and cities that took advantage of its once powerful flow. It was also paddled by the Mississaugas of the Credit after they'd purchased supplies on credit from settlers — giving rise to its name. The Forks of the Credit was also the heart of quarry country in the nineteenth century, known for its large slabs of prized whirlpool sandstone. If you know Queen's Park, Ontario's legislative building in Toronto, you can visualize the beautiful stone blasted out of the hills that surrounded me.

I followed the main BT into the hamlet of Brimstone, once home to quarrymen so tough their penchant for fighting resulted in the village's biblical name. The main BT follows yet another road allowance, this time one that once joined the Forks of the Credit to the village of Cataract through what is now the Forks of the Credit Provincial Park. Along the way, I passed the Dorothy Medhurst Side Trail, named for a keen hiker who once lived nearby. Her daughter was Abby Hoffman, not Abbie Hoffman the activist, but one of Canada's most talented middle-distance runners. One day, when I was riding my horse near Medhurst's home, I came across a lean, long-legged woman leading a goat. It was such an odd sight that I remembered it. Decades later, when I learned Medhurst's daughter was the runner, I put two and two together.

The road led into an open valley, the destination for many years for the Caledon Riding Club's annual Brimstone Ride on Thanksgiving weekend. We'd ride in, tie up our horses and have lunch. My dad made onion soup and heated it over an open fire in a huge cauldron fashioned by the Trimbles. We had McIntosh apples that taught me the difference between the crisp freshly picked ones and the mushy stored ones. Dad set up the soup by the river, and we played in the tufted grass, rolling like wieners down the steep banks next to where today's BT passes by an outdoor bathroom before heading up the escarpment.

Of all the places I've hiked, the Forks of the Credit Park is my favourite. Countless times, I've walked next to the washroom, across the sandy cart track, past the wiener hill, alongside the poison ivy, through a soaring maple forest where white trilliums blanket the forest floor in spring and up the long ascent to the ridgetop. Today, I turned left at the ridgetop and followed the Mill Pond Side Trail. It skirts the valley lip, so you walk almost level with some treetops, then drops down a long set of stairs to the ruins of an old powerplant and waterfall, and crosses over where the dam used to be. The Elora Cataract Trailway and the soon-to-be Credit Valley Trail run parallel to the BT before converging in the village of Cataract. At the intersection of two railways (Credit Valley Railway and the Hamilton North-Western Railway), Cataract was once home to various hotels and bars needed to service those arriving in this transportation hub. Its hills are rich with stories of rushes for gold never found, salt never extracted, Canada Dry water wells and exploding dams. I crossed over the main Credit River and climbed back up the escarpment, then I followed a section of the Trans Canada Trail to the Meadow Trail.

This is my favourite Forks of the Credit Park trail. It dissects what was once pastureland. This hummocky landscape is the western extreme of the Oak Ridges Moraine, for the Niagara Escarpment and the Oak Ridges Moraine collide in the Forks Park. Milkweed and goldenrod, old apple trees, bluebird boxes, Baltimore orioles, eastern meadowlarks and other meadow-loving species find refuge in this vast open landscape partly thanks to a team including local naturalist Don Scallen. They keep the surrounding forest at bay. More recently, Ontario Parks took more drastic steps. It has razed the meadow to encourage growth of a rare tall-grass prairie. This effort is music to my meadow-loving ears. There's a kettle lake where I've spied bufflehead ducks and enormous snapping turtles. White-tail deer abound. On this day, purple lilacs added colour to the vibrant-green, early-season grasses that swayed in the warm breeze.

I paused at the intersection of the Meadow and Ruins trails, the spot where I dream of building a house. From this perch, the meadow stretched away showing off under a deep-blue sky. Farther down the trail, the orange belly of a Baltimore oriole caught my eye. I returned to the main BT as it returned to the ridgetop overlooking maples that reached to the heavens. Ancient horsetails blanketed the sides of the trail as I climbed over a sandy kame. On the far side, tufted mounds of sedge dotted the forest floor as the trail dropped down to course the ridge at mid-tree level. Then it was up again, reminding me that this was the Caledon *Hills* section. (This turned out to be my second hilliest hike along the entire trail.) Then down onto Puckering Lane where I'd met Hoffman and her goat that day long ago and where, today, I did my best to ignore the plethora of No Trespassing signs that flank the road. I'm thankful that Ray Lowes was spared the warnings of video surveillance.

Arriving at McLaren Road, I followed the McLaren Road Side Trail down to the Credit River and then climbed straight up the escarpment — again. Over the railway tracks and I was back into the forest. To my left I caught glimpses of an expanse of fields and forests. Below me was the land-mark "graffiti bridge," soon to be used by hikers rather than trains. Above it was the original site of the Caledon Ski Club. Farther up the mountain there are views of the Caledon Mountain Trout Club.

The McLaren Road Side Trail ended, and I descended back into "the quarry" and then on again to where my car was parked. It had been a hike filled with memories that rushed at me unannounced as I climbed well-known ascents and appeared unbidden as I rounded familiar corners. I love this landscape because of the images it conjures for me of youthful times, but also because I know it so well. I feel secure in Caledon. Being here is like snuggling in bed on a rainy morning. I know the trails, the hills, the trees, its smells and sounds. I fit into this landscape. It's a connection that has taken decades to develop. My ties have evolved over time. I have neighbours who continue to live where their ancestors built the mills and farmed virgin land. I now realize their connections dwell deeper than mine. And what about the Mississaugas of the Credit who travelled the river of my birthplace? Due to enroachments of the settlers and declining natural resources (things I could relate to), they relocated to land adjacent to the Six Nations Reserve near Hamilton in the mid-1800s. In 2010, the Mississaugas of the Credit received $145 million as compensation for injustices inflicted by the Crown in the treaty-making of the late 18th and early 19th centuries. It saddens me to think they needed to break their long relationship to the land. What would it feel like to have Caledon that deeply ingrained in me? What would it feel like to be forced to leave?

Day 17

GLEN HAFFY / SALLY'S & DAVE'S PINNACLES

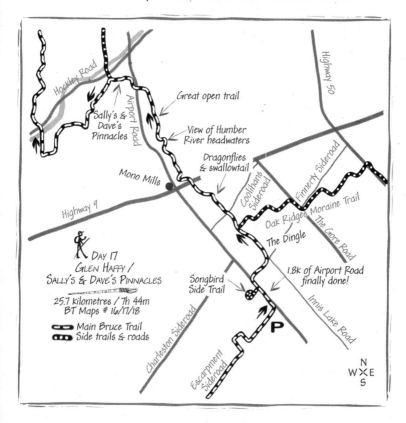

Hockley Road

Great open trail

Sally's & Dave's Pinnacles

Airport Road

View of Humber River headwaters

Dragonflies & swallowtail

Mono Mills

Highway 9

Highway 50

Coolihans Sideroad

Finnerty Sideroad

Oak Ridges Moraine Trail

The Gore Road

The Dingle

1.8k of Airport Road finally done!

Day 17
Glen Haffy /
Sally's & Dave's Pinnacles

25.7 kilometres / 7h 44m
BT Maps # 16/17/18

Songbird Side Trail

Innis Lake Road

Charleston Sideroad

Escarpment Sideroad

P

Main Bruce Trail
Side trails & roads

N W E S

FIELD NOTES

START TIME: 7:10 a.m., Saturday, June 4, 2022

TRAILHEAD WEATHER: cool, crisp, sunny with a stiff breeze

DISTANCE: 25.7 km

ELAPSED TIME: 7h 44m

BT SECTION: Caledon Hills

BT MAP: #16/17/18

MAIN BT WALKED: 26.2 km to 52.0 km

ASCENT: 1057 m / **DESCENT:** 1149 m

SIDE TRAILS: Songbird Side Trail, Hemlock Ridge Side Trail

FLORA/FAUNA OF NOTE: white-tailed deer (*Odocoileus virginianus*)

*In which I relish a Veuve Clicquot hangover before
ley-line energy connects Buddhists to Catholics to Taoists,
and I negotiate dingles, glens and pinnacles to complete
my Caledon Hills end-to-end.*

Yesterday was my 65th birthday. And what a day it was. Alex organized a garden party, an old-fashioned gathering in keeping with his British background and the English garden we inherited from our home's previous owners. A small stone mill, my new home was built in 1857, exactly a century before I was born. White and pink phlox draped over budding peonies below apple blossoms and climbing roses. Shaw's Creek tumbled by filling the air with negative ions. Our secret garden would become a tangle of weeds and ill-tended flowers as the summer progressed, but on this early-June day, it begged to host a vintage event, and Alex pulled it off with grace and charm.

We greeted about 30 of my best friends and family with crystal flutes bubbling over with Veuve Clicquot. We dined at linen-clad tables adorned with spring flowers. Several people roasted me gently as I perhaps drank a little too much bubbly. How could I resist?

≋

Despite my wobbly champagne head, I was up early, eager to get onto the trails on a hiker's dream of a day: brilliant sunshine and cool air. I shivered in the breeze given it was only seven degrees but knew I'd appreciate a gusty wind as the day heated up. I'd planned a linear route since Alex had offered to pick me up at the other end. It included six kilometres of road, two of them along busy Airport Road. This section of the BT was all that stood between me and my Caledon Hills section end-to-end badge.

I set off along a dirt road that offered views of open farm fields with a layered backdrop of green forest upon green forest, each a tone darker than the one before it. Distant peaks of cumulous clouds resembled snow-capped mountains. Among the trees, the Humber River's sinuous tributaries flowed toward Lake Ontario. The Credit River watershed was behind me. The Nottawasaga yet to come. This was my first hike since Queenston where I was walking away from rather than toward home. I related to the title of William Sherwood Fox's 1952 book, *The Bruce Beckons*. A former president of the University of Western Ontario, Fox's poetic prose makes clear the depth of his affection for the Bruce Peninsula. As the story goes, his descriptions so impressed the BT's founders, they named their dream the Bruce Trail. Fox writes, "Happily, it seems to be true that most men, despite the stifling effects of modern life, still keep alive in their souls the [human] race's rare power to perceive in any wilderness — however barren, unfriendly, and unkept — witcheries that beckon to quest and adventure. In qualification of that order The Bruce is indeed extraordinarily rich."

Turning left onto Airport Road, I picked up my pace, anxious to get the next two kilometres under my sandals. Transport trucks, SUVs and pickups roared by. It was surprising how much traffic there was so early on a Saturday morning. I detoured onto the 1.8 kilometre Songbird Side Trail. It demonstrates the BT's policy of acquiring land or access to land along the trail's "optimum" route. Airport Road is part of a long stretch of road walking, which the Caledon Hills BT Club would love to correct. Looking at the BT map, it was clear that when and if that happened, the Songbird Side Trail would be absorbed into the main BT. But for now, it was stranded.

After negotiating scrubby forest, I entered a full-on canopied mature maple bush. It was so dark that if I'd had automatic headlights, they'd have been on high beam. The Songbird Side Trail is what I've dubbed a lolli-loop as you go in along the lolli's handle, skirt the candy and then return via the handle. It was a welcome interlude from road walking and very pretty. Back on Airport Road, I passed the Wat Lao Veluwanaram Buddhist temple. (Wat means temple; Lao refers to the Laotian people who built it and Veluwanaram is the temple's name.) With its typically ornate architecture — all red dragons and gold filigree — it was both intriguing and startling, like the time I saw a live toucan on a palm tree rather than pictured on a cereal box. Later in the day, I walked through the Catholic St. Francis Retreat Centre and the Fung Loy Kok Institute of Taoism. Some people believe the presence of ley lines accounts for the rich collection of spiritual establishments in and around Caledon. Ley lines are believed to be straight energy pathways that link churches, standing stones, burial mounds and other holy monuments. The Camino de Santiago is said to follow a ley line that mirrors the Milky Way.

Almost two hours after starting out, I was relieved to have completed my road walking. Setting the tone, a white-tailed deer did a quick escape as I followed yet another unopened road allowance. The north wind had made it chilly along Airport Road, but it was sheltered and warm down among the trees. The forest was silent. I wondered if the birds and squirrels were sleeping in. I passed through The Dingle, a deep-wooded valley, and entered the Glen Haffy Conservation Area, a glen being a long narrow valley, which in this case was once owned by the Haffy family. When I heard clucking and honking, I figured the nearby farm that kept a collection of exotic birds must still be going strong.

The trail emerged into a field, where I took advantage of a bench overlooking the Humber River watershed from atop Humber Heights. A Canadian Heritage River because of its role as an early transportation route (part of the Carrying Place Trail), the Humber drains into Lake Ontario under an iconic white bridge that you can see from Toronto's Gardiner Expressway. The view before me was uninterrupted by highways or houses or power lines or a mansion built by the rich and famous. I sensed I was crossing an imaginary boundary, this time from semi-rural to rural. Sadly, Caledon was on the wrong side of the divide. It was struggling against the unrelenting pressure of suburbia. Some worried Caledon was destined to become "Brampton with hills." I lamented the Mississauga of the Credit's decision to relocate.

In crossing Highway 9, I'd entered Dufferin County, the domain of William Thorsell, the former editor-in-chief of the *Globe and Mail*. He once told me, "You can still get lost in Dufferin County and be intimidated by the land and sky. Nature balances humanity more evenly there and commands and keeps our attention."

I passed the Oak Ridges Moraine Trail, the Philip Gosling Volunteer Forest and the delightful Darcy's Side Trail, named after a well-hiked Jack Russell terrier, enroute to Sally's Pinnacle. Sally Cohen and her husband, David Moule, are great BT supporters and live nearby. (Dave has a pinnacle too. It's farther along the main BT.) Sally's Pinnacle lies within a climax forest, one that balances between growth and decay, at an elevation of 350 metres. This is almost two hundred metres short of the highest point along the BT (540 metres), but it gives the spot a lofty feel. High overhead, lanky trees swayed in the wind like dozens of arms waving hello. Following the Hemlock Ridge Side Trail down into a BT parking lot on Hockley Road, I noted that the fresh air — and almost eight hours of hiking — had cleared my Veuve Clicquot head. That hiking drug I'd become so fond of apparently has detox qualities too.

Day 18

HOCKLEY VALLEY / ANDERSON TRACT

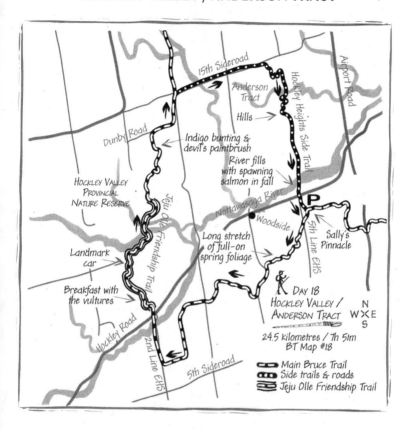

15th Sideroad

Airport Road

Anderson Tract

Hockley Heights Side Trail

Hills

Dunby Road

Indigo bunting & devil's paintbrush

River fills with spawning salmon in fall

HOCKLEY VALLEY PROVINCIAL NATURE RESERVE

Jeju Olle Friendship Trail

Nottawasaga River

P

Woodside

5th Line EHS

Sally's Pinnacle

Long stretch of full-on spring foliage

Landmark car

Breakfast with the vultures

Hockley Road

2nd Line EHS

5th Sideroad

Day 18
Hockley Valley /
Anderson Tract

N W E S

24.5 kilometres / 7h 5m
BT Map #18

Main Bruce Trail
Side trails & roads
Jeju Olle Friendship Trail

FIELD NOTES

START TIME: 7:20 a.m., Monday, June 6, 2022

TRAILHEAD WEATHER: overcast, threatening rain

DISTANCE: 24.5 km

ELAPSED TIME: 7h 5m

BT SECTION: Caledon Hills

BT MAP: #18

MAIN BT WALKED: 52.0 km to 69.3 km

ASCENT: 1118 m / **DESCENT:** 1142 m

SIDE TRAILS: Hockley Heights Side Trail

FLORA/FAUNA OF NOTE: indigo bunting (*Passerina cyanea*), wood thrush (*Hylocichla mustelina*), tall buttercup (*Ranunculus acris* L.), devil's paintbrush (*Hieracium aurantiacum*), oxeye daisy (*Leucanthemum vulgare*), Chinook salmon (*Oncorhynchus tshawytscha*)

In which I dedicate the hike to making a great ride of it.

I dedicate today's hike to Mitzi Lange — a woman who, along with her husband Bob, taught me lessons about how to live. I met Bob and Mitzi in Pátzcuaro, Mexico, where they'd recently bought an ancient ruin overlooking this historic town's chaos of red-tile roofs. In their adopted country, outdoor cafés surround the main square. People meet in this public space and community is made as clouds of luminescent pigeons flow between soaring ash trees.

Mitzi, an accomplished musician, hailed from West Virginia, where her parents christened her Minnie Mae. Bob was a retired doctor. They were vibrant, filled with excitement about this new chapter in their late-70-year-old lives. They hired a young Mexican architect who overflowed with ideas. For three years, they schemed, planned, built and came to know their Mexican neighbours.

I'd recently been in contact with Mitzi who, while as eloquent as ever, relayed sad news. Though he'd seemed fit as a fiddle the last time I'd seen him, Bob had been diagnosed with stage four lung cancer. I felt as if I'd been boxed in the ears. *Not possible*, I thought. I couldn't couple such a vibrant man and this diagnosis.

That morning, I received an email from a mutual friend. Henriette began her note with a birthday greeting. Then this: "I'm sorry to tell you but there has been a tragic event recently that has gripped our community [Pátzcuaro]." In the next line, she mentioned Bob and Mitzi. I prepared for the worst. *How*, I wondered, *could Bob have died so quickly?* I'd corresponded with Mitzi only weeks ago, and though the prognosis wasn't good, there was no mention of imminent death. Then again, I knew that cancer victims often die from related health complications. I read on.

You'll recognise it when you see it.

"Bob and Mitzi were in a horrific car accident near Zacatecas last Thursday afternoon." It wasn't the bad news I'd expected, but how could this be added to such a difficult time for them both? It wasn't fair. Henriette continued, ". . . and Mitzi did not survive it."

Henriette went on with more unsettling details. Unlike in Canada where our system of common law means innocent until proven guilty, in Mexico you are pretty much guilty until proven innocent. Despite the tragedy, and regardless of witness accounts of how the other car veered into my friends, the police put Bob in jail overnight. Can you imagine it? Your wife has just been killed and you are taken away to a holding cell. Worse yet if you happen to be a doctor. It took some haggling for a lawyer to get Bob — who, remember, has stage four lung cancer — released.

~~~

So it was with a saddened heart that I began walking through the Hockley Valley. Overcast skies seemingly ready to burst with tears reflected my mood. Mist enveloped me as I trodded along thinking about Mitzi, her short, curly, blonde hair atop playful eyes. It wasn't hard to imagine her with a guitar despite my never having had the pleasure of hearing her play — and now never would. Some people just have more life than others, more energy, more umph. Their absence creates a larger space that's harder to fill. That was Mitzi.

The forest enveloped me, yet it didn't penetrate. Or it didn't until the trail dropped into a ravine. At the bottom, a stream cascaded down a series of natural ledges forming a sequence of foot-high waterfalls. The crystal-clear water seemed to be having fun, maybe even laughing, as it gurgled its merry way downhill. It reminded me of the life and joy in Mitzi's eyes. Yes, she was gone, but like the water, Mitzi had made a great ride of it.

As I continued along, I began hearing the birds. I imagined they were trying to cheer me up. Spring was slipping into summer, and with it the cacophony of calls that had been keeping me company was diminishing too. At times on my last few walks, I heard no birds at all. But today, the blue jays, wood thrushes, red-bellied woodpeckers and others I couldn't identify were back. I mourned for Bob having to live this tragedy, but I knew the birdsong would have delighted him, had he been along to witness it. The sodden foliage was so fecund, so bursting with life and energy, egging me on, challenging me to live with the courage and verve of my now late friend.

For two uninterrupted hours, I navigated that forested trail. I felt "buried" in nature, enveloped by the maples and cedars. I saw no one. I was alone yet not lonely. When I finally emerged from under that blanket of trees, I followed the trail to the top of a ski hill where I gazed over the rolling landscape of the Hockley Valley. For the first time since leaving Queenston, I encountered livestock. There was a field of sheep below and I could hear lowing cows. I was stunned to realize I'd walked almost four hundred kilometres and this was the first time I'd come across the farm animals that were once so prevalent in this countryside. Many people crave climbing mountains or walking by the sea, but rolling meadows and forests interspersed by old barns and stone farmhouses are my landscape.

I crossed meadows where the birds took it up a notch. I imagined they were celebrating a successful breeding season and heralding a hopeful, happy future. Earlier, I'd watched a woodcock stand guard as her tiny chicks crossed the road. Now I spied meadow birds flitting happily from bush to shrub to telephone wire. I shared their joy at the freedom of this open countryside, the ability to see long distances. Buttercups, devil's paintbrush and daisies had replaced the trilliums and Jack-in-the-pulpit. They seemed happier than their ephemeral cousins which had been trapped under a thickening canopy.

Though similar to the Forks of the Credit, the Hockley Valley is a half-order of magnitude grander. The valleys deeper, the slopes steeper and the trees taller. Often, I walk a 10 kilometre loop following the Tom East, Isabel East and Cam Snell side trails before heading back along the main BT. But today, I followed the main BT to the Hockley Heights Side Trail to complete a 24.5 kilometre loop. It meant I was walking in the reverse direction to my norm — a norm I hadn't previously known I had. Walked backwards, this familiar landscape felt peculiar. I couldn't get my bearings. When I came upon the landmark wreck of car on my right rather than my left, I couldn't turn my brain around despite my knowing the car was exactly where it should be. It was like suffering from vertigo with a bit of amnesia thrown in. I was relieved to pop out onto Dunby Road and regain my mental balance.

Picking up the Hockley Heights Side Trail, I followed it into the Anderson Tract, a municipally owned forest, anticipating its long steep climbs. As I made my way up and down, the sky closed in and those tears finally broke through. The rain never amounted to more than drizzle, so I continued along tired but content among enormous maple trees until I began descending the deserted 5th Line to the Nottawasaga River.

Crossing the bridge just short of the Hockley Road, I recalled walking there one sunny September day a few years earlier. That day, the river churned with enormous spawning adult wild Chinook salmon (their average length is three-quarters of a metre). The sight reminded me of pioneer claims about being able to walk Jesus-like across rivers on the backs of fish. Sparkling, silver-bellied giants who were on their annual one-hundred-plus-kilometre journey from Georgian Bay up the Nottawasaga to spawn in its headwaters.

What a day. It had started with such sadness about the loss of my friend Mitzi yet was ending with so much life. First, all those birds bragging about their breeding prowess and now the memory of these magnificent salmon making their way upstream to lay eggs for a new generation. Not for the first time, I recognized the healing power of nature and thought about the circle of life. I couldn't believe I had the privilege of spending endless days walking along this spine that traverses Southern Ontario. It was day 18 and as the BT led me deeper into rural lands, I felt as though I wasn't simply walking through the forest and across meadows, I was becoming a small part of the landscape. I had a place there too. Maybe there really was a bit of the Niagara Escarpment in my DNA.

Dufferin
Hi-Land
Section

MONO CLIFFS PARK / SPLITROCK

MURPHY'S PINNACLE / MULMUR LOOKOUT

ROCK HILL PARK / KILGORIE / PINE RIVER

Day 19

MONO CLIFFS PARK / SPLITROCK

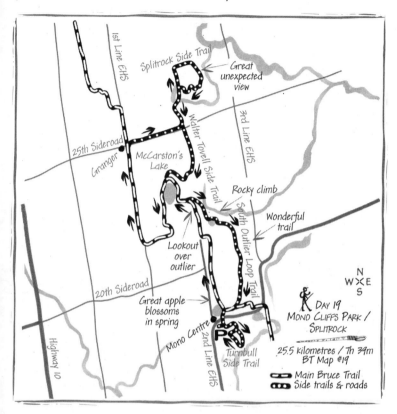

On the map:
1st Line EHS · Splitrock Side Trail · Great unexpected view · 3rd Line EHS · Walter Tovell Side Trail · 25th Sideroad · Granger · McCarston's Lake · Rocky climb · Wonderful trail · South Outlier Loop Trail · Lookout over outlier · 20th Sideroad · Great apple blossoms in spring · Mono Centre · 2nd Line EHS · Turnbull Side Trail · Highway 10

N W E S

Day 19
MONO CLIFFS PARK / SPLITROCK
25.5 kilometres / 7h 39m
BT Map #19

◨◨ Main Bruce Trail
◨◨ Side trails & roads

FIELD NOTES

START TIME: 7:50 a.m., Thursday, June 9, 2022

TRAILHEAD WEATHER: overcast, then sunshine

DISTANCE: 25.5 km

ELAPSED TIME: 7h 39m

BT SECTION: Dufferin Hi-Land

BT MAP: #19

MAIN BT WALKED: 0.0 km to 9.6 km

ASCENT: 956 m / **DESCENT:** 985 m

SIDE TRAILS: Laidlaw Side Trail, Turnbull Side Trail, 2nd Line EHS Side Trail, Splitrock Side Trail, Ralph Tremills Side Trail, Lookout Side Trail, Walter Tovell Side Trail, Carriage Side Trail, South Outlier Connector Trail, South Outlier Loop Trail

FLORA/FAUNA OF NOTE: American crow (*Corvus brachyrhynchos*), eastern white cedars (*Thuja occidentalis*), white birch (*Betula papyrifera*)

In which city slickers put Brampton on a pedestal in the lee of four-hundred-year-old cedars before I fail Peter Cellar's après-hike test.

A walk through Mono Cliffs Provincial Park is always great, but a walk through the park followed by a pint in the Mono Cliffs Inn's Peter Cellar's Pub is greater! It's a cozy spot with a fireplace and a miniature train. Sadly, however, I hadn't planned my après hiking well. I had another obligation, so a great hike would have to do. As I pulled into the parking lot at the Mono Centre's community hall my windshield wipers were slapping time, to quote Janis Joplin. Fortunately, when I set out along the Laidlaw Side Trail enroute to the Turnbull Side Trail it had let up.

I crossed a rolling meadow dotted with apple trees. Laden with moisture, the tall grass obscured the trail. Before long, my shoes, socks and trousers were soaked. The Turnbull Side Trail is another lolli-loop. This time around a pleasant forest, much of it mature hardwoods. The path followed a babbling brook for a time and would make a great after-work stroll with your dog.

I took the Laidlaw Side Trail into the park, where I picked up the main BT. I hadn't walked far when I came across a murder of crows. Because they can be so raucous, crows can be irritating, but they are highly intelligent birds with considerable problem-solving skills. If you ever get the chance, look one in the eye. You'll see it thinking. They are also fierce defenders, known to join forces to mob predators — as in Hitchcock's *The Birds*.

At the top of the cliffs that give the park its name, I admired the vista from a lookout platform. It's a spectacular spot with a view of one of the park's outliers. Vaguely resembling a top hat, an outlier is an area of younger dolostone surrounded by older rocks that have eroded away. I descended a staircase hugging the bluff as it passed through a near tunnel. Ferns cascaded from the moss-coated cliff face. Wafts of the thick peaty fragrance of humus emanated from weeping cracks and crevices. Above me, sinewy eastern white cedars sprouted from the rock — their girths, about the size of my arm, belying their age. The most ancient cedar in the park is almost four hundred years old.

Back up at the top of the stairs, I entered a forest that was bright with white birches, then it was back into the eerie cedars as I climbed to McCarston's Lake. There wasn't a breath of wind nor a ripple on the water. I found a well-placed rock, extracted myself from my backpack and pulled out my breakfast. I wished I'd brought along a thermos of milky coffee. It was so beautiful that I couldn't resist sending a photo to my younger sister in Montreal. As I continued walking, my phone beeped. It was my sister oohing and aahing about the lake. Then she inquired about a trip we were planning. As I walked, we were back and forth for five or ten minutes until I realized I was not taking in anything around me. I had completely lost Jordan. *This is nuts*, I thought. I suggested to my sister that we chat in the evening.

I entered the Mono Tract, one of about a dozen forested areas that make up Dufferin County's 1,066 hectare Dufferin Forest. Then it was a small dirt road bordered by working farms. I could hear cows as I approached Granger, or what's left of it. There was an old red-brick farmhouse and, surprisingly, a Catholic cemetery. In its early days, Dufferin County was dominated by protestants, many of them loyal to the Orange Order. In those days, every village had an Orange Hall and celebrated parade day on July 12. This papist graveyard was a different kind of outlier than the one I'd just admired in the park.

Turning north, I walked to one of my favourite loops: the Splitrock Side Trail. In the parking lot, a fellow hiker was just leaving. "It's very peaceful," he promised. I walked through an old farm field lined on one side with robust maples. The path then made a near 90-degree turn and skirted the top of the escarpment. I didn't notice the sheer cliff until I went to inspect one of the largest white birch trees I'd ever seen. I'd been walking for over two hours since breakfast so I took advantage of a bench with a view. I was halfway through a snack when an energetic poodle came bounding along the trail. Seeing me, she stopped dead, barked a few times as if to say, "What the heck are you doing here?" then turned tail. A minute later, two women and a second dog appeared. I looked at them and they looked at me and we all said, "Well, I don't believe it." One was my university roommate, the other her daughter. We traded stories and I joined them for the remaining portion of the Splitrock Side Trail. It was a nice change to have someone to walk with, but I entirely missed the Narrows Side Trail that follows a deep crevice, despite it being my favourite part of the Splitrock Side Trail. Ah, but it was worth it to gab with my old friend.

Re-entering the park, I followed the Walter Tovell Side Trail. Renowned for having written *Guide to the Geology of the Niagara Escarpment* in 1992, Walter Tovell was the recipient of Ray Lowes's letter about having to release the idea buzzing around his head. At the time, Tovell was president of the Federation of Ontario Naturalists. He was an exceedingly nice man whom I'd had the pleasure of meeting on several occasions before he died.

The Lookout Side Trail climbed to a rocky spot with a sweeping view of farm fields, silos and forest. It was Southern Ontario countryside — the landscape I'd been born into and raised in. As I enjoyed the vista, I heard a man and woman protesting loudly about how terrible the maps were and how they hadn't seen anything and blah blah blah. They asked me what there was to see. I swept my arm out toward the expanse below. "Oh, this is nothing," the woman said. "We've travelled all over the world." They asked for directions to the viewing platform, which I gave them, though I was tempted to send them in the wrong direction.

A few minutes later, I came up behind the pair at McCarston's Lake. This time, they were complaining the trail was too far away from the lake. "Have you been to Heart Lake in Brampton?" she asked. "It's much larger and has a boardwalk around it." Next, they wanted to know why they saw more wildlife on the trails in Mississauga. I explained that in urban settings certain types of wildlife including deer and coyotes are opportunistic; they become accustomed to people so they don't run away. "The wildlife here are wild," I said. I was tempted to add, "and they'll eat you," but resisted.

Shaking my head, I walked on to the Carriage Side Trail and then the South Outlier Connector Trail to the South Outlier Loop Trail. The sun had come out dappling the trail as it followed an old stone fence, lined with maples. I summitted a rocky pitch slowly as I'd been hiking for about seven hours and was getting tired. At the top, I had the same lofty feeling as I'd had on Sally's Pinnacle. I'd found Jordan again. A breeze blew and I felt free.

Day 20

MURPHY'S PINNACLE / MULMUR LOOKOUT

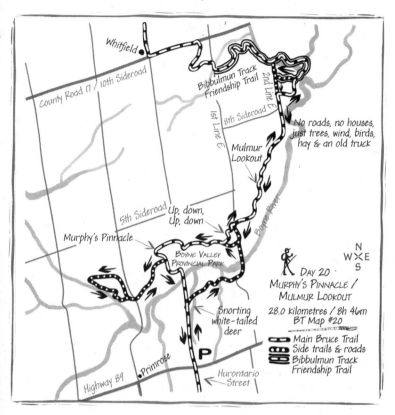

On the map:

Whitfield

County Road 17 / 10th Sideroad

Bibbulmun Track Friendship Trail

2nd Line E

1st Line E

8th Sideroad

No roads, no houses, just trees, wind, birds, hay & an old truck

Mulmur Lookout

5th Sideroad

Up, down, Up, down

Boyne River

Murphy's Pinnacle

BOYNE VALLEY PROVINCIAL PARK

N W X E S

Day 20 MURPHY'S PINNACLE / MULMUR LOOKOUT

28.0 kilometres / 8h 46m BT Map #20

Main Bruce Trail
Side trails & roads
Bibbulmun Track Friendship Trail

Snorting white-tailed deer

P

Primrose

Highway 89

Hurontario Street

FIELD NOTES

START TIME: 7:15 a.m., Saturday, June 11, 2022

TRAILHEAD WEATHER: sunny and breezy

DISTANCE: 28.0 km

ELAPSED TIME: 8h 46m

BT SECTION: Dufferin Hi-Land

BT MAP: #20

MAIN BT WALKED: 15.2 km to 25.4 km

ASCENT: 1235 m / **DESCENT:** 1223 m

SIDE TRAILS: Boyne Valley Side Trail, Mulmur Lookout Side Trail, Boyne Creek Side Trail, Oliver Creek Side Trail, 2nd Line ECL Side Trail, Primrose Loop Side Trail

FLORA/FAUNA OF NOTE: snorting white-tailed deer ("fremitus!" *Odocoileus virginianus*), ruffed grouse (*Bonasa umbellus*)

*In which I recognize writing about a hike and hiking a
hike are not the same before I cruise atop Mulmur's hills
in pursuit of William Thorsell's commanding view.*

Hike 20 — halfway right? Well, not exactly. Over 20 loops,
I'd only covered about four hundred kilometres. My average
length of hike was too short. I wasn't worried about walking
at least nine hundred kilometres to match the length of the
BT, but my goal had been to do it in 40 days. If I didn't, what
was I going to call my book? But there was so much to see.
How could I limit myself to just 40 hikes? I recalled Mary
from Alberta telling me, "I never knew what each day would
be like."

Today's route was still in my home territory. I'd climbed
Murphy's Pinnacle at least a half dozen times and the trails farther north that comprise the Bibbulmun Track Friendship Trail
were especially well known because I recently described this
route in *In The Hills* magazine. My hiking column is a descrip-
tive map. It's the closest I've come to producing a sketchbook.
Problem is I can't draw — or couldn't. But with the help of
some classes, I'm improving. I agree with Alain de Botton.

In his book *The Art of Travel* he writes, "Ten minutes of concentration at least are required to draw a tree; the prettiest tree rarely stops passersby for longer than a minute." Mapping my hikes and writing about them requires an intimacy unparalleled when I only walk a path.

From Hurontario Street, a dirt road that T-bones at Highway 89, the main BT heads north along the old road allowance that was likely closed because it crosses boggy terrain that would have been difficult to negotiate by horse and buggy and even worse by car. No trail user in Canada should take rights-of-way for granted. They are a gift that should be diligently protected from developers, aggregate miners and neighbours who will pave them over and dig them up as fast as you can say "unopened road allowance."

It was a gorgeous sunny morning, cool with a stiff breeze when out in the open. But the trail dipped down into a hardwood forest which was protected from the wind, and I was soon back into that meditative space that I seem to slide into more quickly after four hundred kilometres on the trail. I picked up the Boyne Valley Side Trail. The forest opened into a small meadow where a white-tailed deer leaped to the safety of trees. She snorted angrily, telling me to get the heck away. Likely, she had a fawn. Next a ruffed grouse gave me a start. It was early and I seemed to be taking local wildlife by surprise. I thought of the duo in the Mono Cliffs Provincial Park and their query about why they saw more wildlife in Brampton.

The Boyne Valley Side Trail went straight up, then straight down, then straight up and then straight down, over the road and then down some more to the river. Then it went up a set of switchbacks to the valley's rim. Phew! Following a recently mown, refreshingly level path along the edge of farm fields with the Boyne River Valley stretching out below me, I once again had that I-can-see-now feeling. Meadow birds swooped by riding the thermals created by the cold river. Crickets welcomed the now-warm breeze. I stopped for coffee and breakfast overlooking this vista from the Mulmur Lookout. I waved to a group of about 10 hikers. They would be the largest group I'd encounter along the entire BT. With the exception of parks and popular sites, such as waterfalls, the BT was anything but crowded.

A sign told me this was the Bibbulmun Track Friendship Trail. Walking Australia's one thousand kilometre Bibbulmun Track takes about eight weeks and requires remote camping. The trail leads you to beachheads and through giant karri and tingle trees. I figured that environment would be as alien to me as Southern Ontario's had been to Mary. Leaving the main BT, I turned left onto the Oliver Creek Side Trail, where I stopped beside this sandy-bottomed brook. It marked my turnaround point. I would enjoy the Mulmur Lookout a second time and had the view from atop Murphy's Pinnacle to look forward to.

Red tingle
(Eucalyptus jacksonii)

As I made my way up Murphy's Pinnacle, I met a young couple. We sat on the hilltop with William Thorsell's "commanding view" all around us, discussing the need for a new generation of people to care for existing trails and expand the network. A few drops of rain and an odd crack of thunder cut our conversation short. Leaving my perch, I followed the main BT through a meadow that I recalled as it was where I let my rescue dog Frida off leash for the first time. I had been terrified she'd take off, never to return. But she came back after having a romp, something she wouldn't have done much of growing up a stray in a dense urban city in central Mexico. How would it have felt to her to run free for the first time in her life?

I branched off the main BT, making my way around the Primrose Loop Side Trail. With about half a kilometre to go before returning to my car, the atmospheric pressure dropped, the sky darkened and thunder rumbled ominously. A race against the weather was on. On tired legs — I'd already covered 28 kilometres and climbed 1,235 metres (the most of any on my journey) — I booted it up the hill and crossed the highway with the rain in hot pursuit. I dumped my pack into my trunk and jumped into the driver's seat. Whoosh. Another entertaining — and dry — day.

Day 21

ROCK HILL PARK / KILGORIE / PINE RIVER

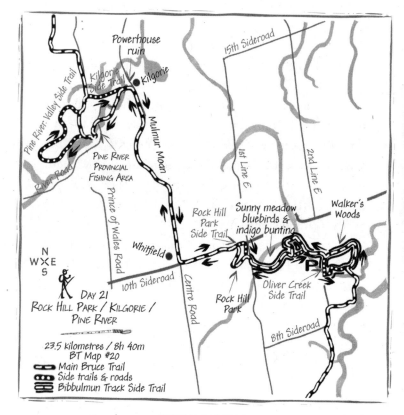

FIELD NOTES

START TIME: 7:45 a.m., Monday, June 13, 2022

TRAILHEAD WEATHER: sunny and gorgeous

DISTANCE: 23.5 km

ELAPSED TIME: 8h 40m

BT SECTION: Dufferin Hi-Land

BT MAP: #20

MAIN BT WALKED: 25.4 km to 37.0 km

ASCENT: 914 m / DESCENT: 905 m

SIDE TRAILS: Oliver Creek Side Trail, David Hahn Side Trail, Pine River Valley Side Trail, Kilgorie Side Trail, Rock Hill Park Side Trail, Moss Haven Side Trail, 2nd Line East Side Trail, Murphy's Pinnacle Side Trail, Primrose Loop Side Trail

FLORA/FAUNA OF NOTE: indigo buntings (*Passerina cyanea*), tree swallow (*Tachycineta bicolor*), bumblebee (*Bombus*)

*In which I realize I don't mind my own company, but I
sure wish I'd had more of Dad's before I rock with Stompin'
Tom, and Mulmur's Moan mass wastes my love handles.*

I've read a lot about how walking is one of the best things
you can do for your physical and mental health. Experts say
that as little as 20 minutes a day reduces the risk of heart
attack and diabetes, helps with depression, improves your
memory . . . You name it, walking helps it. So being hooked
on putting one foot in front of the other on a trail through
forests thick with immune-system-boosting phytoncides
and past waterfalls with feel-good negative ions is high on
the list of good addictions. Besides, walking is inexpensive
and can be done anywhere. Remember 91-year-old Patricia
Stevenson and her pair of retrievers whom I met on my first
day on the trail? Walking sure worked for them.

When I arrive in Tobermory, this journey will surpass
what I've done before. My previous "best" was the 34 days
I spent walking 894 kilometres along St. Frances's route on
the Camino de Santiago in Spain and on to the coast. Some
say everyone walks their own Camino, but I believe the

Camino chooses your walk for you. It was as if this ancient pilgrimage was waiting for me to show up. Every morning I hitched up my backpack and set out. I didn't have a map and there weren't any cellphones tempting me to stay in touch. I simply followed yellow arrows from refuge to albergue across the entire country. I never contacted my partner throughout the entire journey as I wanted a complete break. After I returned home, he told me he'd tracked my progress by monitoring where I was withdrawing money from our shared bank account. But for that month, I was in Jordan, albeit the Jordan of the Camino's choosing.

On my BT journey, I walk day after day for eight or more hours. Just me and the little world around me. Occasionally, I get tired and think it would be nice to be finished for the day, but mostly not. Mostly I amble along lost in my thoughts or in bird calls or in the nature of the forest or that flower. I'd thought I'd want friends to walk with me and though I've enjoyed the times I've been with others, I'm enjoying my own company. I hadn't known I was a solo walker.

Looking back on my notes, I sense a tension has dissipated. After four hundred kilometres, it's hard to recall worrying about whether I love the Niagara Escarpment enough. It's like wondering if you should love your child or your spouse or friends more. For me, the answer, "no," simply isn't an option. I almost always feel as though I'm not doing enough for others. The same applies to the Niagara Escarpment. What more can I do? Then I thought of Bernd Heinrich's desire to love more deeply. I'd thought a lot about my mum over the kilometres, less about my dad. It's not surprising; I knew my mum for six decades, my dad for two. My older siblings got the best of him. By the time I was old enough to appreciate his quiet wisdom, it had been stolen from him — and me. Recently, my eldest sister wrote a poem about Dad that captured my bittersweet memories.

My Father's Walking Stick

Idle now, it leans against the stone
cold fireplace.

Humble in its brevity —
A Malawi tribal cane, its handle barely
Long enough to grasp, a stalk
Of hardwood
Carved in patterns
Intricate and indecipherable.

Where did he get it?
On some long ago safari? I never asked
And so I'll never know.

He brandished it on his daily walks
To the end of our long driveway,
Swinging it with a beguiling
Nonchalance, almost gaily,
Whistling a tuneless tune, off key,
Bereft of harmony, as though
He didn't need support — the illusion
Of stability.

He was nearly blind from a stroke
But never complained. Once,
I found him standing by the mantlepiece
alone — weeping silently.

Dad's walking stick

Like the point of a flaming arrow
Extinguished by the wind
The tip of his stick is blackened, charred
From the long winter hours he sat
By the hearth poking and prodding
The embers, rolling the smouldering logs
Over and over and over
Trying to rekindle
A fire going out.

— Cessie Ross

I can't get past the image of Dad weeping silently by the mantlepiece without my throat catching and my eyes tearing up. He became ill and died so young. I missed the benefit of his wisdom. When asked what I do for a living, I tell people I'm a writer and a "professional hiker." I may not have had the chance to seek Dad's advice on life, but I'm pretty sure he'd admire my choice of vocation.

≈

It was damp in the still-sunless valley when I began walking. Buckets of rain had fallen overnight so the trail was greasy and puddled. It was nothing like Australia's Bibbulmun Track. Summertime hiking is discouraged downunder due to extreme daytime temperatures. I tolerated today's gloom knowing there were open meadows ahead. Climbing out of the valley, I walked through Walker's Woods, a majestic hardwood forest named after Chris Walker, who was a Bruce Trail Conservancy director and trail volunteer. Once again, I was struck by how important this trail is to so many people. So many people, so dedicated to a strip of dirt.

Emerging into the sunshine, I stopped for breakfast, enjoying it with a pair of indigo buntings, a dutiful bumble bee and a tree swallow that had taken up residence in a bluebird house. I crossed the 1st Line East of Mulmur and it was as if I'd been transported back to an earlier hike, maybe the one through the keyhole in Limehouse. Rock Hill Corner, as it's called, is riddled with moss-covered crevices — cracks in the stone that have expanded over time. The cycle of freezing and thawing erodes crevices through a process called mass wasting, which sounded like what had happened to my "love handles." As the crevice erodes, its outer wall thins and begins shedding fragments. They drop to the foot of the cliff forming a talus slope: a mound of rock that skirts the base of a cliff. In this way, the escarpment recedes and is forever changing.

As fascinating as the Rock Hill Corner's geology might be, it's the story of Rock Hill Park that niggled at my memory banks. In 1958, Elwood and Jean Hill began holding country music concerts at their potato farm located pretty much where I was standing. Elwood was a gifted promoter, and soon Rock Hill Park events were attracting thousands of campers and some big-name performers. As the flowerchild 1970s approached, Elwood picked up on the rock 'n' roll craze. In 1969, the same year Max Yasgur hosted Woodstock on his farm, Rock Hill Park was home to the infamous Freak Out concert headlining the rock bands Lighthouse and The Guess Who. As described by Ken Weber in *In The Hills* magazine, thousands of "hippies" turned up for a "camp-in, swim-in, paint-in, dance-in," which proved to be too much for Elwood's neighbours. A law passed prohibiting overnight concerts, but that didn't discourage Elwood. He returned to his country roots and daytime events. In the ensuing decade and a half, crowds of ten thousand or more converged on Rock Hill Park to hear the likes of Willy Nelson, Stompin' Tom Connors, Conway Twitty, Freddy Fender, Hank Snow, Wilf Carter, Tommy Hunter, Barbara Mandrell, Johnny Paycheck and dozens more of North America's biggest names in country music. I'm not sure the von Trapps would approve, but them hills were alive with the sound of country music.

I enjoyed the warm sun on my shoulders as I walked along a paved road toward the shuttered roadside church that is all that remains of Whitfield. Stopping to take a photo, I tried to imagine the scene in the late 1800s when Whitfield had three stores, two sawmills, three churches, a post office, school, lime kiln and two taverns. Not for the first time, I was struck by the industriousness of Canadian pioneers. It took them only a few years to build their cabins, clear farmland by chopping down trees of immense proportions and create working towns. Some had opera houses. I once read that it took a decade for tree roots to rot. Until then, farmers tended their crops among enormous stumps. A sixth-generation Canuck, I'm lucky to have come from such hardy stock.

I arrived at the top of the Mulmur Moan, a long climb down into Kilgorie that I nicknamed in recognition of Vancouver's Grouse Grind. A young runner came loping toward me. I asked him: "Did you run all the way from the bottom?" He nodded yes, shaking his head as if to say, "I know, it's crazy!" Down and down and down I went, arriving in Kilgorie about half an hour later. I passed the white schoolhouse that the Bruce Trail Conservancy once thought of turning into a hostel. Then the trail re-entered the forest alongside the energetic Pine River. While the Boyne ambled along, the Pine galloped. I passed ruins of the old Dufferin Power and Light Company whose turbines were turned by this tributary to the Nottawasaga. The boisterous roar of the post-rainstorm river flooded the valley.

Eventually the trail came to a peaceful lake, part of the Pine River Fishing Area, the breeding grounds for those Chinook salmon I once saw in the Hockley Valley. The sky was blue, the water was mirror-like and the vegetation still had the robust look of spring. As I enjoyed a break, a young family launched a canoe and slowly made their way down the lake. Behind the boat, a subtle wake spread across the water. It was such an iconic Canadian scene that I laughed. A fellow hiker stopped to compare notes. He was walking the BT piece by piece, dropping off a bicycle at the trail's end and then riding it back to the trailhead. We sat for a time, content to enjoy the lake and the perfect hiking weather.

I followed the newly minted Pine Valley Side Trail past four former fishing ponds, which were slowly reverting to marsh. It was so beautiful and felt so remote that I reluctantly picked up the Kilgorie Side Trail to begin my return trip. I had a way to go that included climbing up the Mulmur Moan. Hills aren't my forte, but all the hiking I'd been doing had made a difference. Despite the temperature having climbed to near 30 degrees Celsius, I enjoyed my ascent in the shade. Returning along the road past Whitfield, I ran into Henriette and Bob, more hikers on a piecemeal end-to-end journey. I didn't know it at the time, but 2022 would be a record year for end-to-end recognitions. Some 294 people recorded this goal, more than triple the number in 2010. Compare this to the near two thousand people who complete the 430 kilometre

Pennine Way, Britain's most popular trail. In Canada, walking is not a national pastime as it is in England. On the upside, as I was discovering, crowding is not an issue on the BT except, perhaps, on a sunny Sunday afternoon near a major urban centre or a waterfall. How lucky we are to have all this space. Let's love it to life.

Blue Mountains Section

Day 22

NOISY RIVER TO NOTTAWASAGA BLUFFS

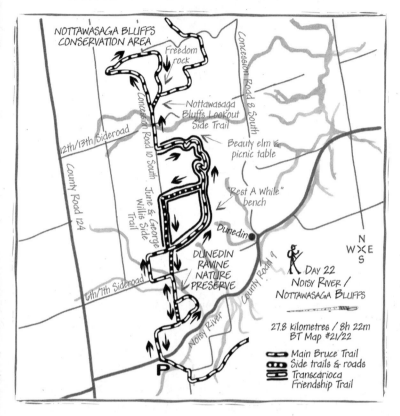

FIELD NOTES

START TIME: 8:30 a.m., Thursday, June 23, 2022

TRAILHEAD WEATHER: sunny, humid & breezy

DISTANCE: 27.8 km

ELAPSED TIME: 8h 22m

BT SECTION: Blue Mountains

BT MAP: #21/22

MAIN BT WALKED: 6.1 km to 22.9 km

ASCENT: 989 m / **DESCENT:** 988 m

SIDE TRAILS: Nottawasaga Bluffs Lookout Side Trail, June & George Willis Side Trail

FLORA/FAUNA: OF NOTE: tall buttercups (*Ranunculus acris* L.), oxeye daisies (*Leucanthemum vulgare*), purple vetch (*Securigera varia*), white clover (*Trifolium repens*) and red clover (*Trifolium pratense*), bird's foot trefoil (*Lotus corniculatus*), Canada anemones (*Anemone canadensis*), baby's breath (*Gypsophila paniculata*), wild roses (*Rosa acicularis*)

*In which there's bad news on the tick front
but a celeb moment, sunshine, open meadows
and dive-bombers save the day.*

I'm back after visiting Alex at his Lodge at Pine Cove on the
French River in Northern Ontario for 10 days. He bought
a wreck of a "camp" in a spectacular setting about 25 years
ago and turned it into one of the province's premier destinations. There are 20 gorgeous cottages, each with a screened
porch overlooking the water. Some have copper bathtubs; all
have fine views of a peaceful setting that makes you proud
to live in this province. I describe his lodge as rustic with
high thread count linens. Breakfast — think freshly baked,
sweet-smelling croissant — arrives at your cottage door in a
wicker hamper; the dining room is a wrap-around veranda
with an outstanding chef from Montreal. You can read a
book, canoe, kayak, swim or simply do nothing. Alex is there
for six months a year overseeing the operation. He virtually
never leaves. I was gobsmacked when he came down to host
my birthday garden party. He's a man lovingly addicted to his

work. I call him my partner with lodge benefits. And oh yeah, he's exceedingly handsome too!

Most mornings, I was in my kayak not long after the sun had risen above the tilting Group of Seven white pines. Slicing through water so smooth that it reflected trees with Robert Bateman's precision, I began my days in mindful peace. Occasionally, I'd see a beaver glide silently by or an otter pop up, its whiskered snout rotating like a submarine's periscope. For 45 minutes or so, I'd dip the blade of my paddle rhythmically, left, right, left, right. Then I'd pull up to the rocky shore of a deserted island, disembark and sit in the sunshine sipping hot coffee I'd brought along in a thermos. When I'd begin my return trip, the water would already be rippling with the slight breeze, upside-down trees distorted, the beavers asleep in their lodges.

≈

My time at the lodge wasn't entirely stress-free, however. After my tick bite in May, I'd taken a single dose of an antibiotic and was symptom-free. No flu, no sore muscles and the bull's eye rash had disappeared. Then, on June 8, my doctor wanted to "discuss my blood test results." Sure enough, I'd contracted Lyme. The tick wasn't just black-legged, it was among the 20 percent of black-legged ticks that carry the offending bacteria. The red bullseye hadn't lied. My doctor referred me to an infectious disease specialist who would decide if I needed to take the next treatment advised for Lyme: a two- or three-week round of antibiotics.

The call ended and I put down my phone. The temperature seemed to drop and then my heart rate picked up. I'd thought I was prepared for this outcome, but it hit me like someone's death you are expecting. You think you are prepared for it but when it comes you realize you weren't. The people I knew who suffered from Lyme disease really suffer. It's a debilitating, life-long ailment that can be treated but never cured.

I did my best to put Lyme disease out of my mind, as there was nothing I could do until I saw the specialist. I took comfort in the fact that I felt great. By the weekend, when I still hadn't heard from the specialist, much less seen him and started the next round of antibiotics, I began to panic. I'm not prone to anxiety, but I really, really, really didn't want to get Lyme disease. I called my doctor, and she came through with the prescription. I filled it, had another blood test and breathed a bit easier. Not out of the water but working on it.

I was halfway through the antibiotics by the time I left the lodge and made the four-and-a-half-hour drive back to Caledon. The specialist had set my appointment for July 6. When I arrived at the trailhead for my first hike post-lodge, I was feeling hopeful. Nonetheless, I tucked my socks securely into my trousers. This was the first of my hikes in the Blue Mountain section of the BT and I'd be staying in the 'hood, as I'd booked four nights in a retro holiday trailer that was parked in a field on Farmer Doug's land west of Singhampton. It was affordable and looked like fun.

At the roadside parking area next to the Noisy River Provincial Park, I met Angela and Annette from Elora. They were hiking south, while I was heading north. In answer to their queries about my being well equipped for a day hike, I explained I hiked for a living. Then, without prompting, they asked, "Do you write the Loops & Lattes guides?" Nodding, I felt like a celebrity. Proudly, they each pulled out a copy of

Collingwood, the Blue Mountains & Beaver Valley Hikes: Loops & Lattes and asked me to sign it. This had started to happen with some regularity since Covid hit. For once in my life, I'd been in the right place at the right time. When virtually every activity except eating, drinking and walking were shut down by the pandemic, people took up hiking. Sales of my guidebooks were already pretty good, but they tripled in 2020–21. In January 2022, Joel Rubinoff wrote an article for the *Record* entitled, "Local hiking guide beats 'Harry Potter' to become indie bestseller." At Words Worth Books in Waterloo, *Waterloo, Wellington & Guelph Hikes: Loops & Lattes* had displaced J.K. Rowling's phenom to become the store's bestselling book ever. At the Bookshelf in Guelph, the same guide was a star. The store's owner told me, "In 2020, it was our bestselling book by far (even beating Barack Obama's book) and is in our top 10 for 2021." I began doing what writers aren't known for: I was making a living.

Books signed for my fans, I set off and it was as if the trail knew it needed to keep my mind off Lyme disease. Between my celeb moment, the ideal weather, the sweeping vistas, the rolling hills, open meadows, airy forests and even the spooky cedar ones, I breezed along. When I stopped and wished there was somewhere to sit, what appeared? A bench, of course. Fittingly, it bore a plaque that read: "Rest A While, in recognition of James 'Dave' Knox, 1944–2021."

I think of spring as being flower season, but all morning I'd been cheered by a summery collection of tall buttercups, daisies, purple vetch, white and purple clover, bird's foot trefoil, Canada anemones, baby's breath and more. Once again, I felt that in comparison with spring ephemerals, these meadow flowers were less complicated. There was nothing sophisticated or shy about them; they exuded happiness.

Oxeye daisies
(*Leucanthemum vulgare*)

I followed the Blue Mountain section's friendship trail:
the Transcarioca Trail in Brazil. When I see Transcarioca, I
always read it as trans-karaoke and feel as though I should
dress like Elvis and break into song. Really, it's a 183 kilometre
route that crosses beaches and passes by Sugarloaf Mountain
in Rio de Janeiro and Corcovado Hill (the one with Christ
the Redeemer on top). It's Brazil's first long-distance hiking
trail and part of the country's plans for a five-thousand-
kilometre coastal route.

I came across a soaring elm tree of remarkable elegance,
bordered on two sides by a riot of wild rose bushes laden with
blooms. This was turning out to be a better hike than I'd remembered. Arriving at the Nottawasaga Bluffs Conservation Area's
parking lot, I began my return journey — first stop Freedom
Rock. Standing on this flat-topped dolostone outlier, bathed
in sunshine, I looked over a band of green trees backed up
against a sky so blue it looked painted on. Freedom Rock is a
mystery. Someone once etched crudely written philosophical

texts into the rock. Before mass wasting — remember mass wasting at Rock Hill Park? — erased them, these slogans were photographed:

TO BE FULLY
EDUCATED ONE
MUST FARM
5 YRS

and

A PESSIMIST A COWARD
AN OPTOMIST A LIAR
A REALIST A HERO

Not your typical graffiti. I recalled my motto — Stay Lost! — that had disappeared from the highway underpass near Hamilton.

On my return journey, I followed a pair of side trails but mostly retraced the main BT. I stopped at the picnic table below the massive elm, admired the wild roses again and took in the vistas. On another unopened road allowance, I heard a lot of cackling. When I stopped to investigate, a tree swallow swooped past me. I ducked, shielding my head. Peering out from below the brim of my straw hat, I saw another bird heading directly for me. It grazed my head before wheeling around like a fighter jet. As I watched it turn, a third bird dive-bombed me or maybe it was the first one coming in for a second go. Cowering, I took cover. The pair were furious, attacking me with determined malintent. I wasn't just reminded of Alfred Hitchcock's *The Birds*, I was living it. This protective behaviour is typical of tree swallows (and red-winged blackbirds) when they fear their young are at risk. I thought back to the swans near Terra Cotta whose similar behaviour had reminded me of my mum.

Getting out of there lickety-split, I continued along in the sunshine. I'd picked a tough route, almost 28 kilometres, for my first hike in 10 days. I was pooped, but looking up the trail and knowing I had five hundred more glorious kilometres of the BT left was like sipping on sloe gin topped off with sparkling water. I felt at ease being back on the trail.

Day 23

NOTTAWASAGA BLUFFS KEYHOLE / MAD RIVER SIDE TRAIL

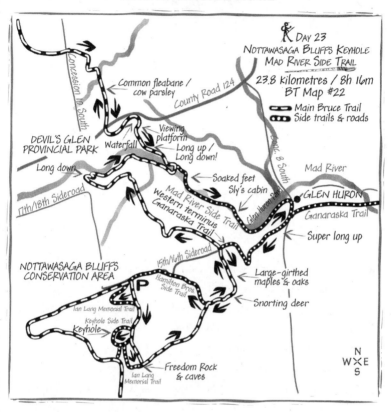

Day 23
NOTTAWASAGA BLUFFS KEYHOLE
MAD RIVER SIDE TRAIL
23.8 kilometres / 8h 16m
BT Map #22
▭▭ Main Bruce Trail
▭▭ Side trails & roads

Concession 10 South
Common fleabane / cow parsley
County Road 124
DEVIL'S GLEN PROVINCIAL PARK
Viewing platform
Waterfall
Long up / Long down!
Long down
17th/18th Sideroad
Soaked feet
Sly's cabin
Mad River
GLEN HURON
Western terminus Ganaraska Trail
Mad River Side Trail
Concession 8 South
Glen Huron Road
Ganaraska Trail
Super long up
NOTTAWASAGA BLUFFS CONSERVATION AREA
15th/16th Sideroad
Large-girthed maples & oaks
Hamilton Bros. Side Trail
Snorting deer
P
Ian Lang Memorial Trail
Keyhole Side Trail
Keyhole
Freedom Rock & caves
Ian Lang Memorial Trail
N W E S

FIELD NOTES

START TIME: 7:30 a.m., Friday, June 24, 2022

TRAILHEAD WEATHER: sunny, coolish, mosquitos

DISTANCE: 23.8 km

ELAPSED TIME: 8h 16m

BT SECTION: Blue Mountains

BT MAP: #22

MAIN BT WALKED: 21.9 km to 34.2 km

ASCENT: 936 m / **DESCENT:** 947 m

SIDE TRAILS: Ian Lang Memorial Trail, Nottawasaga Bluffs Lookout Side Trail, Keyhole Side Trail, Mad River Side Trail, Ganaraska Trail, Hamilton Bros. Side Trail

FLORA/FAUNA OF NOTE: mallards (*Anas platyrhynchos*), eastern meadowlark (*Sturnella magna*), common fleabane (*Erigeron philadelphicus* L.), cow parsley (*Anthriscus sylvestris*, also called mother-die), white-tailed deer (*Odocoileus virginianus*)

In which Farmer Doug welcomes me to his funny farm
before I explore the trail's devilish ways and relate
my Covid-induced brush with civil disobedience.

After completing my hike yesterday, I picked up dinner in
Creemore and arrived at Farmer Doug's at about 6 p.m.
Wearing trousers, a wrinkled collared shirt and a worn base-
ball cap that said Wild Turkey over what was left of his shorn
hair, George, as Farmer Doug was otherwise known, showed
me around his meticulously kept farm. The grass was closely
mown, the old bank barn and brick house were in good shape.
Flowers bloomed in various gardens. Doug didn't strike me as
a local so I asked him about his background. "Ah," he said, "I
was a Toronto hippy. In the 1970s, I bought this old farm."
I didn't think to ask him if he'd attended the Freak Out
concert at Rock Hill, but he seemed the type. "I've tried
everything to make a go of it," he said without remorse. As
we toured his recently white-washed barn, he introduced me
to his donkey. "I had a petting zoo for a while," he volunteered. Nodding toward his long-eared pet, he said, "That's
all that's left of it." We walked toward his house where a pair

of huskies romped in the fenced yard. "I tried dog sledding too." Nodding at the dogs, he added, "That's all that left of it — them and my wife. She came here to run the sledding operation."

He jumped into his vintage red convertible jeep. On the driver's door there was a large round emblem that read: Municipal Area Police. I followed in my car with his 12-year-old border collie, Georgie, trotting alongside. We drove for about a kilometre following a grassy track until we came to a field the size of a couple of football pitches where there were three well-spaced vintage holiday trailers. Each had an outdoor biffy, bottle of drinking water, picnic table and camp stove. I was his only guest. He showed me inside the immaculate trailer, taught me to use the stove and waved goodbye. It was just me, sunshine and the smell of fresh-cut grass.

Clamping with mosquitos

At 6:30 the next morning, dew pooled on the lid of my cooler, and I wished I'd brought gloves. But the stove fired up and I soon had a mug of hot milky coffee in hand. An hour later, I parked at the Nottawasaga Bluffs Conservation Area, where I'd turned back the previous day. I took the conservation area's Ian Lang Memorial Trail to the Nottawasaga

Bluffs Side Trail, which led me to the Keyhole Side Trail, an example of a side trail that trumps the main BT. I clambered over crevices, negotiated tunnels and fit through the keyhole. The sun hadn't reached Freedom Rock, so I looked for caves. Peering into the dark abyss of a big hole in the limestone, I was not tempted to go spelunking. Instead, I found a sunny clifftop where I enjoyed a second coffee.

The trail entered land owned by the Devil's Glen Ski Club, which generously allows the main BT and several side trails to cross it. Thank you Devil's Glen Ski Club (and all other individuals and companies/clubs that allow us to access their land via the BT). The trail zigzagged down to the Mad River. On each switchback, I waded through the same muddy creek, which was tiresome after about the 10th crossing. Then I thought about Philip Gosling bushwhacking through unbroken forest and didn't feel so hard done by.

I had no sooner arrived at the Mad River than I started up the other side of the valley to visit the Devil's Glen lookout. It's a steep climb and with the temperature hovering near 30 degrees Celsius, I was dripping by the time I made it. But the view was worth the effort. I sat in the shade looking over the Mad River valley, a.k.a. Devil's Glen.

In my *Collingwood, the Blue Mountains & Beaver Valley* guidebook, I gave this loop a creepy name: the Mad River in the Devil's Glen Loop. Devil's Glen joins the Devil's Punchbowl on the Niagara Peninsula, the Devil's Pulpit in the Forks of the Credit, the Devil's Playhouse near Owen Sound and the Devil's Monument on the Bruce Peninsula. Each has a story. In *Devil's Glen Country Club*, author Christine Cowley quotes a document written in 1902: "At our feet, below the ledge . . . whole trunks of trees bleached by alternate rain and sunshine . . . formed a waste of utter desolation, so tersely and fitly described by the uncanny name 'The Devil's Glen.'"

The glen sits on the Manitoulin bedrock ledge, the site of a glacial meltwater channel that once flowed along the top of the Niagara Escarpment. Like the Nottawasaga River and the Hockley Valley, the Mad River and Devil's Glen are an example of a misfit river in a re-emergent valley. In geological terms this refers to a valley created by a large river that was blocked by ice during the last ice age. When the glacier receded, a smaller river — a misfit — re-emerged into the incongruously large valley.

Retracing my way down to the Mad River, a tributary to the Nottawasaga, I picked up the Mad River Side Trail. The last time I'd walked it, it was a perfect spring afternoon in May 2020. The first Covid lockdown had been lifted days before and the BT had just reopened. I wasted no time in heading out to work on my Collingwood guidebook. It was like getting out of jail. As I wandered along today, I recalled the joy I'd felt that day. In Bodsworth's 1962 article in *Maclean's* magazine, he wrote about the freedom of walking a trail that stretches on and on. Pre-Covid, no one could have predicted the "on and on" BT would one day be shut down.

When I first learned the conservancy had closed the trail, I was appalled. *Cowards*, I thought. I learned later there were good reasons for the closure, but at the time, I was upset. Yet another wall was closing in. Another restriction. I knew hiking was important to me and that I used the BT a lot, but like so many things, I didn't understand how key it was until it was taken away. I was among those who learned that being outside "in nature" was as important for my mental health as it was for my physical wellbeing.

During the tightest lockdown, Alex and I would sneak past orange barriers to take our shortcut, which crossed public land (not private) to the Caledon Ski Club where hiking trails remained open to members. I had fortunately maintained my membership. We'd stay hidden in the trees at the edge of the Forks of the Credit Road until the coast was clear (no cars coming), as though we were thieves on a getaway. Only then would we pop out of the forest and continue on our way. For variety, we'd walk on back roads, not 100 percent sure this was allowed. We were never stopped, but masked drivers would scowl as they drove by.

We took some delight in defying the rules, as did a friend, who was walking across an open field next to his house during the lockdown, when an OPP cruiser drove by. The cop pulled over, turned on his flashing lights and from the roadside yelled through his blowhorn: "Stop. It's the police. Stop what you are doing. Immediately," or some such. The officer couldn't have known if my friend was on private or public land, and I'm not sure what the charge would have been — illegal hiking? — but my friend's animated retelling of the story proved he too had been enlivened by his brush with civil disobedience.

I'm not prone to breaking rules, especially ones related to hiking. When I come to Trail Closed signs or No Dogs Allowed or Keep Dogs on Leash signs, I obey them (Covid and the Belfountain Park excepted). Irresponsible and thoughtless hikers are a particular problem for the BT because much of the trail crosses private land. Landowner agreements are tenuous. They can be easily revoked. During Covid, many landowners understandably didn't care to have strangers, perhaps Covid-carrying strangers, on their property. The Bruce Trail Conservancy realized the best way to avoid friction was to remove it. Hence their unprecedented, and difficult, decision to close the trail.

The importance of hiker etiquette on a trail, especially one that relies on the goodwill of private citizens, can't be overstated. A blatant example of stupidity are the people who climb the fence to get closer to Hamilton's waterfalls. More often, however, it's small things that result in landowner complaints: walking off the trail, littering, allowing dogs off leash near homes or farms, lighting fires and more. There's a reason why the popular motto "Take only memories (or photos), leave only footprints" (generally attributed to Chief Seattle) is a mantra among hikers. Maintaining positive landowner relations was a founding principle of the BT. In his book, Norman Pearson wrote, "We have always said that the Bruce Trail exists and will only survive by the kind permission of the landowners, and as a result of the responsible good and considerate behaviour of the users."

I passed Sly's Cabin, a replica of the original John Sly lived in from the 1880s until 1920 when it burned down. Sly logged much of the area that is now owned by the Hamilton Bros. Co. An interesting feature of the trail past the cabin is the corduroy road. Corduroy roads are made by laying evenly sized logs across a quagmire, a technique sometimes used on the BT. I admired the millpond that had delighted me in 2020 and wondered if the mallards were the same ones I'd seen two years earlier. Entering Glen Huron, I was struck by the size of the Hamilton Bros.'s building and farm supply operation. There's even a side trail named after the company.

I climbed past Glen Huron's operating water wheel and the old church that's now a private residence. Farther along, the Mad River Side Trail turned right and followed an old road allowance up and up and up. Fortunately, it was forested most of the way. For once I wasn't complaining about shade. At the top, there was a cairn marking the western terminus of the Ganaraska Hiking Trail. It runs from this point to Port Hope.

I rejoined the main BT, following it toward McKinney's Hill (elevation 502 metres) where I startled a deer. She snorted furiously, a warning behaviour similar to when a beaver slaps its tail. Given the time of year, I kept an eye out for a fawn curled up in the grass. I've almost stepped on one a couple of times as their mothers often leave them unattended. There are a number of myths about fawns, including that twins have the same father. Au contraire. Many wild animals, especially birds lack our disdain for philandering. About a quarter of "twin" fawns, have different fathers. Similarly, if you pick up a fawn, leaving your odour on it, its mother doesn't reject it. So, if you make the mistake as I once did and "rescue" a lone fawn, take it back to where you found it. Mum will return and won't be put off by its strange scent. Instead, she'll recognize her offspring by its smell. Fawns may have less odour than adults, but they are not odourless. From a young age they engage in a practice common to white-tailed deer: they urinate on their tarsal glands. Deer recognize each other largely by scent, and the interaction of urine and excretions from their tarsal glands (located inside their hind legs) is key to each deer having a unique smell.

I'm pretty sure I didn't smell like a combination of urine and tarsal-gland excretion, but it had been an unusually hot day for June. I was looking forward to a cold beer and another night at Farmer Doug's.

Day 24

PRETTY RIVER VALLEY / STANDING ROCK

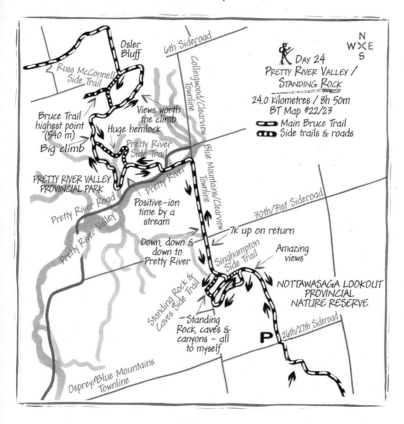

Osler Bluff

Russ McConnell Side Trail

6th Sideroad

Collingwood/Clearview Townline

Day 24
PRETTY RIVER VALLEY /
STANDING ROCK
24.0 kilometres / 8h 50m
BT Map #22/23
▬▬ Main Bruce Trail
▭▭▭ Side trails & roads

N
W E
S

Bruce Trail
highest point
(540 m)

Big climb

Views worth
the climb

Huge hemlock

Pretty River
Side Trail

PRETTY RIVER VALLEY
PROVINCIAL PARK

Pretty River Road

Pretty River Valley

Pretty River

Blue Mountains/Clearview Townline

Positive-ion
time by a
stream

Down, down &
down to
Pretty River

7k up on return

30th/31st Sideroad

Singhampton Side Trail

Amazing
views

NOTTAWASAGA LOOKOUT
PROVINCIAL
NATURE RESERVE

Standing Rock & Caves Side Trail

— Standing
Rock, caves &
canyons — all
to myself

P

26th/27th Sideroad

Osprey/Blue Mountains
Townline

FIELD NOTES

START TIME: 7:30 a.m., Saturday, June 25, 2022

TRAILHEAD WEATHER: beauty, high 32 degrees Celsius

DISTANCE: 24.0 km

ELAPSED TIME: 8h 50m

BT SECTION: Blue Mountains

BT MAP: #22/23

MAIN BT WALKED: 39.3 km to 53.1 km

ASCENT: 1143 m / **DESCENT:** 1123 m

SIDE TRAILS: Standing Rock & Caves Side Trail, Russ McConnell Side Trail, Pretty River Side Trail, Singhampton Side Trail

FLORA/FAUNA OF NOTE: mosquitos (*Culicidae*), maidenhair spleenwort (*Asplenium trichomanes*), wood fern (*Dryopteris carthusiana*), turkey vultures (*Cathartes aura*)

In which I curl up in the backseat of my car before sliding on my backside through Standing Rock's slick, sun-deprived crevices and crannies. Down and up, down and up, down and finally, painfully, up.

When I returned to my lair, I still had the two football pitches to myself. Good for me. Not so good for Farmer Doug. After a quick sponge bath, I let the sun dry me off as I sipped on a cold brew. Afterwards, I had some dinner and spent the evening working at my picnic table. It was luxuriously warm. The sky was cloudless. The smell of recently mown grass reminded me of childhood summers. Birds chattered. Farmer Doug advertised his trailers as "glamping," a combo of glamorous and camping, and so it was. It was like being in the backcountry with a comfortable bed and no heavy backpack. Then dusk arrived and with it, a hatch of mosquitos. Smugly, I retired to my trailer.

I cozied into my bed but was soon shedding blankets. Despite the windows being open, it was warm and airless. I had just drifted off when that dreaded buzz woke me up. Zzzzzzz. I swatted a mosquito that explored my ear. Zzzzzzz. As I rubbed one on my nose, I felt my elbow itch. Zzzzzzz.

Zzzzzzz. Zzzzzzz. I pulled the sheet over my shoulders. *Zzzzzzz. Zzzzzzz.* I hated to turn on the light fearing it would attract more of these pests even though I knew it was carbon dioxide, not light, that attracted them. But I had to check the screens. No holes. I turned the light off figuring they must have come in the door when I'd gone out just before bed. If I was patient, I'd kill the ones inside and have a good night's sleep.

A pesky mosquito

But it didn't matter how many mosquitos I swatted, they kept coming. They bit me right through the sheet, so I had to pull up a blanket despite the stuffy heat. Soon I was sweaty, itchy and wide awake. *Zzzzzzz. Bug repellant*, I thought. I applied it to my shoulders and face. No effect. *DEET*, I thought. I applied it to my shoulders and, yuck, face. *Zzzzzzz. Zzzzzzz.* Finally at around midnight, I gave up. Carrying a sheet, a couple of blankets and my pillow, I climbed into the backseat of my car. I was a bit stiff in the morning, but I'd slept. I had another long day of hiking, so better a few aches and some sleep than no aches and no sleep.

While making coffee, I decided to move out. My sister in Meaford agreed to give me refuge. Blaming the mosquitos on the unusually warm weather, Farmer Doug refunded me for the nights I wouldn't be staying, but refused to return my money for the night I spent in my car. That seemed unfair, but I wanted Farmer Doug to add glamping to his list that included wife, rather than the one that included petting zoo and dog sledding.

♒

Somewhat sleep deprived, I entered a big-bad-wolf (a.k.a dark) forest. Despite clear skies, I could have used a headlamp, reminding me of the Songbird Side Trail in the Caledon Hills section. None too soon, the landscape opened, and I followed a wonderful stretch of trail through an airy maple bush as the main BT paralleled the Niagara Escarpment cliff top in the Nottawasaga Lookout Provincial Nature Reserve.

Ninety minutes into the hike, I left the main BT, opting for the Standing Rock & Caves Side Trail. It's a gnarly 630 metre trail that's tricky but fun. I'd walked it before, but in the opposite uphill and easier direction. That time, I got halfway through before turning turn back due to ice. I only made it when a pair of hikers came along, and we helped each other navigate the slippery conditions. This time, I picked my way among the jumbled boulders and entered the first canyon by sliding down a sweaty flat stone on my backside. The other time I'd been here, my dog Frida tried walking up the same rock, but it was too steep. Grasping desperately with her toenails, she slid back down. Then, she backed up a few paces and made a run for it. Her momentum carried her to the top. Since then, I've learned that she's a climber. If she can't get around a stile, she runs up it and bumps down the other side — a handy skill for a hiking dog.

Despite it being a gorgeous Saturday morning, I had Standing Rock to myself. It was eerie at the base of 10 metre high vertical stone walls coated in moss and festooned with cascading ferns like the set of an Indiana Jones movie. I occasionally glimpsed the distant blue sky as I made my way from one dripping cavern into the next, slipping through slots so narrow my daypack caught on both sides. A dank earthy smell completed the film's backdrop in the sun-deprived cavities. I thought about the mischief that group of mud-caked students I'd observed in the Woodend Conservation Area would have had among these craigs and crannies. Emerging from the labyrinth, I was at the base of Standing Rock, a pillar stranded some 80 metres from the edge of the escarpment. Geology works in mysterious ways.

When I'd explored the Keyhole Side Trail in the Nottawasaga Bluffs Conservation Area, I thought it was like the Limehouse Hole in the Wall on steroids. Now I found Standing Rock and its caverns to be like the latter on LSD. Once again, I was pleased by my side-trail-rich looping version of a BT end-to-end.

The trail descended about 250 vertical metres to the Pretty River. I decided to slow down as my route would take me back up that vertical climb, then down it again and then up it for a final, exhausting time. All on mosquito-interrupted sleep. Despite having completed 23 hikes over more than five hundred kilometres, I still found ascents taxing. I wanted to be fit enough to sprint uphill, but so far slogging was more like it.

I'd hiked much of the Pretty River Valley Provincial Park for my Collingwood, the Blue Mountains and Beaver Valley guidebook, including this section. It was May 5, 2020, a few days before enjoying those mallards on the millpond by Sly's Cabin. It had been a nasty day, overcast, with drifting snow alternating with pelleting rain. But I didn't care. I had a get-out-of-jail-free card. I was so happy to be outside, I didn't notice the weather or, it seems, the long climb. I had no recollection of there even being a hill! Not today. When I came to a babbling brook partway up, I sat down to admire its staircase of foot-high waterfalls, hoping negative ions would take me back to Jordan. If I was tired now, how would I negotiate the rest of this climb, much less the one on the south side of the valley. One step at a time.

After about five kilometres of steady uphill walking, a stretch of heavenly flat trail rewarded me. Then the climb continued. At the top — the real top — my weariness disappeared as I looked over vistas of Georgian Bay, checkerboard farms and turkey vultures soaring on thermals. I saw Old Baldy in the Beaver Valley, where I'd be in several days. It looked a long way away. When a fellow hiker arrived, we were struck speechless by how lucky we were to live in this marvellous place in such a wonderful country and to have the freedom to walk unencumbered.

I picked up the Russ McConnell Side Trail and began my return trip. Down and down, I went, lost in my thoughts. So lost, I bypassed the John Haigh Side Trail, thereby missing the highest point along the entire BT (540 metres). Fortunately, I'd been there before. When I made it back to the Pretty River, I removed my sandals and socks (classy, I know) and soaked my feet. Luxury. I had a bite to eat but could no longer delay my final ascent.

I'd like to say the way up was easier than I'd expected. Truth is, it was a long, arduous struggle. At the top, however, the escarpment came to my rescue with more sweeping views and a fresh breeze that offset the humid heat. I ran into Doug, who was training to walk the West Highland Way in Scotland.

We chatted about his upcoming adventure, and I tried to keep up with him, but he was too fast for my tired legs. I let him walk on, glad that at least for a time, our conversation had been a welcome diversion. Thanks, Doug, and good luck.

Day 25

LOREE FOREST / FLOWERPOTS

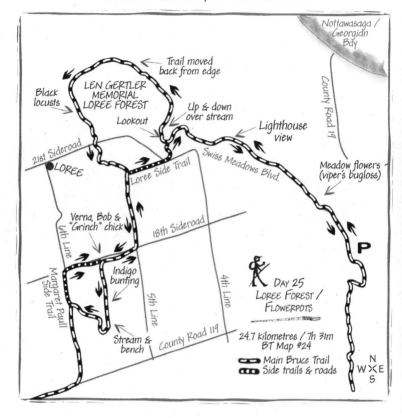

Nottawasaga / Georgian Bay

Trail moved back from edge

LEN GERTLER MEMORIAL LOREE FOREST

Black locusts

Lookout

Up & down over stream

Lighthouse view

County Road 19

Meadow flowers (viper's bugloss)

21st Sideroad

LOREE

Loree Side Trail

Swiss Meadows Blvd.

Verna, Bob & "Grinch" chick

6th Line

18th Sideroad

Indigo bunting

Margaret Paull Side Trail

5th Line

4th Line

Stream & bench

County Road 119

Day 25
LOREE FOREST / FLOWERPOTS

24.7 kilometres / 7h 31m
BT Map #24

⬤⬤⬤ Main Bruce Trail
⬤⬤⬤ Side trails & roads

P

N W E S

FIELD NOTES

START TIME: 8 a.m., Monday, June 27, 2022

TRAILHEAD WEATHER: sunny to start, but clouded up and windy, 18 degrees Celsius, no bugs

DISTANCE: 24.7 km

ELAPSED TIME: 7h 31m

BT SECTION: Blue Mountains/ Beaver Valley

BT MAP: #24

MAIN BT WALKED: 65.2 km to 67.3 km to 0.0 km to 13.3 km

ASCENT: 923 m / **DESCENT:** 928 m

SIDE TRAILS: Margaret Paull Side Trail, Loree Side Trail

FLORA/FAUNA OF NOTE: bird's-foot trefoil (*Lotus corniculatus*), tall buttercups (*Ranunculus acris* L.), crown vetch (*Securigera varia*), viper's bugloss (*Echium vulgare*), oxeye daisies (*Leucanthemum vulgare*), black locust (*Robinia pseudoacacia*), rose-breasted grosbeak (*Pheucticus ludovicianus*), indigo bunting (*Passerina cyanea*), weeping willows (*Salix babylonica*), St. John's wort (*Hypericum perforatum* L.), poison ivy (*Rhus radicans* L.)

In which I learn from my mum about being tethered,
before walking through Len Gertler's forest, and Verna,
Bob and a miniature Grinch capture my heart.

What a difference a mosquito-free sleep and a day off made.
My Meaford sister who saved me from mosquito-hell-in-a-holiday-caravan is the artistic one. Kate lives on what she grows in her garden and spends her evenings painting water-colours, fashioning clothing and canning. She bought a 28 hectare field, dug a pond, planted 22,000 trees and for seven years lived off-grid in a 14 foot by 7 foot (mosquito-free) caravan. Since she moved into the small house she built with her son, Kate's had to get used to the challenges of electricity and running water, a flush toilet and hot shower. I love her soft ethereal way and am secretly pleased I had this excuse to bunk in.

We went for a walk on my day off from walking. We followed a pretty section of the Big Head River, a rambling stream that flows through Meaford into Georgian Bay. Afterwards, we swam and then swam again. In between, our conversation drifted from life and friends to, of course, our siblings and parents. We especially talked about Mum. You'll recall her obituary written by my brother. It continued, "She was an unorthodox but diligent parent, the sort of mother who drove her children just about everywhere, often delivering them to the correct destination at the appointed time." We talked about her life as our mother: a downtown Toronto girl coping with frozen water pipes, vet bills and a husband who aspired to having an estate. When my niece was diagnosed with attention deficit disorder (ADD), a light went on. Clearly Mum had ADD too, something unheard of when she was young. As a student, she was expelled from several schools for her disruptive behaviour, brought on, no doubt, by her inability to concentrate. Mum coped with her ADD by taking copious notes, being beautiful, coy and a great flirt as well as "an unorthodox but diligent parent." Her obituary continued, "She taught her four daughters to protect themselves against the advances of overly amorous suitors by saying, 'Get off my lips, buddy. I gotta spit.'" (True!)

As school-aged kids, we were on our own most mornings, toasting toast and making our bagged lunches. Mum would have already left for Toronto where she had twice weekly tennis matches. She was also a member of the local garden club, sometimes winning prizes for flower arrangements she'd purchased. She could perform a pretty good cartwheel and joined us when we pulled out a skipping rope. Not for the first time, I recognized how like my mum I was — and wasn't. No, I don't cheat at flower arranging, but I have a mild case of ADD, as Alex reminds me. But mostly, I don't like feeling trapped. In some ways, Mum lived my nightmare: she was tethered by five children, nonetheless she coped. I cope too — but by avoiding tethers. I never had children. A dog is the most I can manage, and Alex, though he lives at his lodge for six months of the year. No wonder the free-dom of walking the BT, and doing it in my own looping way, appeals to me. Mum might have become too distracted to walk solo for eight hours a day, but she would have cheered me on along my journey.

〜〜〜

After the heat, it was novel to wear a fleece and be at risk of having the wind steal my hat. I charged along tracing the edge of the Niagara Escarpment. At my feet, Blue Mountain Ski Resort's slopes played out onto a narrow strip of flat land before blending into smoky blue Nottawasaga Bay, a broad inlet of Georgian Bay. Some people suggest Georgian Bay should be a sixth Great Lake and looking at it stretch to the horizon, it was easy to see why. Here, the Niagara Escarpment forms a long ridge that is home to Southern Ontario's best alpine skiing. Blue Mountains, the name of the local municipality and ski resort, actually loaned its mon-iker to the Blue Mountain formation: a regional shale layer likely stained blue by carbon-rich impurities.

Summer flowers were out as I walked for five kilometres along the flat top of the escarpment through meadows slowly reverting to forest given the woody plants that were growing tall enough to begin shading the open field. These were the types of trees and shrubs that Ontario Parks had removed from the Forks of the Credit Park. Nonetheless, I spied bright yellow bird's-foot trefoil mixed with tall butter-cups; red clover; crown vetch; oxeye daisies; St. John's wort, an anti-depressant and anti-inflammatory; and purple viper's bugloss, once used to treat viper bites (rattlesnakes are a type of pit viper). Surprisingly, all these everyday wildflowers are non-native — a reflection of Canada's large immigrant population?

The trail took me down to a small stream in the bottom of a steep-sided valley and up the other side. At the top, there was another vista of Georgian Bay with a thin cloud layer that was quickly filling in the occasional blue gap. Oblique streaks of sunshine illuminated narrow bands of the water's surface, making them sparkle. The wind had picked up so I pulled on my rain jacket over my fleece.

Intermittently, the Niagara Escarpment's characteristic Queenston shale surfaced, making the trail red. The name Queenston reminded me of walking through Queenston in the Niagara section — of Laura Secord, General Brant, the War of 1812 . . . I was recognizing the Bruce Trail Conservancy's depiction of the trail as a ribbon of wilderness linking Niagara's grape vines and suburbs to the Bruce's junipers and black bears. Reinforcing the connection, I ran into a pair of women on the trail — one was the garrulous hike leader I'd met back in Waterdown when I was walking with Gill.

I climbed into the 339 hectare Loree Forest, though it was officially renamed the Len Gertler Memorial Loree Forest in 2007. The Niagara Escarpment Commission, the organization that administers the Niagara Escarpment Plan, made the switch to recognize Gertler for his contribution to the protection of this biologically and geologically significant part of Ontario.

I followed the trail around the Loree Forest, past the Len Gertler Side Trail and the Georgian Peaks Ski Club. Bruised clouds held the promise of *weather*. I crossed from the Blue Mountain section into the Beaver Valley section where I bumped into two of the latter club's volunteers erecting BT signs. We shared a few laughs, and I thanked them for their efforts, not mentioning their work reminded me of the 1971

hit by the Five Man Electrical Band that lamented the proliferation of signs. I'd noticed how signs were proliferating
on the BT, some of them recognizing donors and others
warning of uneven footing or bears in the area. I hoped the
organization wasn't catching a case of sign congestion.

I came to a No Winter Maintenance sign. Beyond it, the
unopened road allowance deteriorated into a track where I ran
into Verna and Bob. In her late seventies, Verna carried a pair
of metal hiking poles. "These old things took me the entire
length of the Bruce Trail," she said. Bob held a wooden staff.
"I carved it myself over the years while waiting for my son
while he attended Scouts." Over a half century or more, it had
turned a rich golden brown, reminding me of my dad's cane.
Verna and I walked along sharing stories only to hear Bob —

Rose-breasted grosbeak
(Pheucticus ludovicianus)

"Come back," he said, beckoning with his staff. He'd spied a tiny chick perched at eye level on a sumac branch. Looking remarkably like a black, white and pink version of the grinch, his scowl was so ugly that this baby rose-breasted grosbeak was cute. He must have fallen from his nest and was too young to fly. We left the wee thing hoping mum would look after it.

I followed the main BT into the forest and then emerged onto a high meadow where I had that top-of-the-world feeling again. The wind made waves in the wild grass where I had hoped to see bobolinks, eastern meadowlarks, Baltimore orioles and other meadow birds. No luck, but I heard the familiar song and glimpsed the blue flash of an indigo bunting. Protected from the wind nearby a trailside stream with a six-foot waterfall and a conveniently placed bench, I took a break. Then it was up and down, up and down until I arrived at the Margaret Paull Side Trail. I had new respect for Verna and Bob. The five-metre-tall flowerpot (a rock formation shaped more like an hourglass than a flowerpot) on my left was the first of several I'd see before arriving in Tobermory.

I took a shortcut on the Loree Side Trail, crossed over a stream and passed by several enormous weeping willows, before retracing my way in. This time, I noted Collingwood's landmark lighthouse. It's no longer in use, but the Nottawasaga Lighthouse Preservation Society looks after this reminder of the days when Collingwood was a major ship-building town. Nearing my car, I ran into two stylish couples whose outfits tended toward bling-bling. They'd seen a sign for poison ivy and were nervous about it as they weren't sure what this nasty plant looked like. I pointed it out, as there was lots in the vicinity. As I walked on, I heard them congratulate each other for having worn long pants. Noting their gold-lamé sandals, I chuckled to myself.

Beaver Valley Section

OLD BALDY / METCALFE ROCK / PINNACLE ROCK
UPPER BEAVER VALLEY / EUGENIA FALLS / HOGGS FALLS
EPPING / JOHN MUIR / FAIRMOUNT SIDE TRAIL

Day 26

OLD BALDY / METCALFE ROCK / PINNACLE ROCK

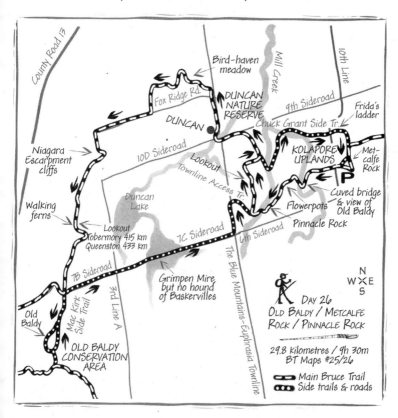

County Road 13

Bird-haven meadow

Fox Ridge Rd.

DUNCAN NATURE RESERVE

Mill Creek

10th Line

9th Sideroad

Frida's ladder

DUNCAN

Chuck Grant Side Tr.

Niagara Escarpment cliffs

10D Sideroad

Lookout

Townline Access Tr.

KOLAPORE UPLANDS

Met-calfe Rock

Walking ferns

Duncan Lake

Cuved bridge & view of Old Baldy

Flowerpots

Lookout
Tobermory 415 km
Queenston 433 km

7C Sideroad

6th Sideroad

Pinnacle Rock

7B Sideroad

Grimpen Mire, but no hound of Baskervilles

The Blue Mountains-Euphrasia Townline

Old Baldy

Mac Kirk Side Trail

3rd Line A

Day 26
Old Baldy / Metcalfe
Rock / Pinnacle Rock

29.8 kilometres / 9h 30m
BT Maps #25/26

OLD BALDY CONSERVATION AREA

N
W E
S

▭▭▭ Main Bruce Trail
▭▭▭ Side trails & roads

FIELD NOTES

START TIME: 7:30 a.m., Saturday, July 2, 2022

TRAILHEAD WEATHER: sunny, breezy, about 25 degrees Celsius

DISTANCE: 29.8 km

ELAPSED TIME: 9h 30m

BT SECTION: Beaver Valley

BT MAP: #25/26

MAIN BT WALKED: 27.9 km to 43.5 km

ASCENT: 1180 m / **DESCENT:** 1186 m

SIDE TRAILS: Mac Kirk Side Trail, Sideroad 7C, Townline Access Side Trail, Chuck Grant Side Trail

FLORA/FAUNA OF NOTE: canola (*Brassica rapa, Brassica napus* or *Brassica juncea*), walking ferns (*Asplenium rhizophyllum*)

In which Canada comes closer to reality before I grace
Old Baldy's pate and attempt to cross the Grimpen Mire.

I stayed at my friend Cheryl's in Thornbury the night before, on Canada's 155th birthday. I hadn't expected my walk along the BT to deepen my understanding of Canada's birth. But the stories that came to life in Niagara made me more aware that the country where my family has lived for six generations was the result of a well-orchestrated, hard-fought battle. Canada's forefathers had their sights clearly set on the goal of independence. They walked a fine line between British dominance and US aggression to achieve confederation. I'm proud of Canada. It's a great nation. But I was becoming increasingly aware of the price paid by First Nations, many of whom were key to Canada gaining its independence. As I walked for long days on a lonely trail, I began to properly process how First Nations were forgotten, cheated or worse once they had served their purpose. The price paid by First Nations was no longer something I sort of knew but didn't want to think about. It was part of Canada's fabric — part of my fabric — and couldn't be ignored any longer. It has been a long time coming, but like me, Canada is facing up to its past. A first step is better understanding.

Pre-Confederation, those living in British North America, as well as Britain itself, were aware of the risk posed by the United States with its policy of Manifest Destiny: that it was America's right to expand across all North America. This ideology didn't only apply to British North America, it justified removing Native Americans from their land, a practice that resulted in many of them fighting with the British against the United States in the War of 1812. When the war ended with the signing of the Treaty of Ghent, neither side declared outright victory, but neither admitted defeat either. The border may not have changed, but Canada stepped closer to independence. The war fuelled national pride, which contributed to the peaceful transfer of power from Britain to North America's new nation, though it took another half century and many of the promises and legal commitments made to First Nations were conveniently forgotten.

≈

I parked at a back entrance to Kolapore Uplands. The BT is among its 50 kilometres of hiking, biking and cross-country ski trails, and Metcalfe Rock is a popular climbing spot. I had a long, undulating walk ahead of me, but I knew it would be a beautiful and varied hike with spectacular views, including one from atop Old Baldy near Kimberley — one of the BT's most iconic landmarks. I was feeling trail-tough, pleased that my right knee felt better than ever despite my having torn the meniscus a year earlier. My core was strong and I'd dropped almost 10 pounds. Long daily hikes were agreeing with me mentally and physically. I remained free of Lyme disease symptoms, so hopefully I'd caught it early enough. I'd know better in four days when I would see the infectious disease specialist.

The trail started as I like it: across a meadow, but before long, I entered the woods, where I crossed Mill Creek (a tributary to the Beaver River) via a handsome curving bridge. I wondered how many streams in Ontario are called Mill and how many lakes are labelled Trout? Then it was up into the Duncan Crevice and Caves Provincial Nature Reserve where there were fabulous clifftop vistas complete with crows in hot pursuit of soaring vultures. This mobbing behaviour is presumed to be an effort by the smaller birds to chase away a larger predator. But naturalist Mark McKellar says mobbing isn't an effective means of protecting vulnerable chicks because the offending bird usually returns. Thinking back on my experience with tree swallows, I begged to differ.

I passed several developing flowerpots; they didn't quite have their characteristic hourglass shape, but, like me, were working on it. I crossed over a small waterfall that I recalled from my Collingwood guide, and suddenly a massive rock blocked my way. From its base, Pinnacle Rock soared overhead, requiring me to step well back to see to the top. Unlike other large rocks, Pinnacle Rock is not an erratic left behind by a glacier; instead, it reportedly let go from the cliff face. I imagined a giant Wile E. Coyote pushing it onto a hapless, though similarly oversized, Road Runner.

As I followed the 9th Sideroad, I inhaled the sweet smell of my childhood emanating from a freshly cut hayfield. Next to it was a yellow sea of canola. Derived from rapeseed by scientists in Saskatchewan, canola (a contraction of Canadian oil, low acid) is a Canadian success. Canada was the first in the world to produce large quantities of a rapeseed that was both healthy (because it contains linoleic vs. erucic acid) and palatable (because it has low concentrations of glucosinolates, which give mustard and horseradish their tangy and often unpalatable flavour).

The trail coursed cliffs that form the east side of the broad Beaver Valley. Well below me, the Beaver River rose up enroute to Thornbury, where it enters Georgian Bay. The main BT dips far to the south before heading north again in a grand V that I'm sure frustrates many end-to-end hikers. As a bird flies, it's about five kilometres from where I had just left the road to where the main BT runs along the opposite side of the valley. But as a BT hiker hikes, it takes two days of strenuous, albeit beautiful, walking to arrive at the same place.

According to a faded sign, I was 455 kilometres from Queenston and only 415 from Tobermory. The reality that these numbers didn't add up to even close to 904 is because the length of the BT has changed over the years. Sometimes, the trail is moved onto its optimum route, other times there may be a change in a landowner agreement or possibly permission to cross land that was previously off-limits. In this way, the BT's length fluctuates. Not including today's hike, I'd covered almost 550 kilometres in 25 looping hikes. So, although I was on track to walk at least nine hundred kilometres, I remained unsure I could do it in 40 hikes. Hmmm. I wasn't certain how I'd deal with this dilemma so in good Jordan style, I figured I'd ponder it when it came to mind.

The trail descended through greasy, green-tinted rocks that reminded me of the Forks of the Credit. Many sported mossy toupées so I was on the lookout for walking ferns. On cue, the characteristic slender leaves of these rare plants appeared. I entered the Old Baldy Conservation Area, having avoided the long detour through Kimberley as I'd walked it before and was already looking at a 30 kilometre day. A couple confused by the discrepancy between their outdated BT guide and the white blazes that directed them down the road, asked me: "Why do the blazes head down?" I explained that I understood there is a dispute between a landowner and the Bruce Trail Conservancy which accounts for the detour. The husband and wife decided it was best to follow their out-of-date guide.

I took the Mac Kirk Side Trail to Old Baldy, where I stopped for lunch atop his head, relishing the view, the sunshine, my hike, my life, the world in general. Examining the map, I realized my route might be considerably longer than 30 kilometres. So, when I spied a shortcut along an unopened road allowance that would save me an hour or more, I decided to give it a try. That infamous question came to mind: How bad could it be?

I started down a track devastated by ATVs, picking my way around metre-deep ruts filled with muddy water. It was slow going but I liked my sneak route, patting myself on the back for finding it. Then I looked up and that fateful question came back to haunt me. As it turned out, it could be bad — really bad. Ahead was the Grimpen Mire, the vast Devon bog populated by the glowering eyes of the Hound of the Baskervilles — or so it seemed despite the blue sky.

Road allowances are left unopened for two reasons: hills or swamps. There was no doubt why Sideroad 7C was not a through road. I dipped my single hiking pole into the mire. The good news was that the water wasn't very deep. The bad news was that the mud was bottomless, deeper than my pole was long. There were a few "stepping islands," each just large enough for me to teeter on in my two sandalled feet.

I hopscotched from one to another until I came to a log bridging an unleapable gap. When I prodded the log, it flipped over, exposing an enormous leech. *Oh good*, I thought, *a hiker-sucking mire of leeches*. I considered turning back, but I was halfway through. If I could make it across this chasm, it looked as if there was a manageable route to dry land. Where was that BT work party when I needed its gallant members?

Using my single pole — thank you god of hiking poles — I pulled the floating log toward me, lodging it into firmer mud. Then I tucked my notebook into my backpack (forgetting that my cell phone was in my rear pocket) and gingerly put weight onto the makeshift bridge. It felt solid — well, pretty solid. Next, I stabbed the foot island up ahead with my pole. It found purchase, tenuous purchase, but purchase. So, there I was all alone with no one having any idea that I had abandoned the BT and was attempting to cross the Grimpen

I walked all 950 km in my Keen sandals & my

Mire in hiking sandals. *This*, I thought, *is not what a certified hike leader is supposed to do*. I was straddling murky water, one foot on the island behind me and the other on a precarious log. My pole was embedded into a mound of sloppy earth, and surely that dastardly hound was waiting to eviscerate a fool like me.

Ever so carefully, I placed my second foot farther down the log. As I shifted my weight onto both feet, I heard a sucking sound as the log lifted behind me and the whole thing began to teeter forward into the abyss. Paralyzed, I watched as my sandalled feet, then my ankles disappeared into the leech-infested muck. *I'm going down*, I thought. On impulse or in desperation, I leaped toward my target: an island no larger than my pair of feet. On landing, I wobbled dangerously almost pitching forward. But my Black Diamond hiking pole saved the day. When I came to rest, my heart was beating thunderous strokes and I was shaking. Breathing hard, I took stock. My shoes and socks were slathered in black sludge, but I couldn't see any leeches. And up ahead? What was up ahead? A straightforward set of stepping islands. I hopped to the first one, then to the next until I was back on dry land. Phew.

≈

The Townline Access Side Trail led me to the Chuck Grant Side Trail enroute to Metcalfe Rock where I hoped to see some climbers. As it was late, I was tired and I'd hiked it before, I reluctantly bypassed the Metcalfe Crevice Side Trail. It's one of the BT's more challenging and fun routes. It packs a lot into 190 metres. Solid shear walls form a 30 metre deep canyon that requires you to scramble over boulders and squeeze through narrow passages. It's not for the faint of heart or dogs. I stopped long enough to watch a climber sashay up a cliff face wedging his toes and fingers into the narrowest of cracks. Then I pushed on as I'd been on the trail for over nine hours and was expected for dinner. When I looked at my GPS, I discovered I'd walked 29.8 kilometres, my longest day yet.

Day 27

UPPER BEAVER VALLEY / EUGENIA FALLS / HOGGS FALLS

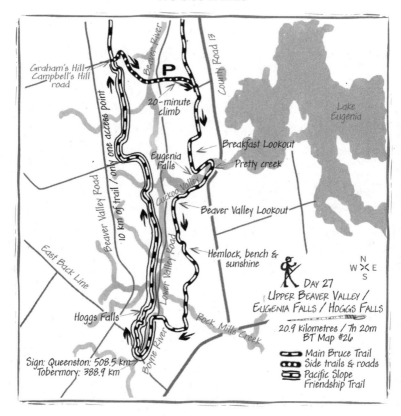

Graham's Hill
Campbell's Hill
road

Beaver River

P

County Road 13

20-minute
climb

Lake
Eugenia

Breakfast Lookout

Eugenia
Falls

Pretty creek

Cuckoo Valley

Beaver Valley Lookout

10 km of trail / only one access point

Beaver Valley Road

Lower Valley Road

Hemlock, bench &
sunshine

East Back Line

Day 27
Upper Beaver Valley /
Eugenia Falls / Hoggs Falls

20.9 kilometres / 7h 20m
BT Map #26

Main Bruce Trail
Side trails & roads
Pacific Slope
Friendship Trail

Hoggs Falls

Boyne River

Rock Mills Creek

Sign: Queenston: 508.5 km
Tobermory: 388.9 km

N
W · E
S

FIELD NOTES

START TIME: 7:45 a.m., Sunday, July 3, 2022

TRAILHEAD WEATHER: gorgeous

DISTANCE: 20.9 km

ELAPSED TIME: 7h 20m

BT SECTION: Beaver Valley

BT MAP: #26

MAIN BT WALKED: 56.8 km to 76.8 km

ASCENT: 861 m / **DESCENT:** 857 m

SIDE TRAILS: Campbell's / Graham's Hill Side Trail, Falling Water Trail, Pacific Slope Friendship Trail

FLORA/FAUNA OF NOTE: black-billed cuckoo (*Coccyzus erythropthalmus*)

*In which I have Eugenia Falls to myself before joining
gold-seeking kooks in the Cuckoo Valley as I combat my
choice of a shady route by regaling the birds with a shaky
rendition of every song I knew about sunshine.*

The weather had been in my favour pretty much since I'd
left Queenston exactly two months ago on May 3. I'd only
pulled out a raincoat on a couple of occasions. Otherwise, it
had been sunny and, with only a few exceptions, not too hot.
The weather in Southern Ontario isn't always agreeable, so
every hike-perfect day is a blessing — and today was another
blessing. It was Sunday on a long Canada Day weekend, so
I worried I'd run into crowds at popular Eugenia and Hoggs
falls, but that would be a small price to pay for the opportunity to explore the Beaver Valley under a chicory-blue sky.

I left my car in the valley bottom on Campbell's Hill
road. This meant I began (rather than finished) my hike with
a 20-minute climb along the Campbell's / Graham's Hill
Side Trail. By the time I arrived at the main BT, my blood
was pumping. I turned south and, entering a dark forest, I
realized I'd made a mistake. Given my day's loop route would
go south up the east side of the valley and then north down

the west side, I'd be longing for sunshine all day despite the cloudless sky. *Grrrr.* There were a lot of trees between me, great views and that big yellow ball of fire. I know my preoccupation with open meadows is obsessive, so I can't fault the Bruce Trail Conservancy for siting its trail inside the forest whenever possible. But couldn't there be a few more nods to people like me and Todd Bordes?

To rub it in, the sun teased me by occasionally settling on a patch of ground or a few leaves. To raise my spirits, I hummed John Denver's "Sunshine on My Shoulders." When that didn't help, I tried "You Are My Sunshine." When my weak-voiced rendition of that Johnny Cash classic failed, I picked it up with the Carter Family's "Keep on the Sunny Side."

After an hour, I climbed to my first lookout where there was yet another well-placed bench. The Beaver Valley Club has turned bench-placement into an art form. I dropped my pack and enjoyed the view while I ate half my sandwich. Trees obscured the sun, but it was airy and brighter. After my break, I skidded down a steepish slope to the Beaver River. I paralleled it upstream for about half a kilometre, crossed a bridge and then walked along as the Beaver cascaded over a series of metre-high drops enroute to the lip of Eugenia Falls. Rather than rushing ever faster toward the 30 metre plunge to the floor of the Cuckoo Valley, the river took its merry time, seemingly unaware of the drama ahead.

A popular tourist spot, Eugenia Falls is important in an industrial sense too. By the late 1800s, five mills and a power plant relied on it. Then, in 1915, Sir Adam Beck, the first chair of the Hydroelectric Power Commission, officially opened the Eugenia Hydroelectric Generating Station. It derives its energy from the Beaver River, backed up as it now is in Eugenia Lake. (Eugenia was named after Empress

Eugénie, Napoleon III's wife.) The innocuous power plant sits at the valley bottom near Kimberley, belying the fact it has the highest head of water of any hydroelectric generator in Ontario. Farther north, the BT passes a pair of large pipes (called penstocks on BT map #26) and two surge tanks (large relief valves that allow the system to burp without mishap).

As I neared Eugenia Falls, the path widened, its rocky, root-strewn surface polished by the footsteps of thousands of tourists. Given its popularity, I was surprised to have the lookout to myself. I could hear the falls before I saw it. As the water, made white by an optical phenomenon known as non-selective scattering, tipped over the precipice, it caught the sun's rays before plunging into the abyss — an abyss once thought to contain gold.

Eventually, I tore myself away, continuing to follow the 28 kilometre Falling Water Trail, which forms a loop along the main BT on both sides of the Beaver Valley from the Valley Crossover Side Trail to Hoggs Falls. Opened in 2008, this project was a dream of the Beaver Valley Bruce Trail Club and encompasses seven waterfalls, including Eugenia and Hoggs, as well as the lovely Cuckoo Valley. Part way down this curiously named glen, I came to a sunny lookout. From my perch, I looked over trees — trees, trees and more trees. There were no roads or houses, no gravel pits, just nature. The Cuckoo Valley's name may memorialize the "cuckoos" who, in 1852, failed to find riches in Eugenia's gold rush. A more likely possibility is because it's home to black-billed cuckoo birds, which don't, as you might expect, say "cuckoo," but do have zygodactyl feet (two toes point forward and two point backwards).

Though largely forested, the trail offered stretches of meadow where I inhaled the sunshine. It took me almost two hours to reach the Lower Valley Road. As I crossed it,

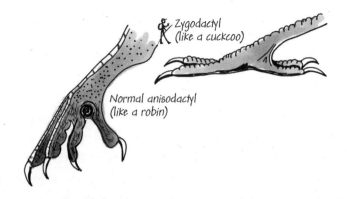

Zygodactyl
(like a cuckoo)

Normal anisodactyl
(like a robin)

I could hear Hoggs Falls. Once again, the trail widened and roots, exposed by busloads of tourists, made for tricky footing. This time I wasn't alone. There were families, groups of friends and a few hikers. I spoke to a pair of young park attendants who were on standby to organize parking, prevent littering and patrol for pranksters. The Boyne River, a tributary to the Beaver, flows over this seven-metre-high cascade that is twice as wide as it is high, making it a sheet waterfall. Before rounding the southern extreme of the Falling Water Trail, I found a peaceful spot on the bank of the river where I soaked my feet.

As I turned north on the west side of the valley, a sign informed me that I was walking along the Pacific Slope Friendship Trail, my seventh. The real thing is a series of paths in Costa Rica's Monteverde Cloud Forest, which reaches down to the Gulf of Nicoya. I've not hiked them but have completed the 260 kilometre Camino de Costa Rica. I crossed the country from the Caribbean Sea (Atlantic coast) to the Pacific Ocean in 16 days. I highly recommend hiking in this Central American country, despite my experience with a group of dysfunctional women, dog snatching and lost hikers.

I followed the trail over a series of short but steep climbs in the deep forest. Fortunately, it wasn't as dim as it had been earlier, and with the temperature still rising, I ambled along contentedly — for a while. The woods alternated between mature hardwoods and scrub softwoods. There were a pair of small waterfalls coated in tufa — a natural cement that looks like natural sponge. It forms when calcium carbonate, the compound associated with the white scale in your kettle, precipitates from water.

What impressed me was that there was only one access point for the next 10 kilometres. This length of uninterrupted trail doesn't (couldn't?) happen farther south, even in Blue Mountains or rural Dufferin. After a few nonstop kilometres in the trees, I began to feel as though I was spending a beautiful Sunday working in a dark office on what should have been my day off. I hummed "Sunshine on My Shoulders" again. Then, thankfully, after passing by the Stew Hilts Side Trail, I emerged from the gloomy depths into a meadow, complete with another irresistible bench. I lay down mimicking a reptile, exposing as much of me as possible to the sun's afternoon rays. Tipping my straw hat over my face, I listened to buzzing bees and chirping meadow birds, the breeze.

Eventually I emerged onto Graham's Hill / Campbell's Hill. Down I went until I came to a newish bridge over the Beaver River. The sun was high in the sky and my car was just up ahead so I followed a path to the riverbank where I freed my feet. With the hot afternoon Sunshine on My Shoulders, I was definitely on the Sunny Side of Life.

Day 28

EPPING / JOHN MUIR / FAIRMOUNT SIDE TRAIL

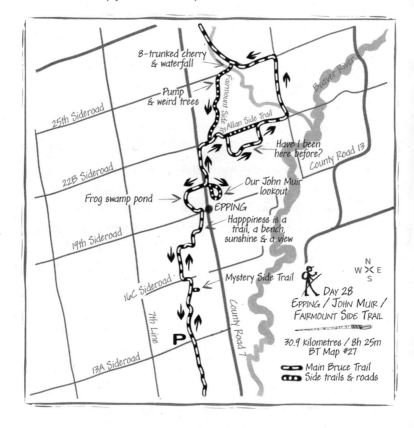

8-trunked cherry & waterfall

Pump & weird trees

25th Sideroad

Fairmount Side Trail

Allan Side Trail

Beaver River

Have I been here before?

County Road 13

22B Sideroad

Frog swamp pond

Our John Muir lookout

EPPING

Happpiness is a trail, a bench, sunshine & a view

19th Sideroad

16C Sideroad

Mystery Side Trail

7th Line

County Road 7

P

13A Sideroad

N W E S

Day 28
Epping / John Muir / Fairmount Side Trail

30.9 kilometres / 8h 25m
BT Map #27

⬤⬤ Main Bruce Trail
⬤⬤⬤ Side trails & roads

FIELD NOTES

START TIME: 8 a.m., Monday, July 4, 2022

TRAILHEAD WEATHER: sun turned to cloud, cool but no rain

DISTANCE: 30.9 km

ELAPSED TIME: 8h 25m

BT SECTION: Beaver Valley

BT MAP: #27

MAIN BT WALKED: 89.5 km to 106.1 km

ASCENT: 1128 m / **DESCENT:** 1121 m

SIDE TRAILS: Mystery Side Trail, Epping Lookout Side Trail, Fairmont Side Trail

FLORA/FAUNA OF NOTE: black cherry (*Prunus serotina*), western yew (*Taxus brevifolia*), brown knapweed (*Centaurea jacea*), musk mallow (*Malva neglecta*), devil's paintbrush (*Hieracium aurantiacum* or *Pilosella caespitosa*), common valerian (*Valeriana officinalis*)

*In which I recall the wildlife-rich Beaver River before I
contemplate the Wood Wide Web, a massive network of
mycorrhizal fungi, and am showered in anti-inflammatory,
anti-tumorigenic and neuroprotective spray.*

I gave into my craving and chose to skip forward to where the
Beaver Valley widens — and lets the sun in. I couldn't face
another day buried in shade. At the valley's edge, I basked in
the morning's glory. The Beaver River flowed below, gaining speed and heft as it coursed through the Beaver Valley
Lowlands, Heathcote and Thornbury enroute to Georgian
Bay. A year earlier, I'd spent three memorable hours kayaking
a section of the Beaver not far from where I stood. Birdlife
was around every corner: green and great blue herons, egrets,
ducks and geese. Afterwards, we jumped into the river's warm
water. The BT might not offer views of snow-capped mountain peaks, but the warm lakes and rivers it passes by offer
great swimming holes. As I skirted the ridgetop through the
Herman McConnell Memorial Forest, I practically skipped
along the level trail. This was my final hike in the Beaver
Valley section. When it was over, I planned to interrupt my
progress toward Tobermory until September when summer's

intense heat would have let up, the mosquitos toned down, and the forest would be slipping into autumn. Until then, I was going to miss these long days on the trail.

I came upon a mystery side trail. It was blazed in blue but had no signs, and it didn't appear on either my BT map or app. *Hmm*, I thought. *Where does it go?* I headed down a steep embankment. About 20 metres later, the mystery trail ended at a small stream that appeared miraculously from between two large rocks. The source. I might not be Dr. Livingston and this brook certainly wasn't the Nile, but a girl can imagine can't she? I scrambled back up and continued with a light step. This was going to be a good hiking day. I could feel it in my bones. If I had Lyme disease, it sure wasn't acting up.

I came across another Beaver Valley bench, which prompted me to begin composing an essay. I called it "The Art of a Well-Placed Bench." My story began: "Happiness is a trail, a bench, sunshine and a view." I would miss these superb resting spots during my break. This one was set into the corner of an open farm field that sloped down to the Beaver River. Behind it, a forest formed a windbreak. From my vantage point, I could see that clouds had amassed over the valley. Today's sunshine would be short-lived. Continuing, I passed a large marsh where my sister and I had walked a few years earlier. We'd joked that every bird we heard was a warbler. "Isn't that a Canada warbler?" I would suggest. "No," my sister would respond. "That's a turquoise-hipped, purple-legged Mexican warbler." It was our nod to how difficult it is even for experienced birders to differentiate between members of this family of passerines — perching birds with anisodactyl feet (three forward and one backward toe) versus zygodactyl feet (two forward and two backward toes like cuckoos).

The sun had disappeared but an open landscape under an overcast sky was preferable to a closed canopy blocking the sunshine. I crossed busy County Road 7 and wandered along the Epping Lookout Side Trail to the John Muir Lookout. The views just kept getting better. Muir spent most of his time in Canada (from 1863 to 1865) living on the Niagara Escarpment. Meaford's 12 kilometre Trout Hollow Trail along the Big Head River takes you to where this famous naturalist lived. Signs point to the location of his cabin and the mill where he worked. After fire destroyed the mill, Muir pulled up stakes and returned to the United States where he founded the Sierra Club. Robert Burcher describes Muir's time in Canada in his delightful book *My Summer of Glorious Freedom.*

I made my way along an unopened road allowance brutalized by ATVs. It wasn't Grimpen Mire II, but the stutter of water-filled ruts made me angry and sad. Where was their respect? I passed The Woods at Kimbercote, a beautiful property where kids attend camps and other programs to learn about nature, outdoor survival, art, music and more. Then I turned north onto another butchered road allowance, following it up a steep incline past a home that made me want to live there. When the trail dipped back into the forest, I remembered to look for an eight-trunked black cherry tree. I admired it before arriving at Webwood Falls and continuing onto the Fairmont Side Trail to begin my return trip. The side trail passes through evidence of an old farmstead, complete with a hand pump that works and a pair of five-metre-tall trees with reddish peeling bark that brought out the dendrophile (tree lover) in me. The first time I saw these eye-catching western yews, I had no idea what they were. But I knew what they weren't: they weren't native to Southern Ontario. From the genus *Taxus*, yews produce a chemical called taxol that is widely used to treat cancer. Fortunately for our supply of yews, taxol is now synthesized in the lab.

I climbed a stile into a cattle pasture and walked behind a collection of barns and other outbuildings. The BT doesn't cross many farms and for good reasons. First, rocks are more prevalent than soil on the Niagara Escarpment, making for marginal farmland. Second, whereas in the United Kingdom walking paths and farms coexist relatively well, in Canada, farmers are less keen to have hikers and their dogs cross their land. The Fairmont Side Trail is a welcome exception. It's off limits to dogs, but open to hikers.

Devil's paintbrush
(*Hieracium auranticum*)

When I returned to the main BT, I had a long walk back along the same route as I'd come in on. Some days that might have bothered me. Certainly, it wouldn't have gone over well just 24 hours ago. But despite the overcast sky and with over seven hours on my feet, I wandered along contentedly with nature and my imagination as companions. It's funny how different one day is to the next. Sometimes I wonder if I'm the same person today as I was yesterday. Who will show up tomorrow? What causes these variations in mood, energy, outlook? We know almost nothing about nature and the cosmos compared to what there is to learn. Only recently, Canadian scientist Suzanne Simard popularized knowledge about the underground system of interconnectedness dubbed the Wood Wide Web in her book *Finding the Mother Tree.* Most of us think of the forest as what we can see. But a third of the carbon in trees is stored underground in roots. Below your feet is an interconnected universe joining fungi to plants and plants to each other that makes humankind's most complex systems of highways or a supercomputer's mishmash of coloured wires look like child's play. This massive mycorrhizal fungi network is estimated to contain up to 150 kilometres of unimaginably minute filaments called hyphae per teaspoon of soil. Together with plant roots, they form mycelial mats through which fungi (mushrooms are the flowering portion of a fungus), trees and other plants share water, carbon, nitrogen, other nutrients and minerals. Some believe trees use this network to warn each other of approaching threats such as insects. What we think of as inert soil is actually a roiling mass of filaments and bacteria working silently underfoot.

Meanwhile, above ground, there are those negative ions I breathe in when walking by waterfalls, and the aerosol oils called phytoncides released by trees. Sometimes I imagine there's an enormous crystal atomizer in the canopy raining down goodness in the form of terpenes that boost my immune system and coat me in anti-inflammatory, anti-tumorigenic and neuroprotective spray. I think everyone is familiar with the tangy smell when you peel a lemon. That's caused by monoterpene limonene. According to the staid American National Library of Medicine, "The therapeutic effects of limonene have been extensively studied, proving anti-inflammatory, antioxidant, antinociceptive, anticancer, antidiabetic, antihyperalgesic, antiviral, and gastroprotective effects, among other beneficial effects in health." Were changes in my mood from hiking day to hiking day the result of differences in a forest's chemistry?

With less than a kilometre to go, I ran into the only other hikers I'd seen all day despite my having covered almost 31 kilometres — my longest day yet. Bittersweet. That was how it felt knowing my next BT hike wouldn't happen for two months. I was addicted to being out there on the trail, addicted to terpenes and negative ions. I was going to miss filling my life with footsteps. Maybe I'd miss myself too.

Sydenham
Section

Day 29

WALTERS FALLS

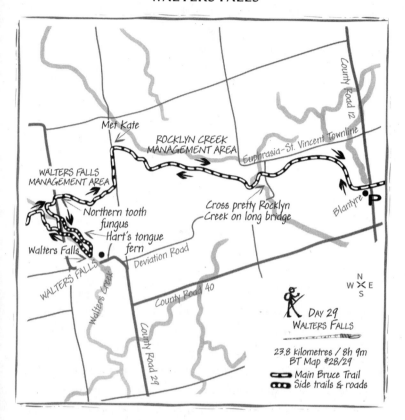

FIELD NOTES

START TIME: 8:40 a.m., Monday, September 5, 2022

TRAILHEAD WEATHER: overcast, maybe rain, became sunny

DISTANCE: 23.8 km

ELAPSED TIME: 8h 9m

BT SECTION: Sydenham

BT MAP: #28/29

MAIN BT WALKED: 0 km to 13.1 km

ASCENT: 722 m / **DESCENT:** 714 m

SIDE TRAILS: Walters Falls Side Trail

FLORA/FAUNA OF NOTE: yellow birch (*Betula alleghaniensis*), northern tooth mushroom (*Climacodon septentrionalis*)

*In which niggling worries mount before fading away under
Frida's tutelage and sister Kate's wintergreen wonder.
And what is that hotel?*

I'd spent most of the last two months with Alex at his lodge.
I kept up my early morning paddling and was otherwise
engaged in writing a major feature story about aggregate
mining for *In The Hills* magazine. It was a demanding article that made my blood boil at times as it involved plans
by a Brazilian multinational with 2021 net revenues of
US$22.3 billion and 34,000 employees worldwide to blast
a hole seven stories deep into Caledon's countryside, not
far from where I lived.

As Labour Day neared, I headed onto the trails at the lodge
to get back into hiking shape and to find some relief from
my research into the pending David-and-Goliath battle over
grey gold between this Brazilian behemoth and a small community not-for-profit: the Forks of the Credit Preservation
Group. Premier Robarts may have hoped that actions taken
as a result of the Gertler Report would temper the drive for
aggregates along the Niagara Escarpment, but the province's

appetite had only grown for a resource we required in ever-growing quantities.

〰

I drove to my sister Kate's near Meaford as I'd arranged to stay with her, and she planned to walk parts of the Sydenham section with me. At 174.4 kilometres, it's the longest of the BT's sections. Along with the northern Bruce Peninsula, it was also the one I knew least well. My return to the trail would be different: I'd be walking with Kate part of the time, and four-legged Frida was ready to go too.

I'd also dodged the Lyme-disease bullet, so that concern was behind me. The combo of the 48-hour prophylactic antibiotic and a two-week round of the same drug had worked. When I saw the infectious disease specialist, he was amusingly disappointed. "You've already taken the antibiotics?" he asked. "Yes," I said. "Do you have any symptoms?" he queried. "No, I don't." He shook his head, "Shoot. I mostly see people who think they have Lyme disease. You actually had it."

〰

I pulled into Blantyre — kilometre zero of the Sydenham section. My plan was to meet my sister at kilometre 7.4 at a pre-arranged time, walk with her to Walters Falls and back again. It was cool and overcast, a dull day, but my spirits were high. Frida was raring to go. We had trouble finding a place to park as the BT lot was chained off. But I managed to squeeze my car onto the little drive into the lot without blocking the way.

Normally, I don't look at my emails when I'm hiking, but my editor, Signe, had asked me to check in about the aggregate story. We were close to press date, so the pressure was on to make sure the plethora of facts included in the four-thousand-word article were correct. Signe had another round of questions, which I answered while Frida sat patiently. I wanted to have the story off my plate so I could get hiking without worrying about it, but it was an important article, the centrepiece of the upcoming issue of the magazine.

By the time I finished responding, it was later than I expected. I was going to have to boot it to make it on time to meet Kate. Checking my route once more, I noticed some fine print on the BT map: "Dogs are not permitted on this section of trail through the Falls Inn property." I looked at Frida. My destination was Walters Falls. It was the point of the hike. I looked at Frida again and decided I'd figure it out when I met Kate. This was not turning out to be the seamless return to the BT I'd imagined.

Finally, I began walking. A hundred metres later, I realized I had set off in the wrong direction. When I turned back toward the car, Frida looked at me as though I'd gone cuckoo. Where were those negative ions and terpenes and whatever other good things nature had divvied out so generously all spring? I took a deep breath. "Don't worry. Be happy. Don't worry. Be happy."

I crossed the busy road and entered a forest, now walking toward Tobermory. The light was flat under the overcast sky. There was a dull silence as though I was in a sound-proof room. I wasn't consciously thinking about aggregates and being late and prohibited dogs, but the weight of these concerns and all the little worries that can add up to stress seemed to be crawling under my skin as though a colony of minute insects had taken up residence. The forest had a bedraggled look. The wild ginger, so robust in the spring, now drooped. The leaves on the trees seemed tired and worn like an old person's skin. They reminded me of how cyclist Sara Dykman described the condition of the Monarchs after they'd completed the long journey from Mexico to the United States: the ends of their wings were shredded, and their vibrant orange and black colouring had faded to a dull taupe and fuzzy grey.

I emerged from the forest at the exact moment my sister arrived. Another couple turned up too. They were hiking back toward Blantyre. Members of the Beaver Valley Club, they told me their club's annual end-to-end hike finished that day in the Blantyre parking lot. When I mentioned I'd parked in the driveway, the husband looked concerned. "I doubt they'll give you a ticket," he said. Of all the days to park in a marginally questionable spot, why had I picked today? I added ticketed car to my list of worries but removed being late. One step forward, one step back. I decided to apply that Mexican philosophy: if you don't like thinking about it, then don't think about it.

Kate and I climbed the big hill on the St. Vincent–Sydenham Townline, and I explained to her that Walters Falls was off-limits to dogs. I abide by the rules when I see BT signs asking dogs be on leash for particular sections of the trail — and I don't bend dogs-not-permitted directives. I knew loose dogs might result in property owners kicking the BT off their land. Kate said she'd hiked this section often and had seen lots of dogs near the falls. "Why don't you check the BT app and see what it says," she suggested. When I did, I discovered that whereas the main BT used to go to Walters Falls, it now stopped short. The Walters Falls

Side Trail replaced the main BT, and it didn't mention dogs. We walked on, hopeful.

It was fun having my "sis" along. We're easy friends anyway, but conversation flows more effortlessly when walking. So effortlessly in fact that I don't remember much about the trail between where we set off until we came to the Walters Falls Side Trail — except for the climb up the blasted hill on the townline. The only sign about dogs was a request to have them on leash, so we continued to the falls. Another worry down.

There was something about Walters Falls that made it hard to embrace. You can only see it by looking down on the rushing water from an overhead platform. While dramatic, this view seemed stilted, an unsatisfactory way to view this 14 m high, double-plunge cataract. But mostly, it was the hotel. I understand the owners put a lot of effort into its design, but it appeared to be a suburban event hall perched on top of the landscape rather than nestled into it. I wondered what John Walter and his wife Elizabeth Payne would have made of it. In the mid-1880s, they harnessed Walters Creek to power a sawmill, woollen mill and a feed mill, which continues to operate on waterpower.

Kate and I headed back into the forest and stopped for lunch. Then we leisurely retraced our route in. When we came across a yellow birch, Kate scratched the bark from a small branch. "Take a whiff," she said. "What does it smell like?" I recognized the odour but couldn't place it. "Think bubble-gum," she hinted. That was all I needed. "Wintergreen," I said. "It smells like wintergreen." In fact, yellow birch doesn't just smell like wintergreen, it contains methyl salicylate, more commonly known as wintergreen oil. And like acetyl salicylate (a.k.a. ASA, or Aspirin), it has anti-inflammatory and anti-fever properties. I stored this knowledge along with burrs being the inspiration for Velcro and that purple trilliums attract carrion-loving pollinators by smelling like and being the colour of rotten meat.

Northern tooth mushroom
(*Climacodon septentrionalis*)

We came across an old sugar maple with a northern tooth mushroom protruding from its trunk. The size and shape of a football, it comprised multiple layered shelves. Once you see one, you won't forget it. They consume the heartwood of their host making the tree vulnerable to being blown down. Tooth-like appendages that produce spores grow on the underside of each of the mushroom's layers, hence its name.

Kate had arranged a meeting with someone for 2 p.m., so she beetled off on a more direct route to her car. Before continuing, I checked my emails to see if Signe had any more questions. She didn't. Another concern gone! Now I only had to worry about a parking ticket. Back on my own with just Frida for company, my shoulders relaxed, and fewer wrinkles creased my forehead. Frida gave me a nudge. "This is more like it," she seemed to be saying. I had about two hours of hiking left. As I moved on, the sun peaked between parting clouds. The forest looked friendlier, and I felt the lightness I'd often imagined over the summer. When I arrived, there was no ticket on my car, nor was there any sign of a BT end-to-end. My guess is it had started, not ended in Blantyre.

Day 30

BOGNOR MARSH / AVALANCHES / CRASHED PLANE / DISAPPEARING WALL

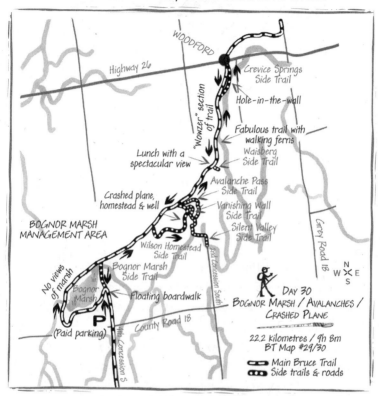

WOODFORD

Highway 26

Crevice Springs Side Trail

Hole-in-the-wall

"Wowzer" section of trail

Fabulous trail with walking ferns

Lunch with a spectacular view

Waisberg Side Trail

Avalanche Pass Side Trail

Crashed plane, homestead & well

Vanishing Wall Side Trail

Silent Valley Side Trail

BOGNOR MARSH MANAGEMENT AREA

Wilson Homestead Side Trail

Grey Road 18

2nd Concession South

Bognor Marsh Side Trail

No views of marsh

Bognor Marsh

Floating boardwalk

P (Paid parking)

County Road 18

4th Concession S

Day 30
BOGNOR MARSH / AVALANCHES / CRASHED PLANE

22.2 kilometres / 9h 8m
BT Map #29/30

Main Bruce Trail
Side trails & roads

FIELD NOTES

START TIME: 8:15 a.m., Tuesday, September 6, 2022

TRAILHEAD WEATHER: clear sunny sky, 25 degrees Celsius (the perfect temperature)

DISTANCE: 22.2 km

ELAPSED TIME: 9h 8m

BT SECTION: Sydenham

BT MAP: #29/30

MAIN BT WALKED: 29.4 km to 41.7 km

ASCENT: 718 m / **DESCENT:** 724 m

SIDE TRAILS: Wilson Homestead Side Trail, Silent Valley Side Trail, Vanishing Wall Side Trail, Waisberg Side Trail, Crevice Springs Side Trail, Bognor Marsh Side Trail

FLORA/FAUNA OF NOTE: Joe Pye weed (*Eutrochium purpureum*), cattails (*Typha latifolia*), dogwood (*Cornus*), maidenhair spleenwort (*Asplenium trichomanes*), Christmas ferns (*Polystichum acrostichoides*), northern holly fern (*Polystichum lonchitis*), walking fern (*Asplenium rhizophyllum*), Canadian yew (*Taxus canadensis*)

*In which a floating boardwalk through a magic marsh
with Frida counting leaping frogs makes me question my
environmental commitment. What is it: environmentalist
or writer? And what about that Cessna?*

I parked in the lot for the Bognor Marsh hopeful my concerns
from yesterday were behind me. I checked in with Signe and
she needed more information, but it only took a few minutes. The magazine was going to press that afternoon, so that
was done. I had no rendezvous with Kate to rush to, there
was unlikely to be an end-to-end on a Tuesday, and when
I was unable to convince the machine to issue me a parking
ticket, I tucked a polite note for the conservation authority
under a windshield wiper. It was an unimaginably beautiful
September day: no humidity, warm not hot, cloudless.

With Frida in tow, I wandered down a vague access road
through a maple forest. Coming out the other end was like
passing through the wardrobe into Narnia. The vast Bognor
Marsh, one of three in the 688 hectare management area,
spread out before me. Resplendent in the morning light, it
offered silence punctuated only by the quack of an occasional
duck. The trees that would once have made this a swamp

rather than a marsh resembled stranded masts marking sunken ships. The low-slung sun illuminated patches of rust, golden and heather-toned grasses that bordered open water. A kilometre away, the backdrop was a bank of green forest rising up the escarpment. Cedars at the wetland's edge gave way to the white trunks of canoe birch, which blended into an upland forest of maples, basswood and beech. Above the treetops it was blue — blue to the heavens.

I stepped onto what I quickly learned was a floating board-walk. When we landed on a firmer walkway, frogs leaped in every direction. Frida didn't know which way to look as they flipped past her snout. We meandered through the wetland on the raised wooden trail. Bliss. *This*, I thought, *is why I hike*. This is what I'm after: this feeling of just me and Frida and the sky and sunshine. The article I'd just written about aggregate mining in Caledon had consumed me for two months. I knew it would be a tough slog when I agreed to write it. The part of Caledon where I was born and live is riddled with pits. The roads jammed with rumbling gravel trucks. Farms torn up, forests bulldozed, meadows flattened, stone and brick cen-tury homes obliterated by companies unconcerned with the environmental consequences or crumbling community spirit.

I knew that writing the story would make me sad, then mad, then sad again when what I really wanted was to escape — doesn't everyone? — onto a hiking trail and find a spot like the Bognor Marsh. But I had a responsibility to write that story. I had the skills, knowledge, contacts and insights. I owed it to the place where I grew up. I'd learned some time ago that while I couldn't do everything to save the environ-ment, I had to do what was mine to do. This article was that; call it payback if you want, but I thought of it as my gift to the Niagara Escarpment and the Credit River. To Caledon.

Nature's beauty is something I think about a lot. In fact, I'd spent most of my career concerned about the environment. I'd sold environmental lab services, published an environmental newsletter, been an environmental consultant, edited Canada's foremost environmental magazine, started an environmental not-for-profit organization, considered running as a Green Party candidate and been a regular environmental commentator on the CBC. Despite spending most of the last decade focused on writing hiking guides, I thought of myself as an environmentalist. So, I was shocked when, shortly after I took a break from the BT in July, a recent acquaintance, Cathy, mentioned she had been surprised to learn from a mutual friend of my environmental resume. Cathy thought of me as a writer. I'd pondered her impression as I might suck on a hard candy, checking it occasionally to see if I could crack it open with my teeth, afraid of swallowing it whole.

The more I thought about it, the more I had to admit I'd drifted from things green. I'd pushed my environmental conscience to the backseat. Truth be told, I intentionally moved away from my environmental activism, environmental consulting and even environmental writing. I continued to worry about my ecological footprint, but I didn't agonize over minimizing my impact on the planet like I once did. I no longer devoured articles about climate change or hung onto the wisdom of David Suzuki, Bill McKibben, Paul Hawken and others. Was writing the odd article such as "Pit by Pit" and loving the Niagara Escarpment enough? Or was I surrendering to the sort of "good life" that John Muir was said to have railed against? I wanted to believe my tactic of focusing primarily on the good, was working, but I wasn't sure. Curiously, my slide from deep to a lighter shade of green paralleled a similar transformation in Caledon.

I followed the main BT for over four kilometres as it circumvented the marsh. I was disappointed that it wasn't possible to see the wetland from the trail since it passed through Joe Pye weed, rushes and dogwood that towered over my head. Eventually, I entered a hardwood forest penetrated regularly by the sun's oblique rays. Though the trail climbed, there was no view. I wondered why the main BT took this detour when it would have made a better side trail. Then again, in the spring, pre-foliage, it would have been spectacular. After another kilometre and a half, I arrived at the Wilson Homestead Side Trail. It was superb: the level path padded with pine needles made me feel as though I wore moccasins. I couldn't hear my own footsteps. I visited John Wilson's farmstead, barn and dug well. I admired the vanishing wall and, of course, the battered Cessna 205, which seemed unchanged since it crash-landed and killed all four of its occupants on September 26, 1970. I continued through the Silent Valley, missing the turnoff onto the Avalanche Pass Side Trail, which I'd fortunately walked previously. It's a fun trail and I was sorry I'd missed it. This series of blue-blazed paths was as entertaining as any of the BT's 450 kilometres of side trails.

I climbed up the escarpment, not suspecting it would be my first of half a dozen similar ascents. The trail skirted the cliff's edge and though I occasionally cursed the trees that blocked the view, I wasn't serious as this was a beautiful stretch of uninterrupted trail. I stopped for lunch at the lookout from the Waisberg Side Trail where I ran into the only other hiker I saw all day. Frida pranced along beside me. I'd forgotten how much more fun it was having her along.

I followed the delightful Crevice Springs Side Trail down and then up the escarpment again before arriving at my turnaround point near Woodford. It had taken me five hours to get this far, and I was pooped — not yet as tough as when I'd finished up in July. Fortunately, my return route was shorter. Envious of Frida's light-footedness, I turned back. A collection of large moss-covered rocks caught my attention. *Walking fern habitat*, I thought. And there they were — a large healthy colony of tip-rooting ferns. I got a kick out of Wikipedia's lingo-laden description of ferns: "A fern (Polypodiopsida or Polypodiophyta) is a member of a group of vascular plants (plants with xylem and phloem) that reproduce via spores and have neither seeds nor flowers." When I studied biology at university, I loved the sound of the words xylem and phloem: two types of vascular tissues wherein one carries water and nutrients up (xylem) and the other carries them down (phloem). Had I thought of it, I might have called a pair of dogs by these biological terms: "Come Xylem. Fetch Phloem."

hat.

toy meets

There's nothing better than a good

I also saw Christmas ferns, northern holly ferns and, a favourite, maidenhair spleenwort fern. A breeze had picked up after lunch and the temperature couldn't have been more pleasant, re-enforcing my decision to avoid Southern Ontario's muggy, buggy summertime heat. There was just the right amount of light warming my shoulders. Perhaps I was experiencing the pleasant aftermath of having put that damned article to bed. I'd had to completely re-write it three times until I finally landed on the message all my research had taught me. Caledon sits on what I refer to as "grey gold." We can't do without aggregates (sand and gravel), but did Caledon have to shoulder such a large share of the damage, and how could we protect ourselves when a multinational Brazilian corporation that has likely never heard of the Niagara Escarpment or the Credit River "owns" the resource? We expect our provincial government to protect the environment and communities from exploitation, but the rules governing aggregates lean heavily in favour of corporations. Queen's Park could at least require project proponents to prove the aggregate they propose to extract is in short supply, but even a demonstration of need has been expunged from Ontario's aggregate policies. And should they be able to clear-cut one-hundred-year-old hardwood forests and demolish heritage houses and barns? This leaves small communities like ours to battle behemoths, as the province, which happens to be the largest consumer of aggregates, lets the parties duke it out.

〜〜

It was after 5 p.m. when I returned to that floating boardwalk in the Bognor Marsh. By then, I'd forgotten about aggregates. There wasn't a cloud in the sky and the air had an autumnal aridness that reminded me of attending the annual Erin Fall Fair, where my favourite event is the heavy horse pull and my favourite fair fare is a cardboard box overflowing with rough-cut fries loaded with salt and cider vinegar.

I walked onto the floating boardwalk, removed my gear and lay down on my back, resting my head on my knapsack. Frida curled up beside me and we listened to the frogs and the birds and the grass rustling in the light breeze.

Day 31

LEBANON MOUNTAIN TRAIL FRIENDSHIP TRAIL / WOODFORD CREVICES

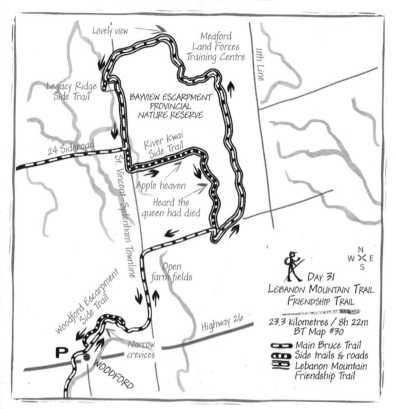

FIELD NOTES

START TIME: 7:45 a.m., Thursday, September 8, 2022

TRAILHEAD WEATHER: clear sky, cool to start, 9 degrees Celsius

DISTANCE: 23.3 km

ELAPSED TIME: 8h 22m

BT SECTION: Sydenham

BT MAP: #30

MAIN BT WALKED: 41.7 km to 56.3 km

ASCENT: 730 m / **DESCENT:** 732 m

SIDE TRAILS: Legacy Ridge Side Trail, Tom Thomson Trail, River Kwai Side Trail, Woodford Escarpment Side Trail

FLORA/FAUNA OF NOTE: white snakeroot (*Ageratina altissima*), eastern wood-pewee (*Contopus virens*), black-throated green warbler (*Setophaga virens*), common self-heal (*Prunella vulgaris*), apples (*Malus pumila*)

*In which a black hole triggers all my senses before I
cross the bridge over the River Kwai, salute Her Maj.
and fail to dig my good teeth into an emu burger.*

I was on my own to start as Kate met me about an hour into
my day's hike. She planned to walk about half of the near
24 kilometre route, which was perfect — sort of like being
married with separate houses. From the community centre
in Woodford, I followed the trail into the forest and immediately climbed up the Niagara Escarpment. By the time I
reached the ridgetop, I'd removed my fleece. According to
the BT guide, there were ruins of a church, barn, cabin and
a lime kiln as well as a disappearing waterfall. I'm not sure
if these things were hidden in the foliage or if I was too
intent on the promised crevices, but I missed them. Instead,
I came to the spooky chasm that Kate had warned me about.
The BT guide suggested anyone who suffers from claustro-
phobia or has a large backpack should take the Woodford
Escarpment Side Trail. Worried that an overhead rock might
come crashing down on her, Kate had elected to meet me
after I'd navigated the chasm.

I'd let Fearless Frida lead the way into a black hole. Even if it hadn't been early in the morning, I doubt light would penetrate this narrow rift. As advertised, I squeezed through narrow tunnels and ducked to keep from banging my head on sharp rocks that protruded from sheer walls. I clambered over slabs of greasy limestone that seemed to have been pitched as by stormy sea. They must have broken away from above, lending credence to Kate's fear. When I emerged, my knees and backside were smeared with green-tinted slime.

I exited onto a dirt road and walked along in the sunshine with soybeans, hay, barns and silos for company. Arriving at our meeting spot before my sister, I had a few minutes to sit down, feel the warm sun on my shoulders and listen to the day wake up. In the distance, a rooster crowed — the universal sound of morning (though it's a myth that roosters only cock-a-doodle-doo to announce daybreak). I wondered if I'd be able to determine whether it was early morning or late afternoon based on what I heard rather than what I heard and saw. I teach a workshop called "Writing With All Your Senses." We are so dominated by sight that we often ignore what we hear, smell, taste or touch. We write about what we see, despite how readily we respond to an old song or the smell of freshly baked bread. When I rave about the sun, it's not the sight of it that I enjoy, it's how it feels.

When Kate arrived, we set off along a farm lane that separated fields of maturing soybeans until we were back into the forest. The trail crossed the Tom Thomson Trail (a multi-use route linking Meaford to Owen Sound) and then swung north. We entered the Bayview Escarpment Provincial Nature Reserve, picking up the Lebanon Mountain Trail Friendship Trail. This 470 kilometre long blazed trail climbs up and down

Lebanon's mountainous spine linking village to village. You can hike it in sections on your own or sign up for the 31-day supported through-hike that takes place in April each year. Lebanon is a country I've long dreamed of visiting. I imagine it as being bathed in a warm yellow light that illuminates a golden landscape studded with statuesque cypress trees. I love Lebanese food: shawarma, falafel, tabbouleh, hummus . . . Despite being able to practically taste those dishes — many of them containing a red spice made from the fuzzy red berries of a Mediterranean species of sumac (vs. Canada's poison sumac) — I returned to the present when Kate and I came to our first vista. We traced the eastern edge of the escarpment overlooking the blue water of Nottawasaga Bay (part of Georgian Bay). For over eight kilometres, we followed an uninterrupted path with the sun streaming through the thinning foliage. The trail was level and smooth. Lebanon could wait. For now, I was content to be where I was.

≈

As we walked, we discussed the importance of having someone you trust to talk to about difficult topics. Subjects prone to misinterpretation or quick value judgments. Kate lived nearer to Meaford, where the roads are mostly dirt and farms are farmed by the people who own them. My sister's neighbour ploughs her drive. She gives him produce from her garden. Meanwhile, in Caledon I was losing my grasp on a similar countryside feel. Included within the Greater Toronto Area's borders, Caledon is next in line for urbanization. The provincially mandated population target is for the municipality to swell to 300,000 residents by 2051 from about 75,000 today. Is it in the best interests of the

Greater Toronto Area and the Government of Ontario to pave over and dig up Caledon? The province reaps financial gains from residential growth through taxation, meanwhile the Greater Toronto Area and, especially Caledon, lose the environmental benefits of greenspace, are robbed of the recreational opportunities available in parks and don't get me going about the costs of crowded roads. Much of Caledon is currently protected under the combined policies included in the Greenbelt Plan, Niagara Escarpment Plan and Oak Ridges Moraine Conservation Plan. Can our collective need for greenspace in the Greater Toronto Area withstand a government-backed drive to house the massive number of new Canadians forecast by our federal government? Will the hills I grew up exploring lose the battle of green versus suburban housing and grey gold? Will a good old country wave from the open window of a battered pickup become obsolete?

I'm not sure why this was the nature of our discussion when we could have been gossiping about our siblings or dreaming of hiking in Lebanon. Maybe walking long distances over several days with the same person results in conversations that move beyond chatting. Maybe yesterday's thoughts about my lapsed environmentalism were under my skin. Maybe that had been what was crawling about when I set off from Blantyre. I'm not a procrastinator, so it wasn't that I'd been putting off thinking about my environmental responsibility. But I'd been busy. Since I'd started writing my Loops & Lattes hiking guides back in 2014, I'd been consumed with the tasks involved: researching routes, hiking them, taking photos, writing up directions, drawing maps, having someone test each route, getting the books edited, designed and eventually printed. Lining up over one hundred stores and cafés to sell the guides, creating a website and an online store, getting publicity, placing ads, giving talks, keeping stores stocked with books, shipping and invoicing and the myriad tasks that it takes to run a small business. This looping journey was proving to be a chance to assess where I was heading. As Dolly Parton said, "Don't get so busy making a living that you forget to make a life." I had satisfied myself that whether I loved the Niagara Escarpment enough was an unanswerable question, but that didn't mean I was doing enough to protect it.

$$\approx$$

We stopped for lunch and then reluctantly headed back along the road. Too soon, we parted company. I picked up the intriguingly named River Kwai Side Trail. The Kwai River flows through Thailand. The bridge, central to the movie *Bridge Over the River Kwai*, was part of that nation's Death Railway. Some 100,000 forced labourers and World War II prisoners of war died constructing it. The trail dropped down, and I crossed a wetland on the River Kwai Bridge. According to Ron Savage's book, *Secrets of Sydenham*, the BT work party that built the bridge arrived upon the name after having to endure one work party member's incessant singing of the theme song from the movie. In a twist of fate, winter's snow proved to be too much, and like its namesake, the BT's River Kwai Bridge collapsed. Unlike its predecessor, however, it was rebuilt in the same locale and no one died in the process.

The trail led to old cattle pasture. It was scrubby with hawthorn and laden apple trees. Fallen fruit mounded up around the base of each tree as though it was talus at the

Wild apple
(Malus pumila)

bottom of a cliff. Branches sagged as if they'd been decorated by an over-zealous child. There were red apples, pink ones, green ones and striped ones, none of which resembled the McIntosh, Red Delicious or Spartans we buy in grocery stores. Our most important fruit crop, *Malus pumila* (sweet apple) is part of the rose family. About half of Canada's 40 registered varieties and the world's 7,500 are found in Ontario, though none of the Heinz-57s in this field would be included in those numbers.

The River Kwai Side Trail continued into another gorgeous hardwood forest dominated by lean maples that had used their energy to reach the light they needed to photosynthesize carbon dioxide into oxygen. Just before I came to the junction with the main BT, my phone buzzed. Most of my notifications were turned off, so I took a look to see what had penetrated the silence. The headline read: "Queen Elizabeth dies at 96." As much as I enjoyed watching *The Crown* and recalled where I was when I learned of Princess Di's death (in a hotel room in the Philippines working on an environmental project), I don't consider myself a monarchist.

But the Queen's death caught me off-guard. It was similarly shocking when my mum died at 94. She'd been around for so long it seemed she'd be there forever. It was an end of an era. I stopped, bowed my head and silently toasted Her Maj.

When I returned to the Woodford crevices, I took the Woodford Escarpment Side Trail. Despite lacking the Indiana Jones excitement of the rocky route, it was lovely, especially given I was tiring. When I emerged onto Woodford's main street, a pickup pulled up beside me. A ruddy-faced man in a sweat-stained cap rolled down his window. "You sure look like someone I saw out walking near here the other day. She had the same straw hat," he said. Coincidently, Kate had mentioned having a long chat a few days earlier with a man driving an ATV. I said, "You didn't happen to run into my lookalike while riding an ATV, did you?" "Sure did," he replied. I told him we were sisters, which prompted him to tell me, "Your sister has great teeth. You do too." He grew up in Woodford. "My dad owned the garage. I live in Bognor now." Then he asked me if I had any more siblings. I held up three fingers. "I'll keep a look out for them," he replied, adding, "Name's Don Bowden." As he drove away, he stuck his arm out the window and gave me a big country wave.

∿

Kate and I had dinner at Meaford's unique Ted's Range Road Diner. Housed in an old Quonset hut with a few picnic tables out front, Ted's is an experience. The extensive menu includes crocodile burgers and kangaroo steaks — though I'm not sure they were for real. But we could have had emu, elk, bison, venison, caribou, muskox or quail. For the faint of heart, there are burgers, steaks, ribs, chicken cordon bleu, French onion soup, Arctic char and just about anything else you might desire. They source local food suppliers when possible and our waiter, Nicole, was a gem. Ted's is Don Bowden's kind of place — ours too — well sort of!

Day 32

THE PALISADES / INGLIS FALLS

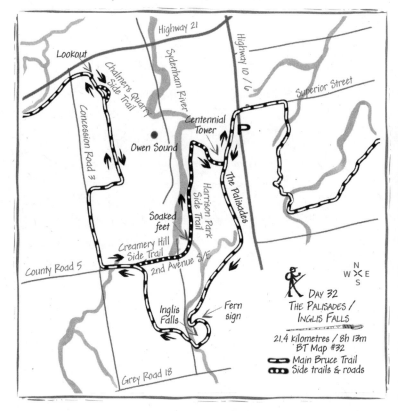

Highway 21
Highway 10 / 6
Lookout
Chalmers Quarry Side Trail
Sydenham River
Superior Street
Concession Road 3
Centennial Tower
P
Owen Sound
The Palisades
Harrison Park Side Trail
Soaked feet
Creamery Hill Side Trail
County Road 5
2nd Avenue S/E
Fern sign
Inglis Falls
Grey Road 18

N W E S

Day 32
THE PALISADES /
INGLIS FALLS

21.4 kilometres / 8h 13m
BT Map #32
Main Bruce Trail
Side trails & roads

FIELD NOTES

START TIME: 8:30 a.m., Friday, September 9, 2022

TRAILHEAD WEATHER: gorgeous, sunny and warm

DISTANCE: 21.4 km

ELAPSED TIME: 8h 13m

BT SECTION: Sydenham

BT MAP: #32

MAIN BT WALKED: 89.2 km to 100.9 km

ASCENT: 704 m / **DESCENT:** 727 m

SIDE TRAILS: Chalmers Quarry Side Trail, Creamery Hill Side Trail, Harrison Park Side Trail

FLORA/FAUNA OF NOTE: blue jay (*Cyanocitta cristata*), disintegrated porcupine (*Erethizon dorsatum*), various ferns

In which we walk with the weight of the Niagara Escarpment bearing down on our left shoulders before Inglis Falls appeals to the maple syrup that courses my veins and the Devil's Playhouse eludes my sleuthing.

I'd been looking forward to this section of trail since a friend had mentioned it. Virginia Heffernan is a geologist and author, and the Palisades in Owen Sound were eye candy for her. Kate was joining me for the first seven kilometres, so we set off together from a parking spot near Centennial Tower in Sydenham, as Owen Sound was originally known. According to the BT guide, local high school students constructed the tower as a centennial project.

Without warning, we found ourselves in the lee of a long stretch of a mammoth, multi-faced cliff. It loomed menacingly above us, blocking out the morning sun. We picked our way through slippery pointed rocks that penetrated the soles of our shoes. Occasionally, we shimmied over boulders wedged between foot-thick white cedars, all the time with the geological weight of the Niagara Escarpment bearing down on our left shoulders. If Kate worried about falling rocks, she didn't mention it. It took us 90 minutes to walk the first two kilometres. But the experience was as sensational as Virginia had promised. When the rocks underfoot let up (though the Palisades continued), we were rewarded with a sponge-like walking surface, the result of hundreds of years of decomposed forest litter. We proceeded stealthily on the soft footing, feeling like early explorers. There were no other people and no sounds except the squawk of an occasional blue jay.

We dropped down to the Sydenham River and then up again enroute to Inglis Falls. Along the way, we passed a sign about local ferns as described by Nels Maher, a naturalist with a particular interest in pteridology, as the study of these seedless vascular plants is known. We proudly ticked off all seven of those listed, including bulblet, hart's tongue, walking, intermediate wood, northern holly fern, ostrich and maidenhair spleenwort fern. The Inglis Falls Conservation Area's mown lawns and paved paths seemed otherworldly after our expedition of the past several hours. But when we walked to the lookout across from the waterfall all thoughts of the Palisades were forgotten. The narrow Sydenham River descended the escarpment forming a spectacular 18 metre "cascading" waterfall. It fanned out into six or seven ribbons that tumbled over rocky ledges with the grace of the Duchess of Sussex's veil.

Kate, who is a fine painter, noted the life-sized mural of the original mill near the waterfall's brim. It was odd, but a clever depiction of times past when Inglis Falls supported several water-powered mills. Peter Inglis replaced a smaller gristmill with a four-story giant in 1862. He also used the river's tremendous power for a sawmill and a woollen mill that produced tweeds, flannels and "rainbow" blankets, so named because they had three coloured stripes (vs. Hudson's Bay blankets' four stripes).

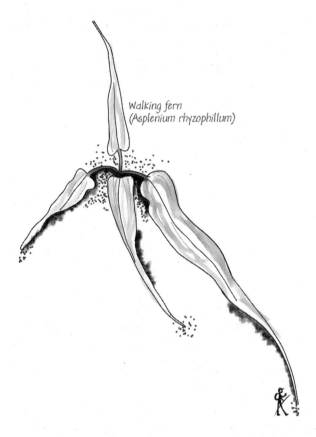

Walking fern
(Asplenium rhyzophillum)

We found a picnic table and had lunch. I'd packed two bruschetta made with Kate's tomatoes, a friend's garlic and a healthy dose of sharp parmesan cheese. The olive oil had soaked into the focaccia, turning my sandwich into an earthy, sensuous piece of autumn harvest. I gave up trying to be polite as the olive oil flowed between my fingers and slid across my palms. Leaning forward, I simply let the juice slide down my chin and drip onto the ground. It reminded me of an episode of *I Love Lucy*. In it, Lucile Ball is in Italy. When she's invited to stomp grapes in a large round wooden vat, the comedian rolls up her bloomers and jumps in. As the fruit pops and the skins ease between her toes, Ball's dismay turns into a slapstick-funny scene.

After lunch, we followed the trail over stiles and across farm fields. All that remained of the canola, so bright and yellow in June, were skeletal stalks faded to a benign beige. Fall was coming whether I liked it or not. But for now, I enjoyed skies so blue, so lacking in the humid haze of summer that my photos seemed tinted. Too soon, we came to the Creamery Hill Side Trail where Kate turned right. We figured we would have covered this distance in a couple of hours, but it had taken us twice that long mostly due to the tough going alongside the Palisades. I continued down a hot road for about two kilometres and then turned into the West Rocks Management Area, where there are great views of Owen Sound. After the morning's combination of walking through a cedar forest, Inglis Falls' mown lawns, farm fields and a dirt road, it felt like I was returning home. The mixed maple forest extends from Queenston to Tobermory, but I never tired of it even if I occasionally grumbled about low light. It's a trait I inherited from my tree-loving dad. He planted twenty thousand trees, giving rise to our farm's name, Woodrising. Maybe we both had maple syrup running in our veins.

I turned back, taking the unremarkable Chalmers Quarry Side Trail. At the Creamery Hill Side Trail where I'd left Kate some time ago, I left the main BT and headed down to the Sydenham River following blue blazes through lush jewelweed. I popped several pregnant seed pods — nature's version of bursting bubble wrap. At the river, I soaked my feet for 15 minutes. I didn't have far to go, but there was a climb ahead, and I had to return along a kilometre-long stretch of that difficult trail below the Palisades.

Turning left onto the Harrison Park Side Trail, I walked along a paved cart path that wound its way through the forest not far from the river and then past a small grouping of suburban houses. Continuing straight ahead, I passed through thick foliage and had that Narnia wardrobe feeling again. The path squeezed between enormous boulders. I had to scramble as I neared the main BT. Fortunately, the sun was now behind me and light illuminated the rocks and trees. It felt airy and bright and cool — so different from the heaviness of the morning. I turned right on the main BT, heading away from my car. I hoped to find the Devil's Playhouse, a series of "rooms" with sheer 20 metre high walls favoured by rock climbers. I traced the base of the cliffs tripping over loosely strewn talus for half a kilometre before I gave up the search. Satan would have to wait for another time.

Day 33

LINDENWOOD MANAGEMENT AREA / MYSTERY CABIN

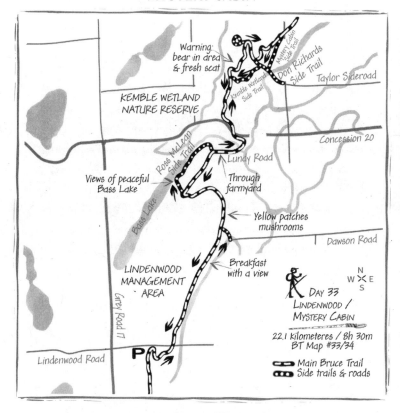

FIELD NOTES

START TIME: 8:45 a.m., Saturday, September 10, 2022

TRAILHEAD WEATHER: sunny and hot

DISTANCE: 22.1 km

ELAPSED TIME: 8h 30m

BT SECTION: Sydenham

BT MAP: #33/34

MAIN BT WALKED: 128.4 km to 140.7 km

ASCENT: 702 m / DESCENT: 671 m

SIDE TRAILS: Ross McLean Side Trail, Mystery Cabin Side Trail, Don Richards Side Trail, Kemble Wetland Side Trail

FLORA/FAUNA OF NOTE: green heron (*Butorides virescens*), Canada geese (*Branta canadensis*), leopard frogs (*Lithobates pipiens*), green frog (*Lithobates clamitans*), bracken ferns (*Pteridium aquilinum*), sensitive ferns (*Onoclea sensibilis*), yellow patches mushroom (*Amanita flavoconia*)

In which I pace the cage before Bruce Cockburn's
outbound stage carries me to Ursus americanus *and*
the Bruce is no longer beckoning.

With a brilliant sun climbing the eastern sky, I drove to the trailhead near Lindenwood, while listening to a best of Bruce Cockburn collection. In 2012, when I was the editor of *Alternatives Journal*, Cockburn received Earth Day Canada's Outstanding Commitment to the Environment Award, and I interviewed him. I was curious to know how he came up with songs like *When a Tree Falls*, in which he describes what's happening to the rainforest as a lobotomy. I asked him how he combines his music with his activism. Cockburn explained, "I see it. It's visual. It starts with words."

About three songs in, a tune began with a sequence of quiet, rhythmic notes. Behind Cockburn's precise picking, there was the occasional slide of a bass guitar. A simple melody with complex words, poetry really. When the tune ended, I hit repeat. It wasn't an environmental ballad, but I listened to "Pacing the Cage" over and over. "Sometimes you feel like you've lived too long / Days drip slowly on the page / You catch yourself / Pacing the cage."

In a 1999 interview, Cockburn explained to Susan Adams Kauffman that he wrote the song when he felt as though he was in a trap. "I'm thinking more of finding yourself in a place that you've willingly waltzed into," he said. "Suddenly, you realize it's not such a good place to be, and it's hard to find your way out, hard to know where the next step is supposed to go."

When I've contemplated changing my life in the past, I've learned that it's other people who slow my transition. This can be good as it makes me less likely to act impulsively, but it can drag out the process. It can cause me to feel as though I'm "pacing the cage." I like to start things. Malcolm Gladwell, the Waterloo-born author of countless bestselling books, including *Outliers: The Story of Success,* popularized the notion of the "10,000-hour rule." Gladwell posited that to gain genuine expertise in something you need to do it for at least ten thousand hours, an amount of time roughly equal to five years of 40-hour work weeks. Perhaps coincidentally, five years is about how long I last in a job. I jump in with both feet, give it my all and then the burn in my belly begins to wane.

It had been seven years since I began working on my Loops & Lattes hiking guides, two years past my best-before date. I'd produced six books in six years. It had been an intense, rewarding journey — and an unexpected success. Covid (and Alex) had induced me to keep on with my hiking guides. The extra couple of years of "stickwith-itness" was a financial miracle; it "tipped" the brand, to use another Gladwell term. Loops & Lattes became a household name among Southern Ontario hikers. I received countless notes from people who told me their guidebook had "saved" them during the pandemic. "With the province going into stay-at-home lockdown just after Christmas," wrote one person, "this book was an absolute godsend." Another said, "Congratulations for opening up a world of beautiful trails and inspiring us to walk them." And still another: "We have felt more connected to the earth than ever, hiking through the seasons, watching the colours change . . ."

I'd hoped the books would inspire people to get out hiking, but they were doing more than that. People were falling in love with the outdoors. As the BT's founders knew and the Senegalese forestry engineer Baba Dioum told the audience of an environmental conference in 1968: "We will conserve only what we love . . ." I was proud of the books and their unexpected effect. But I was pacing the cage. My 10,000 hours of writing hiking guides were up.

My 33rd BT hike began with the last stanza of Cockburn's song on repeat inside my head: "Sometimes the best map will not guide you / You can't see what's round the bend / Sometimes the road leads through dark places / Sometimes the darkness is your friend / Today these eyes scan bleached-out land / For the coming of the outbound stage / Pacing the cage."

〰〰

The trail quickly took Frida and me up onto the Niagara Escarpment, where I once again skirted the cliffs with the sun showering me in light. By 10 a.m., it was over 20 degrees Celsius and the humidity was rising. I stopped atop a rocky ledge overlooking a lone farm where Dawson Road abuts the escarpment. The barn was well maintained and had a working silo. A tractor had left fresh tracks through a slurry of muddy manure to a triplet of farm fields, their crops recently harvested. Beyond the patterned rows of shorn wheat was an expanse of trees that extended until way, way in the distance I recognized the escarpment's hump that's dominated in winter by ski lifts. It was hard to believe I'd come so far. Maybe I was already on Cockburn's outbound stage. Maybe I was hiking my way out of a rut and into a new beginning.

I took the Ross McLean Side Trail, following it down to Bass Lake. The forest's perfect reflection in the tranquil water reminded me of Alex's lodge. I longed to paddle away in my kayak, exploring the lake and massive marsh. Now on the Bruce Peninsula, I felt the transition. South to north. Rural to wilderness. The Bruce no longer beckoned; I'd arrived.

At the Kemble Wetland Nature Reserve, Canada geese heralded autumn with the same assuredness as the rooster I'd heard announce morning while waiting for Kate a couple of days earlier. It might be summertime warm, but fall was around the corner. Moving away from the marsh, I found myself in scrub land where I had to duck under apple trees laden with fruit. I kicked an odd apple, which Frida picked up and gnawed on until I sent another one skidding down the path. I began crushing the caramel-coloured rotten ones underfoot. Just in time, I noticed that what at first glance appeared to be a pile of decomposed apples was nothing of the sort. It was a steaming mass of fresh poo decorated by apple seeds. Two strides farther there was a similar deposit, then another. I froze. The air I inhaled took all sound with it. I didn't need an expert to tell me this wasn't coyote scat. I was a long way from anywhere. Alone. I tightened my rein on Frida and began talking to her, whistling, singing. I walked farther, holding my breath while simultaneously belting out a tune and listening for cracking branches or other signs of *Ursus americanus*. A shiny new Bruce Trail sign nailed to a tree caught my attention. Caution, it read, Bear in Area. I sang louder. About two hundred metres and 10 hours later, the trail dipped back into the woods where there was another bear warning sign, this one facing the opposite direction. It seemed I'd passed through unscathed. My heart rate steadied; I breathed easier.

In truth, I shouldn't have been so afraid. Encounters with black bears on a hiking trail on the Bruce Peninsula in a field of apples not long before hibernation shouldn't be surprising. Moreover, fatal attacks are so rare that walking among *U. americanus* is far safer than driving my car. And while grizzly bears are known to viciously protect their cubs (70 percent of human deaths caused by *Ursus arctos horribilis* result from this behaviour), black bears aren't similarly inclined. With black bears, the risk arises if you come between one, especially a pregnant sow, and its food. We may joke about women's cravings while with child, but according to an Ontario government website, a black bear must consume twenty thousand calories a day, the equivalent of four hundred apples, to prepare for hibernation. Sometimes, that quantity might be hard to come by, but this year, a bear could consume that many in an hour. Over 90 percent of a black bear's diet is plant-based. Of the 10 percent that comes from animals, most is derived from eating insects, including ants, wasps and bees. It seems Pooh wasn't only after the honey.

I stopped for lunch atop a rise in the trail. Trees obscured the view, but there was a light airiness to my perch. Frida lay down and slept while I rested. When we carried on, I walked alongside a natural stone wall decorated with maidenhair spleenwort, moss and other ferns before arriving at the Mystery Cabin Side Trail, my turnaround point. The side trail dropped down, passed by the foundation of the mystery cabin, and I noted that anyone who lived there would have had an impressive view from their front step. The Mystery Cabin Side Trail led to the Don Richards Side Trail and to the Kemble Wetland Side Trail before hooking back into the main BT — thereby, much to my relief, avoiding the Caution: Bear in Area stretch.

I occupied myself by paying attention to ferns and mushrooms. I added sensitive and bracken ferns to my list of these feather-like plants that represent new beginnings for some Indigenous people. I'd now identified nine of 50 types of ferns that have been identified within the Niagara Escarpment Biosphere Reserve. It's also home to about one-quarter of Canada's endangered or threatened species. I identified an eye-catching yellow patches toadstool. It's one of about 150,000 species of fungi that taxonomists have described and one of a possible 3.5 million thought to exist. Like so many of nature's treasures, mushrooms are proving to have characteristics that humble humankind. One species can break down plastics in weeks rather than years. Over three hundred of them are known to be hallucinogenic. Acid produced by another is used to make Lego. And a white button mushroom (*Armillaria ostoyae*) in Oregon is the largest living organism on the planet. It covers almost one thousand hectares and is estimated to be over eight thousand years old.

One of my goals when I set out was to get to know the Niagara Escarpment better, with the hope, as Baba Dioum believed, it would help me love it more. I was confirming that by walking the BT on my own for day after long day, I was developing a deeper intimacy with the landscape. Borrowing the British concept of "hefting," the more I learned about the Niagara Escarpment's flora and fauna, its geology, its rivers and valleys, the more attached I became. Like cattle and sheep who are hefted to their farm, I was becoming less likely to wander away and more apt to find my way home.

Day 34

KEMBLE MOUNTAIN

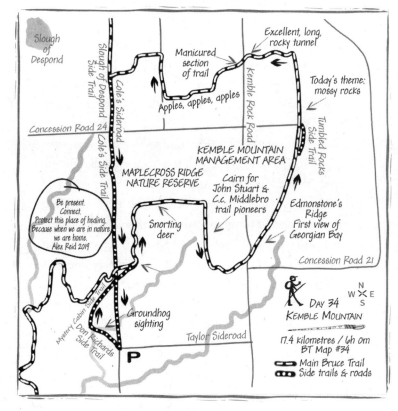

Slough of Despond

Slough of Despond Side Trail

Cole's Sideroad

Cole's Side Trail

Manicured section of trail

Excellent, long, rocky tunnel

Apples, apples, apples

Kemble Rock Road

Today's theme: mossy rocks

Concession Road 24

Tumbled Rocks Side Trail

KEMBLE MOUNTAIN MANAGEMENT AREA

MAPLECROSS RIDGE NATURE RESERVE

Cairn for John Stuart & C.c. Middlebro trail pioneers

Be present. Connect. Protect this place of healing. Because when we are in nature we are home. Alex Reid 2019

Snorting deer

Edmonstone's Ridge First view of Georgian Bay

Concession Road 21

Mystery Cabin Side Trail

Don Richards Side Trail

Groundhog sighting

Taylor Sideroad

P

Day 34
KEMBLE MOUNTAIN
17.4 kilometres / 6h 0m
BT Map #34
Main Bruce Trail
Side trails & roads

FIELD NOTES

START TIME: 9:30 a.m., Wednesday, September 14, 2022

TRAILHEAD WEATHER: overcast and cool

DISTANCE: 17.4 km

ELAPSED TIME: 6h 0m

BT SECTION: Sydenham

BT MAP: #34

MAIN BT WALKED: 140.7 km to 152.9 km

ASCENT: 608 m / **DESCENT:** 642 m

SIDE TRAILS: Don Richards Side Trail, Mystery Cabin Side Trail, Tumbled Rocks Side Trail, Slough of Despond Side Trail, Coles Side Trail

FLORA/FAUNA OF NOTE: groundhog (*Marmota monax*), wild grapes (*Vitis vulpina*), blue albatrellus (*Albatrellopsis flettii*) or maybe Hypocreaceae, aborted entoloma (shrimp of the woods, *Entoloma abortivum*), white-tailed deer (*Odocoileus virginianus*), bear or cow?

*In which a whistling pig gives us a start before
I fail to believe that a bear encounter is more authentic
on my own. I refuse to take nature for granted and
give a nod to my dad's legacy.*

Less than two hundred metres in along the Don Richards
Side Trail, a smallish brown animal came barrelling down the
path toward Frida and me. When it saw us, it careened left,
leaving us to wonder if we'd just seen a groundhog. The largest member of the squirrel family, groundhogs are hopelessly
cute. Endearing photos of them with yellow daisies protruding from their mouths attest to their herbivorous nature. Less
heartwarming is seeing one munching on your garden lettuce.
Also known as whistling pigs or land beavers, groundhogs go
to sleep in October and don't wake up until Groundhog Day
(February 2) — or later. While hibernating, their heart rate
slows to five beats per minute from 80, and their body temperature cools to near freezing. When I was a kid, groundhogs
were plentiful — then coyotes arrived and decimated the population. It was good to have caught a glimpse of this character.

I followed the Mystery Cabin Side Trail in the opposite
direction of my last hike. When it intersected with the main

BT, I went north into the unknown. It's comforting to revisit a familiar trail, but I like entering new territory — especially on my own. In *The Art of Travel*, Alain de Botton wrote, "Our responses to the world are crucially moulded by whom we are with; we temper our curiosity to fit in with the expectation of others." For a pure experience, de Botton prefers to travel on his own. I'm not sure that my solo journeys are more authentic, but I certainly see, hear and feel more when I'm not distracted by company. People, particularly women, raise their eyebrows when I tell them I mostly hike on my own. "I couldn't do that," they say. I realize that walking solo isn't for everyone, but if they gave it a try, they might be surprised at what they learn about themselves. A walk in the park is great therapy — better even if the absence of company forces you to converse with yourself — and better again if you have a few adrenalin-producing moments to make you feel alive.

〰

I entered the MapleCross Nature Reserve, enroute to the Kemble Mountain Management Area. I was encountering more of these "parks," that were there to protect nature, not provide recreational opportunities. On my last hike it had been the Lindenwood Management Area with its vast wetlands. I'm not sure how much management goes on, but the protection from human encroachment offered by this designation shouldn't be underestimated. Creation of the Forks of the Credit Provincial Park was first suggested in 1968. It took 17 years to receive this designation. Now, these 282 hectares of protected land form an island of green within an ocean of aggregate mines peppered with housing "developments." Looking around, it was hard to imagine a similar fate for Kemble Mountain, but it took forward thinking to push for the Forks Park in the 1960s, and if the mad rush to grow Canada's population continues, Algonquin Park maybe become a similar oasis. We take nature for granted at our peril.

Wild grapes
(Vitus riparia)

September is normally a great month for fungi, but it had been so dry they were scarce. I was surprised by a cluster of small white ill-formed mushrooms. Commonly known as shrimp of the woods, their less appealing name is aborted entoloma. Given their moniker, I presumed these mushrooms encouraged miscarriage. But I was wrong. Some fungi, including this one, become misshapen — they "abort" — if grown close to honey mushrooms. The stem and cap of the aborted entolomas turn into the popcorn-like white balls that I saw. Good to eat, but funny to look at.

Frida and I startled a deer before we came to a cairn situated in a thick forest. It was erected in 1975 to recognize two prominent Sydenham section members: John Stuart and C.C. Middleboro. They were referred to as "trail pioneers," which made me try to imagine the forest where I stood as they would have known it almost a half century ago. Rather than being wilder, it was likely more tame. Tamed by axes and chainsaws, horse-drawn ploughs and tractors. Although the Bruce Peninsula's black bear population is threatened by human contact, black bear habitat in more southern parts of the province is expanding because so much agricultural land has been abandoned. In addition to the expansion of natural forests, reforested areas are evident along the BT. They are the result of massive initiatives offered by the Ontario government in the 1960s and beyond. My dad paid two cents a seedling for the twenty thousand trees he planted. I admire the rows of now mature red pines and black locusts alongside the road outside Belfountain. They are my dad's legacy.

Soon I was atop Edmonstone's Ridge on a parcel of land sold by Robert Samuel Edmonstone to the Grey Sauble Conservation Authority according to a plaque. I had my first lookout for the day. Below me the forest gave way to farm fields, and in the near distance Georgian Bay. The combination of agricultural land, forest and water made for a spectacular sight. I had lunch with the view.

The outer edge of the woods where I sat was becoming increasingly airy as the lush spring leaves aged like an elder's skin. It wouldn't be long until the light would turn to a buttery yellow under a canopy of orange and red foliage. But as the trail delved deeper into forest's core, the light dimmed and green returned. I gave the 830 metre Tumbled Rocks Side Trail a go. A sign described it as "a more challenging alternative route." After passing through a narrow crevice, I scrambled over the promised tumbled rocks. Then I climbed to the top of Dodd's Hill before dropping down onto Graham's Hill Road along a damp trail bordered by ferns cascading from moss-covered rocks. Was this the BT or the West Coast Trail?

After a stretch of road, I entered cow pasture that reminded me of the apple-rich bear territory of my last hike. This time, I was more sanguine, or I was until Frida had a good bark and something big took off from behind an apple tree. It made too much noise to be a deer, so it might have been a bear, surely it was a cow. The apple trees let up and I breathed easier as I crossed wide-open fields. Before I popped out onto the road (a.k.a. the Slough of Despond Side Trail), I was humbled by the message on a trailside plaque. It read:

Be present.
Connect.
Protect this place of healing
Because when we are in nature,
We are home.
Alex Reid 2019.

Day 35

SKINNER'S BLUFF / BRUCE'S CAVE

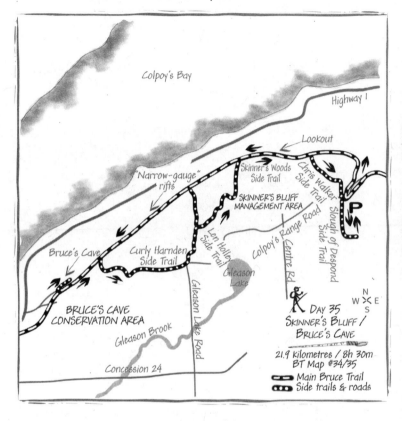

FIELD NOTES

START TIME: 9:15 a.m., Thursday, September 15, 2022

TRAILHEAD WEATHER: mixed cloud, cool, perfect hiking temperature

DISTANCE: 21.9 km

ELAPSED TIME: 8h 30m

BT SECTION: Sydenham

BT MAP: #34/35

MAIN BT WALKED: 158.1 km to 166.6 km

ASCENT: 700 m / **DESCENT:** 714 m

SIDE TRAILS: Bruce's Caves Access Trail, Curly Harnden Side Trail, Len Holley Side Trail, Chris Walker Side Trail, Slough of Despond Side Trail, Skinner's Woods Side Trail, The President's Path (touched it!)

FLORA/FAUNA OF NOTE: porcupine (*Erethizon dorsatum*), eastern white cedars (*Thuja occidentalis* L.)

In which I become a member of the Moses family before old
codgers cling to the escarpment's cliffs, Bruce lodges in jail
and the scum and filth in the badness of the ground doth
ariseth many fears in mine soul.

I stayed overnight at the Country Sunset B&B with Cecilie
and Bill Moses. What a great service they provide. It's not
fancy, but it felt like home. I had my own bed/sitting area
where both Frida and I were welcomed. In fact, when I drove
into Owen Sound for dinner, Cecilie kept Frida for me. How
often does that happen at a hotel? I gave Bill a ride into
Owen Sound so he could pick up his truck at the repair shop,
but nothing is ever simple, is it? His truck wouldn't start.
Fortunately, I had booster cables. By the time Bill's vehicle
was going, I felt like an integral part of the Moses family.

Next morning, Bill joined me while I enjoyed a dark-
roasted brew. He pulled out a tome of a book called *The*
Vascular Plants of the Bruce Peninsula by Joe Johnson. "Do
you know this book?" he asked. When I shook my head, he
explained that Johnson, a 40-year Wiarton resident, had
written it. "Joe had an unusual attention to detail," Bill told
me. "You could say he was obsessed with vascular plants."

(Vascular plants such as flowers and trees have tissues — remember those dogs named xylem and phloem? — that conduct nutrients, water and other compounds. Ferns are vascular, but seedless; whereas fungi, lichens and mosses are not vascular.) Johnson's obsession made it hard for him to know when to stop. Furthermore, his manuscript was hand-written. Bill worked tirelessly, finally wrestling what the author wanted to say into the book he was showing me with obvious pride. Johnson's (and Bill's) work was especially useful since it could be compared to vascular-plant research documented by P.V. Krotkov in the 1930s, thereby giving scientists an idea of the change in local flora. I wished I could have stayed longer, but Kate was about to arrive. We were heading out together for my seventh and final hike in the Sydenham section.

Kate followed as I drove to where we planned to drop her car. It was one of those days when the sun's reflection on the film that builds up on the inside of your windshield is a problem. We continued along Colpoy's Range Road. On the BT map, it looked like a normal road, but it was little more than a cart track that put my Mazda hatchback to the test. It took us longer to get to the trailhead than planned and then 10 minutes into the walk, I realized I'd forgotten a walking pole and we had to double back. Would this hike ever get going?

For seven uninterrupted kilometres, the trail followed the escarpment's edge through the Skinner's Bluff Management Area. Tucked into the end of Colpoy's Bay to our left we could see Wiarton, a town whose name was popularized in Stan Rogers's ballad "White Squall," in which he refers to a red-eyed Wiarton girl. We looked out over Whitecloud, Hay and Griffith islands. The latter, all 930 hectares of it, is owned by the Griffith Island Club, a private sport-shooting resort with accommodations and other amenities related to hunting.

Like most of the Niagara Escarpment's cliffs, this one along Skinner's Bluff is populated with gnarly white cedars. Known as the tree of life, they contain vitamin C — the cure, Indigenous people taught Jacques Cartier, for scurvy. After the glaciers receded, white cedars were largely shaded out by the incoming hardwoods. But these tough old codgers refused to capitulate. Some of them clinging to the edge of cliffs for almost two thousand years, their octopus-like roots finding purchase in the smallest cracks in walls of solid limestone. It wasn't until almost 1990 that we learned from University of Guelph professor Douglas Larson and his colleague Peter Kelly about the tremendous age of these unassuming trees. They grow so slowly that one described and photographed by Larson and Kelly that germinated in AD 688 appears to have a diameter of 10 centimetres or less.

Kate and I descended the escarpment and then doubled back in the lee of the cliffs along the Bruce's Caves Access Trail within the Bruce's Caves Conservation Area. We picked our way through the escarpment's iconic green-tinted rocks, making slow progress. With no idea of what to expect of Bruce's Caves, we were wowed when we came upon a great gaping chasm seemingly held up by a central, hourglass rock column. In a photo, Kate is dwarfed by the grand opening. The caves are the result of weathering and post-glacial lake levels, but I liked the story of Robert Bruce, the man behind the caves, as opposed to Robert *the* Bruce, the 14th century King of Scotland. Bruce's-caves Bruce arrived from Scotland during the Crimean War (1853–1856). Settling near Wiarton, he worked construction and kept to himself. In summer, he lived on his 120 hectare property that included the caves. In winter, he moved into town where he paid rent for a "room" and board in the local jail!

After exploring the cave, we found a picnic table where we had lunch before turning around. This was the end of the Sydenham section for us. We retraced our way back along the BT until we arrived at the Curly Harnden Side Trail, which we followed to Kate's car. It took us through a hard-wood forest, much of it along what the BT guide refers to as a cart path but is likely an old logging road. We took advantage of the double track by walking abreast for a change. Unlike the trail along the cliff's edge, the cart track was heavenly as it was mostly devoid of the ridged rocks that tire out my feet. Today wasn't the first time I appreciated the relatively smooth surface of a logging road — and it sure wouldn't be the last.

North American porcupine
(Erethizon dorsatum)

I was sad when we parted company. The last few days had tempered my claims about preferring to walk solo. As de Botton suggests, having Kate with me changed things, but isn't that part of the travel experience too? Isn't seeing something through someone else's eyes its own form of curiosity? One's not better; it's different. Kate and I travelled at the same speed, seemed to get hungry at the same time and we learned more about each other despite having been sisters for a long time. I felt teary as I walked along the Len Holley Side Trail, especially glad to have Frida bounding alongside me.

I passed through more thick forest feeling deflated until I returned to the main BT and lookouts over Colpoy's Bay and the islands. I liked seeing the same view in the afternoon light. I snapped some comparative photos and continued on. I picked up the Chris Walker Side Trail recalling having walked through Walker's Woods back in the Dufferin Hi-Land section. That man sure got around. I returned to my car where I'd intended to continue for another 90 minutes on a six-kilometre loop along the Slough of Despond Side Trail and then back on The President's Path. But the September sun was already low in the sky, and I had a two-hour drive home. Instead, I followed the Slough of Despond Side Trail as far as The President's Path and turned around, entirely missing the point of this excursion. I had wanted to see the wetland that shared its name with the one described by John Bunyan in his 1681 book, *The Pilgrim's Progress*. Curious to understand why it's considered one of the most important theological books ever written, I'd recently read it. In *The Pilgrim's Progress*, the protagonist sinks into the Slough of Despond (a.k.a. the swamp of despair) weighed down by the immensity of his sins. Bunyan wrote, "This miry slough is such a place as cannot be mended; it is the descent whither the scum and filth that attends conviction for sin doth continually run, and therefore is it called the Slough of Despond: for still as the sinner is awakened about his lost condition, there ariseth in his soul many fears, and doubts, and discouraging apprehensions, which all of them get together, and settle in this place; and this is the reason of the badness of this ground."

Yikes. The Slough of Despond made my imagined Grimpen Mire near Old Baldy seem like a lark. I wondered why Grey County had so nameth this slough, but the local archivist could not telleth me. It is a badness of ground that I doth shall see one day hence.

Peninsula Section

Day 36

WIARTON / SPIRAL STAIRCASE / COLPOY'S BAY

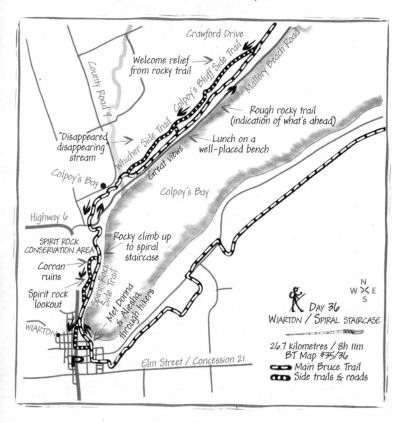

FIELD NOTES

START TIME: 8:30 a.m., Monday, September 19, 2022

TRAILHEAD WEATHER: clearing skies after thunder and lightning and rain

DISTANCE: 26.7 km

ELAPSED TIME: 8h 11m

BT SECTION: Peninsula

BT MAP: #35/36

MAIN BT WALKED: 0 km to 12.9 km

ASCENT: 770 m / **DESCENT:** 786 m

SIDE TRAILS: Colpoy's Bluff Side Trail, Whicher Side Trail, Spirit Rock Side Trail, Wiarton Side Trail

FLORA/FAUNA OF NOTE: purple asters (*Symphyotrichum ontarionis*)

In which the Bruce beckons, the smell is not an eel, and pit
vipers are not found amid the alvar's clints and grikes.

When I drove into Wiarton, the early morning thunder and
lightning had let up. A misty haze hung like gauze before a
blue-sky backdrop. Clearly it was foggy fall, the season when
air near the ground cools and becomes saturated with moisture, making driving tricky. The sun was doing its best to
"burn off" the fog by raising the air temperature sufficiently
to un-saturate it. I followed the main BT along Wiarton's
beachfront, greeting campers as they emerged from their
tents. Continuing along a small road past the town's water
works, I entered the Spirit Rock Conservation Area.

I was familiar with this section of trail as I walked from
Wiarton to Cape Croker in 2018 in advance of writing an
article about the South Peninsula section for the *Bruce Trail
Conservancy* magazine. Research for that story made me
understand what "the Bruce" meant to the trail's founders.
Yes, it was a nod to James Bruce, the eighth Earl of Elgin and
Governor General of the Province of Canada from 1847 to

1854, after whom the peninsula was named. But "the Bruce" was code for "wilderness," and the trail led them there. The Bruce beckoned the trail's founders just as it had William Sherwood Fox, the author of *The Bruce Beckons*.

≈

As I paralleled Colpoy Bay's shoreline, the clouds thickened and became an intense stormy grey. I smelled what I knew was geosmin, the chemical we perceive as having an earthy smell and associate with rain. Sandwiched between the bank of thunderheads and the dark cliffs of Skinner's Bluff, a band of sunshine sent rays of light streaming across the corduroy ripples of Colpoy's Bay. The inky water sparkled. It was a toss-up whether I'd be hiking in rain or sun.

The trail led me along the shoreline through yet another cedar forest before turning up hill through yet more slippery rocks, wet from the morning's rain. Soon I came to what I'd been anticipating: the spiral staircase. Yes, a six-metre-high, rusty-red metal spiral staircase. I wondered if the similar curved conveyance that had once provided the Morningstar family with access to Twelve Mile Creek in Niagara had inspired this unusual feature. Fortunately, Frida is not put off by metal stairs and she bravely made her way up. (Dog owners be forewarned, many canines wouldn't attempt these stairs.) I continued through forest before being treated to a long stretch of open trail across scrubby meadow. The wind had picked up and the clouds were dashing across the sky. It had become a blustery, woollen-sweater day. The air was crisp. It smelled like the leaf piles parents rake only to have their kids jump into them. The changes that occur as trees hunker down for the winter help create that familiar odour, but mostly it comes from decaying leaves. For me, it's the smell of family walks on Thanksgiving Day.

The trail took me through the pretty village of Colpoy's Bay. Farther on, a sign swung in the breeze. Etched into it was a poem by William Wordsworth. His words added to the slight melancholy that accompanied the smell of pending fall:

> With an eye made quiet by the power
> Of harmony, and the deep power of joy,
> We see into the life of things.

Wordsworth's peaceful message was offset by signs opposing a "smelly fish plant." The term smelly, I presumed, embodied both the risk of odour and the possibility of sketchy deal-making. In 2021, the local council approved an application for an on-land Atlantic salmon farm. It proposed to grow 15,000 tonnes of salmon per year, which would require it to treat and recirculate 1,300 litres of water from Colpoy's Bay — *per minute.* The ongoing battle reminded me of my isn't-it-someone-else's-turn response to the blasting quarry proposed for my backyard in Caledon. I wondered if there wasn't some way forward that didn't pit quarry or fish plant against community, and life's essentials (aggregates and food) against nature in expensive, acrimonious conflicts.

The ongoing battle is a marked change from how things were in less crowded days. In 1906, Wiarton "beat out" Southampton, Owen Sound, Collingwood and other larger towns by "winning" the government contract to build a fish hatchery. It stocked Georgian Bay with trout, splake and other species for 85 years. Somehow the business survived when invading sea lamprey devastated the bay's population of native lake trout and white fish. The alien species arrived from far afield via waterways such as the Welland Canal, back in Niagara where I'd walked about 30 hikes ago. Commonly, though erroneously, called eels, sea lamprey are eel-like, parasitic creatures that have been largely eliminated from Georgian Bay by various eradication programs. They are not to be confused with the Great Lakes' four native species of lamprey: foot-long chestnut and silver varieties, which are parasitic and can leave deep scars on host fish, and six-inch-long American brook and northern brook lamprey, which are non-parasitic.

Leaving the sweeping view of Colpoy's Bay, I followed a rocky, forested, foot-fatiguing trail. It was a relief to find a bench at the Whicher Side Trail. I enjoyed lunch and my feet were happy to have a break. The rocks kept up until I reached the turnaround point of my day's journey at the Crawford Road Side Trail. It led me to Colpoy's Bluff Side Trail — an oh-so-welcome relief. It was another blessedly smooth cart path that led me to the Whicher Side Trail, which was also kind to my feet. It opened into a meadow where I came upon the disappearing stream mentioned in the BT guide. Given the dry conditions, it seemed to have disappeared some time ago. I inspected several gravestones as I detoured through Colpoy's Bay Cemetery and waited while Frida stopped for a drink from pretty Colpoy's Creek. I step-stoned a line of flat-topped rocks separated by narrow crevices, recognizing it as alvar (a rare limestone plain comprising clints [flat limestone rocks] and grikes [cracks between the clints]). *This feels like snake territory*, I thought. No eastern massasauga rattlers appeared, though I was now in or near the territory of these threatened venomous pit vipers, a description that makes them sound scarier and more aggressive than they are. Ontario's only venomous snake is about half a metre long and rarely strikes unless it's threatened. Bites are rare, normally well under 10 per year according to the Toronto Zoo. (Alberta has prairie rattlesnakes, BC has northern Pacific rattlesnakes and Ontario and Quebec used to have timber rattlesnakes, though they've been listed as extirpated [locally extinct] since 2001. All are pit vipers, which means they have heat sensors between their nostrils, which they use to locate prey.)

Re-entering the Spirit Rock Conservation Area, I picked up the Spirit Rock Side Trail and visited The Corran Ruins. Formerly a 17-room mansion built by Hestor and Alexander McNeil in 1882, it was destroyed by fire and purchased in 1976 by the conservation authority. The side trail led me to the lookout. Some claim that when conditions are right, a woman's face is reflected on the cliff face below the ledge. I continued to the highway and down the hill into Wiarton. It was only 4 p.m. so I had a look around this pretty town before I picked up a bear bell for Frida. Skeptics say rather than warding off bears, it calls them to dinner.

When I returned to my car, there was a woman sitting at a picnic table soaking her feet in a tub of water. Parked nearby was a white transit van with its door open. Inside I spied a well-used backpack and a pair of muddy hiking boots. I asked the woman if she was hiking the BT. Donna was from Ottawa. Together with her daughter, Alesha, she was 34 days into their end-to-end journey. Donna told me, "The Beaver Valley section almost killed me. Up and down. Up and down." The mother and daughter were staying in their van and using trail angels when possible. I'm a trail angel for the Caledon Hills section. The job involves providing hikers, mostly those completing the entire trail, with transport from their vehicle to the trailhead. "I don't think there are any trail angels north of here," I said. Donna replied, "We'll figure something out." She sounded exhausted by the thought. We shared a few stories, then I left her to her foot bath, not mentioning the rocky trail ahead.

Day 37

JONES BLUFF / CAPE CROKER / NEYAASHIINIGMIING

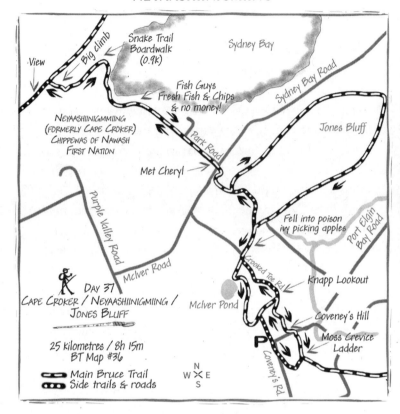

The map shows handwritten labels:
- View
- Big climb
- Snake Trail Boardwalk (0.9k)
- Sydney Bay
- Sydney Bay Road
- Fish Guys Fresh Fish & Chips & no money!
- Neyaashiinigmmiing (formerly Cape Croker) Chippewas of Nawash First Nation
- Park Road
- Jones Bluff
- Met Cheryl
- Purple Valley Road
- Fell into poison ivy picking apples
- Port Elgin Bay Road
- McIver Road
- Crooked Toe Rd.
- Knapp Lookout
- Day 37 Cape Croker / Neyaashiinigmiing / Jones Bluff
- McIver Pond
- Coveney's Hill
- Moss Crevice Ladder
- 25 kilometres / 8h 15m BT Map #36
- Coveney's Rd.
- Main Bruce Trail
- Side trails & roads
- N W E S

FIELD NOTES

START TIME: 8:30 a.m., Tuesday, September 20, 2022

TRAILHEAD WEATHER: thick fog clearing to blue skies and an unseasonably warm temperature

DISTANCE: 25 km

ELAPSED TIME: 8h 15m

BT SECTION: Peninsula

BT MAP: #36

MAIN BT WALKED: 21.5 km to 36.2 km

ASCENT: 830 m / **DESCENT:** 853 m

SIDE TRAILS: Coveney's Side Trail, Knapp Side Trail, Snake Trail Boardwalk, Jones Bluff Side Trail, McIver Side Trail, McIver Pond Side Trail

FLORA/FAUNA OF NOTE: poison ivy (*Rhus radicans* L.)

In which I snake through a wetland recalling orchids once visited; drool over hot, crisp, golden, battered white fish dipped in homemade tartar sauce and fresh-cut french fries sprinkled with salt and malt vinegar and relive spirited battles once won — and lost.

When I looked out from my room at the modest Bear Tracks Inn in the morning, I was greeted by soupy orange fog that bled quickly to grey. It obscured the sun: a white ball of roiling molten gases rimmed by a shimmering mustard-yellow halo. Enroute to the trailhead, I drove through alternating shafts of blinding sunlight and patches of dense fog.

In *The Bruce Beckons*, Fox wrote, "[If] the visitor delights in rough wild tracts of land and water and is eager to wander-long among uncouth scenes, he is ready to fall in love with The Bruce." I associate the word *uncouth* with a bad-mannered person, so it seemed an odd adjective to choose. But the archaic definition describes uncouth as a place that is "uncomfortable, especially because of remoteness or poor conditions." I'd already encountered bears and worried about rattlesnakes. I'd experienced long sections of uninterrupted trail. Today, I would follow a six-kilometre loop around Jones Bluff. It wasn't the longest continuous stretch I'd covered, but it might qualify as a "rough wild tract," as suggested by Fox.

I picked up Coveney's Side Trail, following it to the main BT, where I encountered my first obstacle of the day: the Moss Crevice Ladder. Squeezed into a slim gap between rocks, the narrow passageway was more staircase than ladder. Frida bounced down without incident. It set the tone for the better part of the hike: lots of rocks, moss and scrambling. The temperature rose quickly and when I arrived at Knapp Lookout, it was hard to imagine there'd been fog. I gazed over Colpoy's Bay and the three islands — White Cloud, Hay and Griffith — that I'd looked upon only a few days ago from across the water.

I was meeting my friend Cheryl Mitchell for the latter half of the day's hike, so I took the shortcuts on the way to Neyaashiinigmiing (Cape Croker) so we could walk around Jones Bluff together. Knapp Side Trail followed the delightfully named Crooked Toe Road through a forest and past a lovely log home. It was buried in the trees, too dark for reptilian me, but in winter it would be an oasis. On the side of a paved road bordered by yet more apple-laden trees, I spied a beauty on a low-hanging branch. As I reached for it, Eve-like, from the edge of the ditch, my feet went out from under, and I slid on my backside down a bank into a patch of poison ivy. Whoops.

Fortunately, I was wearing socks and long pants, so it was only one forearm that slid through this ubiquitous nasty plant. Somehow despite all my years of hiking, I've either avoided coming into contact with it or, though it's unlikely, I don't react to urushiol oil. Since almost everyone is allergic to this compound (also found in poison oak and staghorn sumac), it's likely the former. I didn't have any warm soapy

Poison ivy
(Rhus radicans L.)

water to wash with so I applied the antimicrobial lotion I now carry in my backpack since Covid seemed to make it indispensable, unsure if it would help. Hopefully, I hadn't bruised or broken any stems, as simply brushing against the leaves doesn't expose you to the problematic oil. The local tourism association writes that poison ivy is "fairly common" on the Bruce Peninsula. I beg to differ; it's rampant.

Unexpectedly, I came across Donna and Alesha's white van, so I tucked a note under the windshield wipers, wishing them a good journey. Soon afterwards, I followed the long road into the 210 hectare Cape Croker Park, part of the Chippewas of Nawash Unceded First Nation's Neyaashiinigmiing reserve. I passed the entry gate and wandered through the lovely campground, emerging at a beach on Sydney Bay. Customers were already lined up at the Fish Guys Fresh Fish & Chips trailer. It was early for lunch, so I decided to stop in on my return as I'd be coming back this way in about an hour's time. Neyaashiinigmiing means "point of land surrounded on three sides by water," and if you look at the 6,300 hectare reserve on a map, you'll see why. It extends farther into Colpoy's Bay than any other point along the eastern shore of the Bruce Peninsula, which makes it the perfect place for the Cape Croker Lighthouse. About one-quarter of the band's 2,800 members live on the reserve, which, along with two smaller reserves, is what remains of the First Nation's traditional lands. On the band's website, they explain that their territory once included the entire Bruce Peninsula as well as an additional 800,000 hectares south of it. In yet another linkage, Chief James Nawash, after whom the First Nation is named, fought alongside Shawnee Chief Tecumseh against the Americans in the War of 1812.

I realized the presiding governor general while the First Nation was negotiating Treaty 72 — the one that some claim ceded much of its (and the Saugeen First Nation's) traditional lands— was James Bruce, after whom the peninsula had been named. I had further discovered that in 2021, Parks Canada began referring to the Bruce Peninsula as the Saugeen Peninsula, which I presumed was related to the ongoing lawsuit launched jointly in 1994 by the Chippewas of Nawash and the Saugeen First Nation. They claim damages for alleged improprieties committed by the Crown while negotiating Treaty 72 in 1854. In 2021, the justice hearing the case agreed that Crown negotiators breached the "honour of the Crown." An out-of-court settlement between these First Nations and Bruce County have led some to believe that a land transfer might be an outcome of the land claim with the remaining defendants, the federal and provincial governments.

〰

I was excited to revisit the nine hundred metre Snake Trail Boardwalk, the BT's longest. According to Tom Hall from the Peninsula Club, it took three years to build during which a core group of about 12 volunteers bonded into the Order of Muddy Boots. Continuing on, I had views of Canada geese congregating on peaceful Sydney Bay to my right. To my left was a wetland that looked very different from the one I'd walked through for that magazine article. It had been June and I recalled my delight at seeing my first showy lady's slipper. Yellow and pink varieties hadn't prepared me for these aptly named beauties with their pale pink bulbous labella, white petals and sepals. I'm not sure my pleasure matched John Muir's though. He's reported to have claimed that seeing his first calypso orchid (in Niagara) was one of the two happiest moments of his life — I never discovered what the other one was.

I began the steep four hundred metre ascent to Sydney Bay Bluff through slippery moss-covered boulders. All morning, I'd been looking at the sheer cliffs anticipating (dreading?) the climb. The incline was gradual at first and then entered a boulder field where the fun began. Whereas a straightforward climb up a steep hill can be a grind, negotiating a tricky path, sometimes using my backside as an extra appendage, is entertaining. I'm careful when walking solo, so I'm slow, but this was my kind of trail, not unlike the Metcalfe Crevice Side Trail in the Beaver Valley. I was nose to rocks spray-painted with a thick layer of spongy moss as I progressed. Together with the rich peaty soil littered with miniature cedar cones, the moss emitted an earthy aroma as familiar to me as woodsmoke. Finally, I made it to the base of the metal staircase that scaled a sheer wall to the Sydney Bay Bluff — my final ascent.

The slatted metal stairs looked painful for dogs, and as I was only going to the top to see the view and then returning, I left Frida tied up below. Once I was out of sight, I could hear her whining. I called out encouraging words, hoping they would relieve her concern. From the clifftop, I gazed over Sydney Bay and the solid block of green forest that made up the vast First Nation. Clouds zoomed toward me as I perched on a rocky ledge. I looked forward to what lay ahead on the Bruce but was apprehensive too — a combo that W. Sherwood Fox would have respected. I was venturing into territory unknown to me along the most rugged sections of the BT. This was the Bruce, the wilderness that entranced and motivated the BT's founders.

Frida greeted me as though we'd been separated for hours or days. We made our way back down through the slippery mossy boulders (not as fun as climbing up). Just before returning to the Snake Trail Boardwalk, I ran into a group of BT hikers and their guide. For the third time, I came across the same leader I'd seen near Waterdown and again in the Blue Mountains section.

As I approached the Fish Guys Fresh Fish & Chips van, I smelled the aroma of deep fat frying and picked up my pace. Then a cold-sweat-inducing thought crept from my loins, up my back and landed between my shoulder blades. *No, it couldn't be*, I thought. I checked my pockets just in case. But it was true. For the first time in 37 hikes, I'd left my wallet behind. There would be no fish and chips for lunch. Ouch. My sandwich would have to do. But it was no substitute. All I could think about was hot, crisp, golden, battered white fish dipped in homemade tartar sauce and fresh-cut french fries sprinkled with salt and malt vinegar.

After lunch, I walked back through Cape Croker Park and made my way up the long hot road, where I could see Cheryl waiting in the distance. I'd walked 13.5 kilometres and would walk 11.5 more. Cheryl and I met years ago on a tennis court and that sport turned us into great pals. We were doubles partners for a long time, playing in tournaments as far away as Montreal and Vancouver. But it was on the singles court that we had the greatest fun and our most spirited battles. Occasionally, the outcome caused Cheryl to throw her racquet. But we always shook hands at the end of a match. Cheryl is naturally fit and fleet-footed. At net, she can change direction in mid-air while simultaneously switching her racquet from her right hand to her left to put away what should have been my clear winner. We were evenly matched when playing against one another for "fun," usually splitting sets. But in a tournament, I was out of my league. I seldom won a game, much less a set when the outcome mattered to Cheryl.

As we walked around Jones Bluff through Neyaashiinigmiing — the point of land surrounded on three sides by water — we overlooked Sydney Bay, then Georgian Bay and then Colpoy's Bay. We chatted, catching up on what was new with friends, family and partners. In a flash, we'd completed the six-kilometre loop. We passed by the apple tree where I'd had my brush with poison ivy, then detoured to McIver's Pond through — yeah! — a meadow. When we came across a sign promising a water pump in one hundred metres, we took the bait and pumped enough to satisfy Frida. When we returned to the main BT, who did we run into but Donna and Alesha. It reminded me of when I walked the Camino de Santiago de Compostela. Sometimes I arrived at a refugio for the night only to run into someone I hadn't seen in several days.

The mother/daughter duo planned to enjoy dinner at the Fish Guys Fresh Fish & Chips. *Grrrr.*

At five, we arrived at my car. I was tired, but Cheryl, true to form, was just warmed up. She followed me back to the Bear Tracks Inn where we had dinner and clinked glasses to old times and good tennis matches.

Day 38

HOPE BAY / RUSH COVE / JACK POSTE

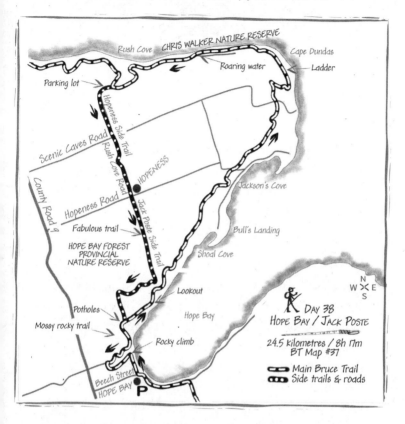

FIELD NOTES

START TIME: 9 a.m., Thursday, September 22, 2022

TRAILHEAD WEATHER: cool, overcast, rain threatening, then sunshine

DISTANCE: 24.5 km

ELAPSED TIME: 8h 17m

BT SECTION: Peninsula

BT MAP: #37

MAIN BT WALKED: 44.1 km to 61.7 km

ASCENT: 827 m / **DESCENT:** 856 m

SIDE TRAILS: Rush Cove Road, Hopeness Side Trail, Jack Poste Side Trail

FLORA/FAUNA OF NOTE: devil's paintbrush (*Pilosella aurantiaca, Pilosella caespitosa*), juniper (*Juniperus communis* L. var. *depressa* Pursh), Canadian lousewort (*Pedicularis canadensis*)

In which Gill proves urban trails and the BT are rocky
hills apart, leaving me to find hope-ness in Bruce's role in
Canada being the oldest continuous democratic federation
in the world, to lament treatment of Indigenous Peoples
and to fall in love with Jack Poste.

I took yesterday off to catch up on my note taking. In the late afternoon, my friend and book designer Gill Stead arrived to join me for the next three hikes. Gill hiked with me in Waterdown and was back again for more — good sport that she is. Gill braved a fun race called "Current to Killarney Canoefest" in 2019. About a dozen of us paddled nonstop for six hours in Alex's 10 metre long Montreal canoe. We launched from Little Current on Manitoulin Island and made our way across Georgian Bay's open water to the town of Killarney in the eponymously named provincial park. We were short by about six paddlers, so we didn't get a break for the entire crossing. Like I said, Gill's a good sport.

After dropping a car, we arrived in Hope Bay where a chilling mist obscured the view, the campground and beach. We noted the village was devoid of the No Parking signs that had proliferated during the pandemic. It was good to feel welcome. We walked through the village and into the

Hope Bay Forest Provincial Nature Reserve along a rocky path that headed up a steep incline. It was a tough start. Gill had been walking up to 15 kilometres at a stretch, but mostly on urban trails. This was different. "How are you doing?" I asked. A sigh was her breathy response. While Cheryl and I had walked around Jones Bluff on a level path almost devoid of rocks, they came on strong near Hope Bay and didn't let up. Up and down, up and down we went over slippery moss-covered boulders. We were both glad we'd brought along hiking poles. At the Jack Poste Side Trail, nearly perfect cylindrical glacial potholes greeted us. I'd seen these natural phenomena near Hilton Falls when I walked with Susan on that crazy derecho day. Like me, Gill was surprised to see what rocks swirling around in water can do given time.

We made it to the cliff's edge where it was fun to see Georgian Bay through Gill's eyes. She was amazed and daunted by the string of bay upon bay upon bay up the shoreline and out of sight. The hills weren't as big as they'd been in earlier sections where cumulatively I'd climbed more than seven hundred metres most days, but the rocks demanded our attention. It was hard on our ankles and feet. We took a break on a flat cantilevered clifftop and then continued to the junction with the Hopeness Side Trail. Gill was fading and with some prompting admitted her legs had that jelly-like feel, which is no fun. When I explained that her car was only three kilometres away if she took the side trail, she perked up. With two more days of hiking ahead, Gill reasoned it was best to not push it. I watched her trot away with a lightness to her step that hadn't been there moments before. Fortunately, I had faithful Frida to keep me company for the next 19 kilometres.

BT volunteers have worked their magic again. Thanks. Nicola

It was already 1 p.m., so I picked up the pace despite the trail becoming trickier. I was feeling rushed, worried about making it back to my car before dusk, concerned I might twist an ankle, wondering if there was a bear or a rattlesnake around the next corner, feeling responsible for Gill's jelly legs. "Stop it," I said to myself. "Let it go." Slowly, I switched my focus to the views, the forest, Frida. When the trail headed down to the water, I'd mostly shed my angst. As Frida scampered down a near vertical ladder, I was once again thankful for her agility. The trail continued to parallel the water, but on a lower level in a more arid environment. Yellow and orange devil's paintbrush sprouted from cracks between flat limestone slabs. These prolific, brightly coloured flowers are thought to have acquired their name because you'll have a devil of a time getting rid of them once they become established. There were swathes of juniper hugging the ground, their gin-flavouring berries almost as plentiful as the apples I'd been scavenging. I identified Canadian lousewort, a semi-parasitic plant as it nicks nutrients from the roots of its neighbours. A wort is a plant once thought to be good or valuable, versus a weed, which was bad or harmful. Some worts were named because they looked like a human organ (e.g., liverwort) and, at the time, the thinking was that any plant that looked like an organ must be good for it (not true). Some worts had medicinal properties (e.g., St. John's wort), whereas it was believed that a lousewort transmitted lice (plural of louse) to cattle.

When I made it down to Rush Cove, Georgian Bay was pounding the stony shore with relentless white-capped waves. They crashed, exploding into frothy spray that shot high overhead. This was more like the great lake described by Stan Rogers in "White Squall" — the one that can go from calm to one hundred knots in a flash. I stood mesmerized by the intense drama of the scene with Frida tucked behind me, her tail between her legs as though heeding Rogers's warning. A sign telling me I was in the Chris Walker Nature Reserve broke my contemplative mood. *That guy is everywhere*, I thought. Nearby a solitary BT plaque made me chuckle. It read: "Walk with a cautious step for we are not masters, only custodians." The thought of mastering Georgian Bay or the four-hundred-million-year-old Niagara Escarpment was laughable. After a quick lunch, I turned back along an abbreviated route to Hope Bay.

The main BT followed the road up the escarpment. When the white blazes branched onto what had been the Barrow Bay Side Trail, I stuck with the Rush Cove Road

Side Trail's blue slashes and then continued along Rush Cove Road to the Hopeness Side Trail. Hopeness appears on maps, but there isn't much there besides the single farmhouse that escaped demolition by Dow Chemical. According to a website called Finding Hope Ness, in the 1960s, Dow bought most of the land in the vicinity planning on mining magnesium-rich rock. The company offered farmers $5,000 each for their farms and most accepted despite bitter family disputes. Dow tore down the historic barns and near-century homes, destroying the rural community, and then abandoned the project for reasons I was unable to uncover. Now called the Hope Bay Forest Nature Reserve (the lone farmhouse excepted), the land is again the focus of a struggle as the reserve is included in the Saugeen Ojibway Nation's Treaty 72 land claim. It heralds changes that are in store for the Niagara Escarpment, the Bruce Peninsula and the BT as all levels of government in Canada come to terms with Indigenous land claims.

Local resident Phil McNichol who is the author of Finding Hope Ness, writes, "My home and property are surrounded on three sides by [the land claim] . . . Am I worried about that, for my sake, and the sake of my family? Not really. Despite the dishonourable way they were treated, over and over again, since before 1836, the Saugeen/Nawash people [the Saugeen Ojibway Nation] chose the path of peace in the courts of their historic oppressor to seek justice. That was, and remains, a huge expression of hopeful trust in the current legal processes of the Crown and Canada, as well as the inherent justice of their cause."

This expression of hopeful trust brought to my mind the First Nations Peace Monument I visited at the DeCew House Heritage Park in Niagara. The Wampum Belts engraved into that memorial seek peace and reconciliation. In 2021, former senator Murray Sinclair, who headed up the Truth and Reconciliation Commission, spoke at Queen's University. He told the audience that getting to the truth was hard "because there were so many people who just didn't believe that it [residential schools] could happen in this country." But, he warned, ". . . getting to the reconciliation [a harmonious relationship] is going to be harder." To get to reconciliation, Murray believes Canadians must "learn how to talk to, and about, each other, with greater respect than has been the case in the past."

Canadian historian John Ralston Saul has written extensively about Indigenous Peoples. Recently, he wrote in the *Globe and Mail* that the situation for First Nations in Canada is "the single most important unresolved flaw in our nation." He suggested that every citizen needs to commit to this issue "if Canada is to function as a place of justice." Even though Canada has this dark history, Saul commends the country for being "the oldest continuous democratic federation in the world," something he credits, in part, to James Bruce, the man after whom the peninsula was named. Better known as Lord Elgin, Bruce was Governor General of the Province of Canada from 1847 to 1854. During that time, Bruce signed the Bagot Report, which eventually led to the creation of the residential school system about 35 years later. Along with Robert Baldwin, an anglophone, and Louis-Hippolyte LaFontaine, a francophone, who jointly led what's often referred to as Canada's first responsible government (one that is responsible to its citizens rather than the Crown), Bruce rallied for a nation built on nonviolence, two peoples (French and English) and immigration. The threesome became friends who risked their lives to do it. Canada was a violent place throughout the pre-Confederation days as those "two peoples" battled for control. In 1849, protestors razed the legislative buildings in Montreal (the seat of government at the time). Fire broke out after rioters tossed lit torches that ignited gas lines broken by the bricks and stones they pelted at St. Anne's Market, home to Legislative Council and Assembly of Canada. The melee resulted after Bruce signed the Rebellion Losses Bill, which compensated French Canadians for damages suffered during the 1837 rebellion, and enraged Canada's elite. But unlike William Lyon Mackenzie, who decades earlier had agitated for responsible government, Canada's new leaders opted for a peaceful response. This nonviolent approach has become deeply seeded in the country's ethos.

Canada would be a different place today had Baldwin, Lafontaine and Bruce strived for a nation built on three rather than two peoples. But despite that lost opportunity, the three leaders passed an astounding array of legislation intended to result in a fair and just society. Saul wrote, "What they put in place are the legal and social foundation of Canada today." Among others, the measures they passed into law encouraged immigration, toll-free roads for the poor, official bilingualism, independent judges and a public school system. The trio wrested power from Britain, setting Canada on its way to becoming an exemplary democracy — all under the watchful eye of the like-minded ruling monarch, Queen Victoria.

On Finding Hope Ness, Phil McNichol remarked on the Saugeen Ojibway Nation's choice of "the path of peace in the courts of their historic oppressor to seek justice." While processing land claims has been slow and governments haven't shown much appetite for settling them, First Nations have mostly trusted the courts, eschewing violence. It takes a strong democracy to withstand the political pressures that can derail an independent judiciary. The system isn't perfect, but Canada is demonstrating that its long history of democracy means it's up to the challenge. It's noteworthy, that the just society Baldwin, LaFontaine and Bruce orchestrated and risked their lives for is the reason the Saugeen Ojibway Nation can trust the courts.

Despite James Bruce's role in establishing a resilient democracy, it's more likely the BT's founders landed on the name Bruce because of William Sherwood Fox's enthusiastic descriptions of the peninsula in his book, *The Bruce Beckons*. Nonetheless, the speech BT founder Norman Pearson made on the BT's 30th anniversary captures James Bruce's spirit as well as that of Canada, the trail and the William Claus Wampum Belt. Pearson said, "Recently, authors have talked about the power of the sovereign individual, and the huge energy which is released when such individuals co-operate . . . Their rewards lie in sharing with all future mankind the beauties of the Niagara Escarpment."

Since walking through Hopeness and in light of what I've come to understand about reconciliation, I've begun referring to the peninsula as the Saugeen Bruce.

〰

The Hopeness Side Trail and, especially, the Jack Poste Side Trail offered welcome relief from the morning's rocks as it followed yet another blessed cart path. I proclaimed out loud and for all the bears and rattlesnakes to hear: "I love Jack Poste" or at least I love his trail. When I re-entered the woods, brilliant sunshine streamed through the trees, the sky was a deep blue and there was no wind. Bliss. I wished Gill were experiencing this. I was drenched in "hopeness."

Day 39

LION'S HEAD

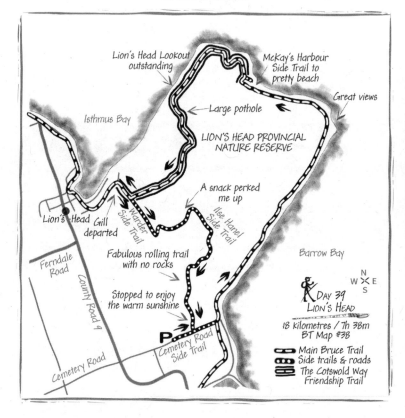

Lion's Head Lookout outstanding

McKay's Harbour Side Trail to pretty beach

Great views

Isthmus Bay

Large pothole

LION'S HEAD PROVINCIAL NATURE RESERVE

A snack perked me up

Lion's Head

Gill departed

Warder Side Trail

Ilse Hanel Side Trail

Barrow Bay

Fabulous rolling trail with no rocks

Stopped to enjoy the warm sunshine

Ferndale Road

County Road 9

P

Cemetery Road Side Trail

Cemetery Road

Day 39 Lion's Head

18 kilometres / 7h 38m
BT Map #38

Main Bruce Trail
Side trails & roads
The Cotswold Way
Friendship Trail

FIELD NOTES

START TIME: 9 a.m., Friday, September 23, 2022

TRAILHEAD WEATHER: lovely sunny day shaping up, 9 degrees Celsius

DISTANCE: 18 km

ELAPSED TIME: 7h 38m

BT SECTION: Peninsula

BT MAP: #38

MAIN BT WALKED: 69.6 km to 81.6 km

ASCENT: 532 m / **DESCENT:** 546 m

SIDE TRAILS: Cemetery Road Side Trail, Ilse Hanel Side Trail, McKay's Harbour Side Trail, Lion's Head Pothole Side Trail, Warder Side Trail

FLORA/FAUNA OF NOTE: common loon (*Gavia immer*), bearberry (kinnikinnick, *Arctostaphylos uva-ursi*), porcupine (*Erethizon dorsatum*), white birch (*Betula papyrifera*), purple asters (*Symphyotrichum ontarionis*)

In which Gill's in for a dime and a dollar, Lion's Head
outshines itself even if its image has eroded over time,
I cross the nine hundred kilometre threshold and
want the BT to never never.

After another enjoyable meal at the Bear Tracks Inn's friendly restaurant, Gill woke up ready to hit the trail again. Her option was a 12 kilometre stretch all the way around Lion's Head Provincial Nature Reserve. I'd walked it before on a dull November day with Alex, so I knew it was a spectacular route under an overcast sky. I expected it to shine even brighter given the day. With zero humidity, we were going to see for a long way from atop Lion's Head.

The Cemetery Side Trail took us to the Ilse Hanel Side Trail and onto the main BT. For the next nine kilometres it was views, views, beaches, a porcupine and more views — first looking over our right shoulder into the rising sun above Barrow Bay, then gazing over the ocean otherwise known as Georgian Bay. We skirted the escarpment's cantilevered crags soaring near the clouds along a rough but level trail. Unlike the day before when we had the mossy, wet ups and downs, this was similar to my walk around Jones Bluff with Cheryl — with more dramatic vistas. We were always on a precipice overlooking turquoise water. These were the series of cliffs that had impressed Gill yesterday — the ones featured in so many tourism brochures for the Saugeen Bruce Peninsula.

Bearberry (kinnikinnick)
(Arctostaphylos uva-ursi)

We began seeing small-leafed, low-lying bearberry with its red currant-like fruit. Then we clambered down to McKay's Harbour where we stopped to enjoy the sunny sandy beach. I'd loved this spot when Alex and I visited it, thinking it would be a great place to camp for a few nights. When we turned back to the main BT, an enormous porcupine blocked our way. In typical fashion, it didn't budge, which might account for the falsehood that porcupines are easy to catch — and eat — if you are lost in the woods, and are therefore protected in Ontario, which they are not. They are Canada's second largest rodent and like beavers, the country's largest, their ever-growing orange front teeth contain iron. When Kate and I walked near the Palisades, we came across a pile of quills shaped vaguely like a porcupine. It was as if the rodent had melted like the Wicked Witch of the West in the Wizard of Oz. The quills, some 30,000 per porcupine, which despite the myth are not fired at an aggressor, are used in Indigenous quillwork. A gorgeous — and painstakingly slow — artform, quillwork involves using dyed porcupine quills to decorate buckskin clothing, birchbark boxes, medicine bundles, moccasins and more.

Back atop the escarpment, we rounded Lion's Head Point on our way to Lion's Head Lookout. We were now following the Cotswold Way Friendship Trail, number nine of nine of these "sister" paths. (A 10th was added in 2023.) I'd love to walk the Cotswold Way someday. It's a 164 kilometre footpath that runs from Chipping Campden to Bath in England and, surprising to me, is younger than the BT. Its 50th was in 2020, whereas the BT crossed that threshold three years earlier.

In my opinion, the BT guide understates the beauty of Lion's Head Lookout. A "spectacular view over Isthmus Bay" doesn't do it justice. From our vantage point we could see the massive cliffs we'd just walked over as well as those yet to come. In between was the town of Lion's Head, a popular tourist spot snuggled into a well-protected cove. The Lion's Head moniker doesn't come from a bird's eye view looking down on the square isthmus, which separates Barrow Bay from Isthmus Bay. Instead, photos taken in the late 1880s show that Point Hangcliff at the peninsula's southern tip as seen from the village once resembled the profile of a lion. Over time, erosion has erased the likeness, but the name remains.

Once past the lookout, we were on the main access trail from Lion's Head. It filled up with view-seekers, many of whom stopped us. "How much farther is it?" they moaned. Most had underestimated how difficult it is to walk for 2.5 kilometres along a relentlessly rocky trail. Hat's off to those who made it. "They're the real hikers," suggested Gill. On that note, Gill began to fade too. She even passed up the detour onto what must be the BT's shortest side trail: the five-metre-long Lion's Head Pothole Side Trail. It leads to the base of what is surely the BT's largest pothole.

When we arrived at Gill's car, I hung around long enough for her to drive away. When she stuck her arm out the car window and gave me a big old country wave, I had that lonely feeling again. I was cheered, however, knowing I was close to exceeding nine hundred kilometres on the trail — the distance covered by those who hike the BT from end to end; I'd lost 10 pounds and was hiking tough. But these accomplishments were bittersweet. I was perilously close to Tobermory and, like not wanting to finish a good book, I didn't want this journey to end. I'd become addicted to whatever compounds long days on the trail dished out. I dreaded the thought of having to sit indoors behind my computer. Was being tied to that keyboard what had me pacing the cage?

I retraced the main BT to the Warder Side Trail enroute to the Ilse Hanel Side Trail. When I exchanged white blazes for the blue ones, it was like breathing fresher air. It was a relief to be away from the crowd. When I ignored the sections of the BT that attracted view-seekers, I'd only encountered a handful of fellow hikers. Despite the BT running through Canada's most densely populated province, often close to large urban centres, the trail was often lonely. I know that writing about hiking encourages people to explore trails, but more role models are needed — hikers from different age groups and ethnicities. More group hikes, better access to trails, even courses about how to hike. During the pandemic, when some trails became overused, I know the odd person blamed my hiking guides for the crowding. I assured them the opposite was true. The books moved people away from the main routes, such as the Lion's Head access trail I'd just escaped. The books introduced trails that were previously unknown, trails that were often right outside the hiker's home. It's not enough to simply draw a line on a map and tell people it's a trail, go walk it. Yet this is what most trail websites and government brochures do. If you've never hiked before and grew up in a culture that didn't include walking through a forest or where forests were littered with unexploded land mines, it takes a helping hand.

~~~

The Ilse Hanel Side Trail, like the Jack Poste Side Trail, received my joyous exclamation of devotion. The near stoneless trail rolled through a mature forest interspersed with white birch. I admire these trees for their role in canoe making, letter writing, construction of komatiks (a.k.a. dog sleds) and fire lighting. But I take them for granted. Today, I observed how their albino-white bark livened their fellow grey-trunked forest mates, much as a pinch of salt makes a meal sparkle.

When I returned to the Cemetery Side Trail, I sat down on a wooden bench that was drenched in sunshine. Purple asters perked up the dry grasses that rattled in the warm breeze. The heat had revived bees, and I could hear their bzzz, pause, bzzz, pause as they passed from bloom to bloom. Closing my eyes, I lay back on the bench and Frida curled up in the warm grass. My uncluttered state of mind reminded me of Neverland and Peter Pan, the boy who wouldn't grow up. I felt the same way about walking the BT. Couldn't it go on until never never?

Day 40

CAPE CHIN / DEVIL'S MONUMENT / OTTER LAKE

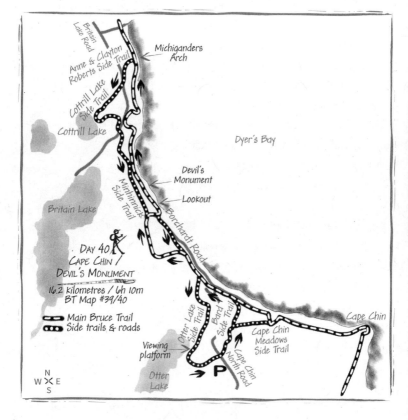

FIELD NOTES

START TIME: 8:45 a.m., Saturday, September 24, 2022

TRAILHEAD WEATHER: cool 9 degrees Celsius, promising rain

DISTANCE: 16.2 km

ELAPSED TIME: 6h 10m

BT SECTION: Peninsula

BT MAP: #39/40

MAIN BT WALKED: 106.5 km to 114.9 km

ASCENT: 442 m / **DESCENT:** 446 m

SIDE TRAILS: Cape Chin Meadows Side Trail, Bard Side Trail, Devil's Monument Side Trail, Anne & Clayton Roberts Side Trail, Cottrill Lake Side Trail, Minhinnick Side Trail, Otter Lake Side Trail

FLORA/FAUNA OF NOTE: white ash (*Fraxinus americana*), poison ivy (*Rhus radicans* L.)

*In which the devil helps me contemplate 40 days and
40 hikes thanks to Christian beliefs about the number 40,
Noah, his ark, Cockburn, Lopez, de Botton, Muir, Thoreau
and even Madge — you're soaking in it.*

I had expected Gill to bow out of today's hike, but nope; she
was up for at least part of it. "Yahoo," I said, as we clinked
cups of coffee. At the trailhead just north of Cape Chin, we
discovered the main trail now followed the chin right down
to its whiskers. This meant there was a new loop around the
cape. I figured I'd add it to the end of my day.

Cool, overcast weather had replaced yesterday's brilliant
sunshine. We followed the Cape Chin Meadow Side Trail
and then picked up the Bard Side Trail. When we arrived
at the cliff overlooking Dyer's Bay, Gill remarked on how
quiet it was. The roar of crashing waves was gone. "So, this,"
I remarked, "is what Simon and Garfunkel meant by the
sound of silence." The water's intense blue was now a steely
grey-green except for a fringe of turquoise that lapped onto
the bleached shale beach. Sunlight backlit a layer of fractured
clouds that congregated above us and then thinned into the

distance as if someone had been tugging at the hem of a too-small wool sweater.

The Devil's
Monument

We passed Gill's car where we'd dropped it in the Devil's Monument parking lot enroute to what an interpretive sign bills as the peninsula's "only documented Nipissing-level stack or flowerpot." When Lake Nipissing covered the area thousands of years ago, it was 17 metres higher than today's Georgian Bay. At 14 metres, the Devil's Monument easily wins the contest for tallest flowerpot. Its iconic shape is the result of water eroding the stratified rock's base, leaving the harder dolostone cap. We followed the Devil's Monument Side Trail down a set of metal stairs (with Frida once again tied to a tree) to view the stack from below. It soared overhead, more pulpit-like than monument-esque. It wasn't difficult to imagine Satan pontificating from this lofty perch.

Rescuing Frida, we made our way to a lookout, where we took a break along with a half a dozen other hikers.

Afterwards, Gill had to return to her car, leaving me on my own — again. Just as she was getting her hiking legs under her, we ended our three-day adventure. Feeling teary-eyed, I gave my friend a big hug and watched her disappear. I remained where I was, not yet ready to leave the Devil's Monument. Gill's departure had put me in a contemplative mood. I'm not religious, but today was day 40 of what was supposed to have been 40 days and 40 hikes. I'd intended the book's title to be a play on the rain that fell on Noah and his ark for 40 days and 40 nights. I'd since learned that the number 40 has far more significance in Christianity than a popular biblical story in which God eliminates the world's evil in a planet-wide flood. In particular, the temptation of Christ came about after he spent 40 days and 40 nights fasting in the desert — a period now recognized as Lent when Catholics give something up. On the 40th day, Satan appeared before Jesus but couldn't convince him to abandon God and worship the devil instead.

While planning my routes through the Sydenham and Peninsula sections, I'd decided to add two hikes. There was just too much to see. So, it was by happenstance that rather than arriving in Tobermory, I found myself face to face with the Devil's Monument on day 40. Was it coincidence that for Christians, 40 signifies new life, new growth, transformation and a change from one task to another?

I'd asked myself if I loved the Niagara Escarpment enough. Did I love it as much as Pati loved the Sierra Gorda in Mexico? As I trundled down the BT, I'd recognized that it wasn't about volume of love; it was about depth of under-standing and what you did with that love.

The celebrated American nature essayist Barry Lopez referred to deeper knowledge as syntax. In his recently published, posthumous book, *Syntax of the River*, Lopez wrote, "I think when you're young you want to learn the names of everything. This is a beaver, this is spring Chinook, this is a rainbow trout, this is osprey, elk over there. But it's the syntax that you really are after. Anybody can develop the vocabulary. It's the relationships that are important." I likened it to my efforts to speak Spanish. I could memorize the entire dictionary and conjugate verbs fluently, but that didn't mean I could speak Spanish, and it certainly didn't mean I understood its nuances.

Coincidentally, Lopez has been studying the river featured in his book for — here's that number again — 40 years. Like Lopez, I'd been learning the syntax of my local environment in Caledon for at least four decades. I hadn't studied it with Lopez's single-mindedness, and I still tended to simply name things, but I'd walked Caledon's hills and valleys, could trace the course of "my" river, knew where and when to find yellow lady's slippers and walking ferns. I was able to write "Pit by Pit," that four-thousand-word article on aggregates, because I saw the connections. I brought the ideas together and arranged them in a way so others could understand them too. I had the syntax — *syn* meaning together and *tax* (or *tactics*) meaning arrange.

I also knew Caledon's public trails. I didn't need a map to find my way, and I had a unique ability to connect the trails into loops. The years I spent hiking with the Caledon Countryside Alliance on Sunday mornings honed this skill, and it had been the impetus behind my first guide, the one that described Caledon's loop routes.

Unfortunately, I don't have God's power, so 40 days and 40 hikes didn't banish the world's evil. But I was seeing more connections: the ongoing presence and vulnerability of our hardwood forest, the impact of the Welland Canal on Georgian Bay's fish, efforts of peace and reconciliation with Indigenous Peoples, aggregate mining, Queenston shale, cliffs, limestone, indigo buntings . . . But what struck me most was my increased understanding of the important role the BT plays in protecting its host, the Niagara Escarpment. The simple act of having the path run along unopened road allowances and other rights-of-way had undoubtedly contributed to these linkages remaining in the public domain. But this didn't get to the essence of the what the BT does for the escarpment. For most people it's easier to love, fight for and protect a trail than it is to love, fight for and protect a landscape. There are exceptions, of course, but think of the Appalachian Trail or the Cotswold Way. News that these trails were being damaged or interrupted due to a housing development, a mine or a quarry would raise the ire of not just local residents who may be immediately affected; it would catch the attention of people who have walked, will walk or dream of walking these iconic routes. Moreover, these landscapes have gained international recognition in large part because of the trail that crosses them. Of course, the housing development, mine or quarry would also affect the landscape the trail passes through: the Appalachian Mountains and the Cotswolds, but somehow (locals excepted), it's harder to feel passionate about or even imagine this impact on a landscape. It's as if a trail is a panda bear or an elephant. Campaigns to protect their habitat don't focus on saving the bamboo or savannah, they focus on the iconic animals.

The same is true of the Bruce Trail. I'd wager that far more people know about the Bruce Trail and have a pretty good idea that it runs across Southern Ontario than could tell you what the Niagara Escarpment is, where it's located and why it should be protected. I wish the BT's founders had called their dream the Niagara Escarpment Trail. Nonetheless, after half a century, the BT has become an integral part of Ontario, and politicians are wise to not fool with it. In other words, the BT is the poster child for the Niagara Escarpment.

Ray Lowes, the father of the BT, sensed this opportunity. Often described as a dreamer who left the limelight to others, Lowes was a crafty salesman who supported himself during the Dirty Thirties by selling brooms and Christmas cards door to door in Hamilton (before becoming a metallurgist with Stelco). Lowes wrote in poetic prose, but he always had his endgame in sight. In 1963, he contributed to *The Bruce Trail News*: "[H]ere stands a rugged beautiful continuum of rocks, waterfalls, greenery and 'recreational opportunity' that must be preserved for us and for the future."

He continued, "The Bruce Trail is the chain that at once binds this potential into a unified whole; that brings the very existence of a unique resource sharply to the attention of a population used to taking things for granted; that, when it is built and being used will inspire a desire to protect and preserve from further encroachment a green belt across the province which could be our pride in future years."

Yes, Lowes wanted a trail free of No Trespassing signs. But he also understood that the broader public had to share his belief in a ribbon of wilderness, so he cajoled them into doing so. Muir inspired Lowes. Remember, the American's mission, according to his biographer, was to save "the American soul from total surrender to materialism." Lowes used his dreaminess to soften his message about our shared responsibility to nature. But he never let up. His contribution to *The Bruce Trail News* continued, "We are poor indeed if we are so grasping for every dollar that we cannot afford this narrow strip of land across our Province for the good of all."

Muir went on to become the father of the Sierra Club, Lowes the Father of the Bruce Trail. I wish I'd met him.

Lowes's dream diluted over the years. The erosion picked up momentum when the then Bruce Trail Association shifted to describing itself as a hiking group to differentiate the BT from the Niagara Escarpment Commission and its ongoing struggles. The BT's leadership at the time feared that because landowners confused the two groups, they would stop allowing the BT to cross their private property. It wasn't for another three decades, long after controversy surrounding the Niagara Escarpment Plan had died down that the Bruce Trail Association re-established its important role in conservation. David E. Tyson wrote in his book, "The Bruce Trail Association was founded by four naturalists who wanted to promote the preservation of the Niagara Escarpment. However, over the years the association came to be thought of as a 'hiking' group by many people and our main focus on conservation was being lost." Tyson quotes David Moule, who never gave up on the conservation vision: "Hiking," according to Moule, who allows the BT to cross his land in the Hockley Valley, "is what we do when our work is done."

Lowes died on August 7, 2007. Five months earlier, the Bruce Trail Association changed its Letters Patent and became the Bruce Trail Conservancy. Preservation of the Niagara Escarpment is no longer ancillary to hiking. The conservancy is one of Ontario's largest land trusts. With its new tagline, "Preserving a ribbon of wilderness for everyone, forever," the conservancy has returned to its roots. It embraces the role of the trail in protecting the escarpment.

Thinking back to what I could do for the landscape I'm hefted to, I recalled Cockburn's song about pacing the cage. Maybe, it occurred to me, I'm already on that outbound stage. I'm not a Christian, but maybe my choice of the title *40 Days & 40 Hikes* wasn't just because it's catchy. These thoughts brought me back to Lowes. As I got up from where I'd been sitting, I asked myself: What would Lowes recommend I do for Caledon? Hitching up my backpack, I realized that by landing on the right question, I had the first of my answers: I wasn't doing enough. My friend Cathy's surprise to learn about my environmental resume had been a call to action.

〰

I walked on to Michiganders Arch. Enroute, I leapfrogged a group of five women out for a few days on the trail. Dressed in long hiking pants, socks and hiking shoes, they pulled off the trail to let me pass. On a hunch, I asked them if they knew what poison ivy looked like. "No," they admitted. Feeling like Madge whose manicure customer was horrified to learn she was soaking in "it" (dish detergent), I pointed out that they were standing in "it" (poison ivy). They leaped back onto the trail. With visions of the short-shorts-clad young woman near Tiffany Falls and the gold-lamé-sandalled ones near Blue Mountain, I congratulated these women on their hiking attire, assuring them they were okay, but suggesting they avoid touching their clothing.

After peering through Michiganders Arch onto Dyer's Bay, I turned back along the Anne & Clayton Roberts Side Trail. Though the sun had been peeking through over Georgian Bay, the clouds closed in, the temperature dropped and the light faded as I walked inland through a spruce forest. I missed Gill. The Cottrill Lake Side Trail branched off, leading me to the promised lake and wetland. With rain threatening, I admired the view and quickly continued to the Minhinnick Side Trail. It paralleled the main BT following a welcome cart track. Clear of the dense forest, it was a brighter sort of autumn day. I could practically smell decomposing leaves and taste crisp McIntosh apples. The bees so active yesterday, must have been sleeping.

I slipped by the Devil's Monument Side Trail and followed Borchardt Road, where it was even cheerier. Might I avoid the rain? I was relaxed and even a bit proud of myself. Earlier in the hike, I'd surpassed that critical 902 kilometre mark. I still had two hikes to go before Tobermory, but they felt like freebies. The pressure was off. Answers had come. When I walked the Camino in Spain, four of us continued walking past Santiago de Compostela for three days until we reached the Atlantic coast in Finisterre — land's end. Those final three days were the best. I felt carefree as though my job was done and I was on vacation. As a reward for having surpassed the full length of the BT, I gave myself permission to not walk around Cape Chin if I didn't feel like it when the time came. If I didn't continue, I would only cover 16 kilometres, my shortest hike since the Niagara section.

I took the Otter Lake Side Trail. Entering a small woodlot, I spied an enormous ash — a loner amid ancient maples. With so many of these previously prolific trees having succumbed to the emerald ash borer, this beauty was a welcome and perhaps hopeful sight. I popped out into the sweet fragrance of a recently cut hayfield. The trail alternated between open fields and alvar, where I entertained myself by trying to avoid stepping on the cracks, I mean grikes, without breaking my stride (or my mother's back).

From a viewing platform, I looked over Otter Lake set within an enormous marsh. Inland again, the clouds had thickened, and the air stood still: The calm before the storm? All I could hear were Canada geese. I thought about Barry Lopez. In his book he wrote about the difference between silence and stillness. At that moment, what I experienced was stillness. Then I realized I was in love again — the third time in three days. I loved the Otter Lake Side Trail. Not for the first time, I thanked the Bruce Trail's founders, the staff and volunteers who created and maintained such an amazing network of side trails, some 450 kilometres of them. Today, I'd linked a long section of the white-blazed main BT with five blue-blazed side trails to form a large loop.

I left the lookout, following the trail across more meadows. I chatted briefly with two hikers, the first I'd seen in an hour or more. When I heard a car drive by, I knew I was closing in on civilization. Time to decide: Would I round Cape Chin? I played eeny, meeny, but remained undecided. When I stepped onto the road, great plops of rain began pockmarking the fine dust that coated my car. By the time I'd stuffed my pack into the trunk, ushered Frida into the back seat and climbed behind the wheel, the rain was coming down so hard I worried I'd need an ark. My Cape Chin decision had been made for me.

Day 41

HALFWAY LOG DUMP

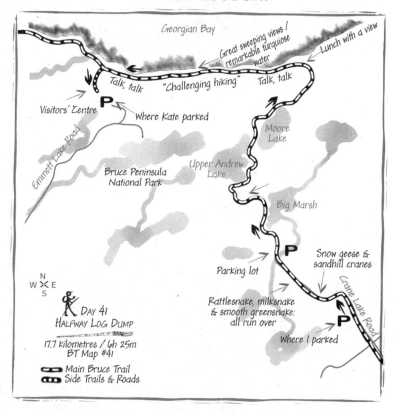

Georgian Bay

Great sweeping views / remarkable turquoise water

Lunch with a view

Talk, talk

"Challenging hiking"

Talk, talk

Visitors' Centre

P

Where Kate parked

Emmett Lake Road

Bruce Peninsula National Park

Upper Andrew Lake

Moore Lake

Big Marsh

P

Snow geese & sandhill cranes

Parking lot

Crane Lake Road

Rattlesnake, milksnake & smooth greensnake: all run over

P

Where I parked

N W E S

Day 41
HALFWAY LOG DUMP

17.7 kilometres / 6h 25m
BT Map #41

▭ Main Bruce Trail
▭ Side Trails & Roads

FIELD NOTES

START TIME: 8:45 a.m., Thursday, October 6, 2022

TRAILHEAD WEATHER: fairly warm, about 15 degrees Celsius, overcast, rain threatening

DISTANCE: 17.7 km

ELAPSED TIME: 6h 25m

BT SECTION: Peninsula

BT MAP: #41

MAIN BT WALKED: 127.9 km to 142 km

ASCENT: 380 m / **DESCENT:** 383 m

SIDE TRAILS: High Dump Side Trail

FLORA/FAUNA OF NOTE: massasauga rattlesnake (*Sistrurus catenatus*), milksnake (*Lampropeltis triangulum*), greensnake (*Opheodrys vernalis*), snow geese (*Anser caerulescens*), sandhill cranes (*Grus canadensis*), ducks, eastern gartersnake (*Thamnophis sirtalis sirtalis*)

In which I toss my notebook to the wind as my sisters and I delight in our members-only club before we witness the demise of slithering serpents in search of brumation.

When I learned my younger sister who lives in Montreal was coming with her family for Thanksgiving, I hatched a plan. "Dori," I said, "Why don't you come a few days early and walk with me for my last two hikes into Tobermory?" It didn't take any convincing. "Yes," Dori said. Next, I invited Kate to come too. She had a commitment on day two, but said she'd join us for the first hike and would drop us off on the morning of the second before she headed home. *This is amazing*, I thought. Could there be a better way to be ushered into Tobermory than with my sisters? Plus, it solved a dilemma: The last stretch into Tobermory lacks side trails. It was best done as two linear hikes with car drops. It wasn't until after they'd agreed to accompany me that I read the BT guide to them: "The section between kilometre 135.9 and 146.5 is considered to be the most challenging hiking along the entire length of the Bruce Trail. Be prepared!" Cellphone reception was intermittent, it was remote, and the trail went through territory known for bears and rattlesnakes. By then it was too late though. They'd already said yes.

More than a week after I sat overlooking the Devil's Monument contemplating my journey and vowing my last two days on the trail would be freebies, I picked up Dori at the GO station in Brampton. Off we drove in brilliant sunshine. We had had summertime weather since my last hike and as we pulled out of the GO station parking lot, my thermometer registered 27 degrees Celsius. We called Kate to let her know we were enroute and would meet her at the Buddha Bing hotel in Tobermory in about three and a half hours. After checking in, we planned to head off for dinner.

Younger by five years, Dori had started a new career that summer as a guide with Vermont Bike Tours. She led some deluxe trips mostly around Banff and Canmore. She'd enjoyed every minute of it and had just landed a winter gig leading ski tours that followed the "Powder Highway" in British Columbia. After more than a decade operating her own successful, high-end maple syrup business (she won every award possible), she was content to be an employee. "They just tell me what to do and where to do it," she explained. "I love it."

As we headed north, clouds blocked the sun. By the time we met Kate at the Buddha Bing, it was raining. At the Crowsnest Pub, our waiter told us, "You can have anything on the menu as long as it isn't made with lettuce or tomatoes. We're out." Despite these omissions, we had a decent pub meal — I guess. I was so caught up in the fun of sitting there with my two sisters that I didn't pay much attention to the food.

The next morning, we had coffee and scones. Blood is thick between us: we're early risers, coffee drinkers and happy hikers. Our other sister and brother are more inclined to sleep in, and while active, wouldn't have embraced what was in store. We dropped a car at the Halfway Log Dump parking lot and drove to the trailhead on Crane Lake Road. At under 18 kilometres, we didn't have a particularly long way to go, but it included seven kilometres of the tough section mentioned in the BT guide. With the recent rain, it would be slippery. I decided to carry two hiking poles instead of one — now possible since I'd put my notebook away.

We left my car three kilometres short of the Crane Lake parking lot because the puddles straddling the road made me worry about flooding. After piling out, we hoisted our packs and with Frida in tow, we were off. It was cloudy, threatening more wet stuff, but for now the rain was in check; soon we were down to our shirt sleeves. Up ahead, there was something on the road. As we got closer, it looked like a snake. Cautiously we approached and indeed it was a dead massasauga rattler. Massasaugas are threatened in Ontario and the Saugeen Bruce Peninsula is one of their last strongholds. We felt saddened by this loss, but it was a rare opportunity to see a rattlesnake up close. It was fatter and shorter than we'd expected, and we could see why their markings are described as resembling a

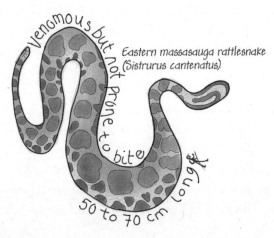

Venomous but not prone to bite

50 to 70 cm long

Eastern massasauga rattlesnake
(Sistrurus cantenatus)

figure eight. We made out the rattle. If we didn't already know we were in snake country, this discovery and Kate's regular squeamish reminders removed all doubt.

Half a kilometre later, we saw something else that looked like a snake. Once again, we cautiously approached. It was about the same length, but slimmer, and between its dark markings it was a shimmering silver where the massasauga had been a dull beige. It was a mouse-eating eastern milksnake, non-venomous, but crafty — and dead. They imitate rattlesnakes by using their tails to "rattle" dry grasses. Then, around the next curve there was a smooth greensnake. Half the length and girth of a milksnake and mini compared to a massasauga, its diminutive size and tropical-parrot shade of green mean it's my favourite slithering serpent. It had also been run over. This trio of dead snakes is evidence of just how vulnerable they are to road traffic, especially in fall when looking for somewhere to brumate — the form of hibernation practised by cold-blooded animals such as snakes.

When we heard loud honking, we looked up. Overhead, a pair of snow geese were coming in for landing on a nearby lake, presumably enroute from the Arctic to the southern US. Smaller than Canada geese, these monogamous birds are easy to identify when they are snow-phase morphs. The black tips of their wings contrasted with their sparkling white bodies. Blue-phase snow geese are mostly blue-grey. Like eye colour, genes determine whether a snow goose is white (recessive gene) or blue (dominant gene). Variants interbreed, though they tend to hook up with their own kind unless raised with a brood of mixed goslings, in which case colour doesn't seem to matter.

No sooner had the snow geese landed than we heard the unmistakable call of sandhill cranes. The first time I heard them was near Cape Croker. That day, I was walking through an open field when from up ahead came this raucous other-worldly sound. When I realized the noise was coming from a bird of Magic Johnson proportions, I deduced it must be a sandhill crane, but I'll never forget that sound. The All About Birds website describes it as a "loud, rolling, trumpeting" call that can be heard from miles away.

We were following a seven-kilometre stretch of the main BT through the Bruce Peninsula National Park toward the shoreline. While Parks Canada hadn't changed the park's name, it described it as being in the traditional territory of the Saugeen Ojibway Nation. Walking mostly through forest, we skirted several lakes: Big Marsh, Upper Andrew and Moore, where hundreds of ducks congregated in preparation for their trip south.

With six decades of shared memories, we had lots to gab about in that easy way of siblings when there's no need to explain inside jokes or temper good-humoured cajoling. Oftentimes, we finished each other's sentences. We teased Dori for being short, Kate for being a typical middle child and me for being outspoken. We explored the lives of our absent brother and sister without worrying that our comments would be taken out of context, and caught up on the latest news about our collection of nieces, nephews and grandnephews. One of us would mimic our mum or dad or Aunt Sybil and the other two would chuckle. There was a lot of "Do you remember . . ." Walking at the same speed, wanting breaks at the same time and even seeming to pee with similar regularity, we marched down the trail as the only members in a members-only club.

When Frida's barking interrupted our chatter, we thought bear, but it was a couple with their dog. They cautioned us of a massasauga up ahead that had struck at their pooch (but missed). We paid more attention to where we put our feet but never encountered the snake. At 11 a.m. when we arrived at the cliffs overlooking Georgian Bay, we turned west toward Tobermory. Beyond a seemingly endless series of bluffs, the BT's northern terminus was out of sight. We lost our sunny skies as we followed the headland, but the iconic fringe of turquoise at the shoreline didn't let up. This Caribbean shade of bluey-green is the result of "whiting." It occurs when fine particles of limestone or dolostone are suspended in the water and reflect blue and green light.

The trail morphed into the rocky beast the BT guide had warned us about. We scrambled over ledges, oftentimes sliding down on our backsides and occasionally lending each other a hand to make getting up easier. We made slow but steady progress, stopping regularly to ooh and aah at the views. High above the beach, we followed the long arc of a bow-shaped bay. We kept reminding each other to keep an eye out for slithering, rattling reptiles, but it turned out Dori and I weren't much good at it. With me in the lead and Kate pulling up the rear, Dori and I heard Kate screech. She'd almost stepped on a snake that Dori and I had blindly walked right over. In our defence, it was a garter snake and not a rattler. But this time it was alive, albeit drowsy in its shady bed.

The hours rolled by as we negotiated the tricky footing, growing quiet as we concentrated on the trail. Our feet fatigued but it wasn't as tough as we'd expected given the dire warning. Almost too soon, we arrived at the Halfway Dump Side Trail. The curious name comes from this spot being a drop-off for lumber as the cliffs part here, making the shoreline accessible. It's a popular place to go "bouldering," wherein people climb the area's huge boulders without ropes but with a large crash pad set out below to cushion their fall.

We were surprised by the size of the Halfway Log Dump parking lot and its attractive building with washrooms and running water. The north Saugeen Bruce Peninsula has become a popular playground, no longer the uncouth landscape Fox knew. More unexpected, at only 380 metres, our day's cumulative ascent made it the flattest hike of my entire journey. Still high from our hike, we climbed into Kate's car and headed back to Tobermory for a celebratory dinner.

Day 42

TO TOBERMORY

Day 42
To Tobermory

23.9 kilometres / 9h 38m
BT Map #41/42

Main Bruce Trail
Side trails & roads

Georgian Bay

Tobermory Harbour
FATHOM FIVE NATIONAL
MARINE PARK

Viewing tower
Dunks Bay
Little Cove
Talk, talk, talk, talk!
Driftwood Cove
The Grotto &
the Natural Arch

Northern terminus
"Challenging
hiking" con't

Tobermory
LITTLE COVE
PROVINCIAL
NATURE RESERVE
Large
sinkhole
Cyprus
Lake
Cameron Lake
Halfway Dump Road
P

Highway 6
Emmett Lake Road
BRUCE PENINSULA
NATIONAL PARK

Lake Huron

FIELD NOTES

START TIME: 8:45 a.m., Friday, October 7, 2022

TRAILHEAD WEATHER: overcast, 5 degrees Celsius and blustery

DISTANCE: 23.9 km

ELAPSED TIME: 9h 38m

BT SECTION: Peninsula

BT MAP: #41/42

MAIN BT WALKED: 142 km to 167 km

ASCENT: 720 m / **DESCENT:** 772 m

SIDE TRAILS: High Dump Side Trail

FLORA/FAUNA OF NOTE: striped maple (*Acer pensylvanicum*)

In which there's perfection.

We were up early again, coffeed, fed and on the road as the morning failed to shed the gloom that had arrived with a blustery cold front. As promised, Kate was driving Dori and me to the Halfway Log Dump parking lot so we could walk the 24 kilometres into Tobermory and the northern terminus. We chatted about what fun we'd had the day before, but there was a pall over our discussion. Since Kate wasn't accompanying us, Dori and I didn't want to go on about today's hike, and I think Kate was feeling sheepish for not agreeing to come along. Her commitment for the day had been postponed, so she really didn't have a reason not to.

Filling an awkward silence, Dori broached the elephant in the car: "Kate," she said, "why don't you come?" Now Kate is the kindest of our siblings. She's the one we elect when someone in the family needs to have a delicate conversation with someone else in the family. But I know that if you want Kate to do something, don't push her. I added, gently, "It would be great if you were there when we get to the end of the trail." As this idea sunk in, I hoped Dori would leave it alone. But no, I could see that our most enthusiastic sibling was about to say more. *Shoot*, I thought. *Dori don't blow this. Don't push her.* Then Dori said, "Kate, you don't have to stay the night; you can drive home after the hike." Kate hadn't slept well at the Buddha Bing. She hadn't complained, but she mentioned it, which meant it was a problem. I breathed in, hoping this option would tip the scale. The conversation died after our encouragement. We continued in pregnant silence.

Kate pulled up to the trailhead and we all got out. Once Dori and I had our backpacks on and Frida was on leash, we turned to Kate to give her a big hug. There was something about the way she looked at us that caused both Dori and me to blurt: "Kate. Come." A big smile spread across her face. "You don't mind waiting while I switch into my hiking pants?" she asked. "Of course not," we chimed. In no time, she'd changed, packed her knapsack and donned her hiking poles. The members-only club would live for another day.

I'd lamented the change from blue skies, but this day was wonderful in a different way. It was cool and blustery, brimming with energy. After a short walk to the shoreline along the Halfway Dump Side Trail, we turned toward Tobermory, continuing to follow the beastly section for another three and a half kilometres. Once again, the trail was easier than the guidebook promised. Sure, there were rocks and a couple of spots where we had to scramble using our hands, but it was more fun than bother, plus the view of what appeared to be white beaches ahead drew us on.

We could make out the Fathom Five islands and felt our progress toward the northern terminus. It would be the end of my loopy route, which I'd started back on May 3 when the trees were bursting with new growth, and birdsong filled the forest. How different it was now. Today was all about autumn, the promise that winter wasn't far off. The changing of the seasons, golden and red leaves, the smell of smoky fires and the taste of hot tea. A bittersweet feeling nipped at my euphoria. I knew that I'd "come down" in the days ahead. I brushed it aside though; today was celebratory. Here I was with two of my siblings. They were as excited to be part of my final hikes as I was to have them along. We all realized how lucky we were to be such good friends. Though there has been turmoil, we remain a tight family. We clambered along, taking photos of one another. We were awed by the natural arch and the grotto, as well as the lookout over Indian Head Cove. We agreed that this hike was something — easily one of the best along the entire BT.

Four hours after we'd hit the trail, we stopped at a protected spot and tucked into our sandwiches. Checking to see how far we'd walked, I'd expected we covered 10, maybe 12 kilometres and that we were about halfway to our goal. When I realized we were only a quarter of the way there, I thought, *Yikes, at this rate, we aren't going to arrive in Tobermory until after dark.* "Hey, you guys," I said, "we've got to pick up the pace — a lot." Off we went with new determination. Great sisters that I have, they relished this new challenge.

We didn't stop as often, but there were views that had to be admired. We made our way along what we'd thought from a distance was white sand but turned out to be smoothly rounded, bleached rocks, two or three feet in diameter. I was amazed at how an obvious path can be worn into such an unforgiving surface. The footing was tricky, but I found myself almost running. I love stepping from large beach rock to large beach rock. I look for the flattest tallest stones and keep the momentum going. When Dori, who always walks faster than I do, said she couldn't keep up, I was flattered. Now at "sea" level, we had to dodge the spray as a moody Georgian Bay crashed onto the rocky shore. Maybe it was the day or the active water, but we were full of spunk. I recalled my favourite scene from The Chronicles of Narnia. In *The Lion, the Witch and the Wardrobe*, Aslan (the lion) returns from death and goes on what's described as a "romp" around Narnia with the two girls, Lucy and Susan, in tow. The children run and run and run fuelled by some super-power so their feet hardly touch the ground and they never tire. That's how I felt. The miles melted away.

Speeding along at almost five kilometres per hour, we came ever closer to Tobermory. We concentrated on covering the terrain and our thoughts as we admired Loon Lake, moved inland to avoid Driftwood Cove and then rounded Little Cove, where we came to Little Cove Road, our first road in almost 17 kilometres of trail. We nearly missed our next turn as there was a new section of the main BT that shortened our route by at least a kilometre. Maybe we would make it to Tobermory before dark after all. We continued around Dunks Bay and into Fathom Five National Marine Park. Here, the trail was wide and soft underfoot, giving our feet the relief I'd come to equate with a cart path.

We arrived at a lookout tower, where Kate announced, "No way. There's no way. I'm not climbing all those stairs. My knees hurt." Dori concurred. But I couldn't not go up. I knew there would be breathtaking views from the top and though I might visit this tower again, what I saw and how I reacted to it today could never be repeated. My response to everything that had happened all day was affected by my sisters being there. I decided de Botton was wrong. He inferred that if your curiosity was altered by the presence of others, it's less genuine. I disagree. Had I experienced this day on my own, or even if only Dori had been along, it would have been different, but no less authentic. Some things are meant to be shared. They are the things you recall when you get together days or months or years later. "Remember that time you stripped down to your underwear and changed your pants in the Halfway Log Dump parking lot?" I wasn't just falling deeper in love with the Niagara Escarpment, its flora and fauna, even its rattlesnakes and black bears, I was falling more in love with my sisters too.

I offered to climb up the tower on my own if they'd keep Frida, but, of course, my sisters being my sisters, they weren't going to be outdone. Leaving my ever-patient pooch tied to a bench, we clambered to the top. It was totally worth it. From this vantage point, we identified several of Fathom Five's 22 islands, including popular Flowerpot Island. After skirting the shore of Georgian Bay for so long, we looked out over Lake Huron, of which Georgian Bay is but a small part. Our eyes followed the contour of the Niagara Escarpment as it dipped underwater. I knew it would reappear in about one hundred kilometres as Mnidoo Mnising (Manitoulin Island). Then it would swing in a large arc across the top of Lake Michigan, before forming the Garden and Door peninsulas and petering out near Chicago. In my mind's eye, I traced its 1,609 kilometre horseshoe-shaped path from upper New York State, into Canada at Niagara Falls and then all that way across Southern Ontario to where I currently stood. The Niagara Escarpment: L'Escarpement du Niagara to franco-phones, Gchi-Bimadinaa (The Great Cliff That Runs Along) to the Anishinaabe, and Kastenhraktátye (Along the Cliffs) to the Kanyen'kehà:ka.

I thought of the erosion that scoured the less hardy Queenston shale that lay below a dolostone cap that formed cliffs made of rock that was more than four hundred million years old. I acknowledged that some forces are just too big to properly fathom. Walking most of Niagara Escarpment's length in Canada had brought me closer to it, more familiar with it, more respectful. My syntax was much improved though incomplete as it always would be. I would never stop learning about the Niagara Escarpment, never stop wondering if I was doing enough to protect it and my beloved Caledon. I heard the *Chi-Cheemaun* ferry sound its horn as it arrived from Mnidoo Mnising. I liked to think it was welcoming me to the northern terminus, but knew this journey had no end.

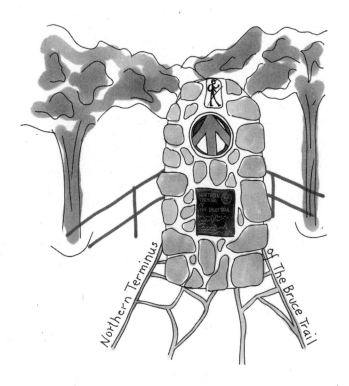

EPILOGUE

It was 6:15 p.m. with darkness closing in when the three of us arrived at the northern terminus. The cairn looked remarkably like the one I'd admired so many kilometres before in Queenston. We took photos as we congratulated each other with big hugs. I thanked them both again and again, and threw in some pats for Frida. She'd been a trooper, walking contentedly for hour upon hour with no idea of where we were headed or how long she'd be on the trail. Imagine a human doing that. I'd covered over 950 kilometres in 42 self-supported loop hikes over three months.

As I discovered along the way, the northern cairn in Tobermory wasn't the end of my journey, it was a new beginning. In the aftermath of my long walk, I left the cage and climbed aboard the outbound stage. With better syntax, including a deeper understanding of the relationship between the BT and the Niagara Escarpment, and with Ray Lowes whispering in my ear, I arrived at what I could do to help protect Caledon. I'm developing Caledon's Way.

It's an idea that had been rattling around in my brain since I wrote *Caledon Hikes* in 2014. One of the routes in that book is the Grand Caledon Tour. It connects several of Caledon's villages in a 121 kilometre loop that follows the Niagara Escarpment as well as the Oak Ridges Moraine. It even touches the Peel Plain, the rich farmland that is so threatened by sprawl in Caledon's southern reaches. Recently, development of a pair of new trails in Caledon has been announced. They will connect two more of Caledon's villages and add another 30 kilometres to the loop, making it about the same length as England's famous Cotswold Way.

A long-distance, inn-to-inn trail is unheard of in Canada. But Caledon's unique collection of small villages, natural rolling landscape and its existing network of paths make it an ideal place for this Canadian first. Caledon's Way will link village to village, celebrating the beauty of these historic hamlets as well as the splendour of the forests, rivers and valleys that lie in between. It will be my way of using my skills and energy to create something that will bring joy and the colour green back to the community. It will be Caledon's geography of hope. One day, it may even become Caledon's panda bear, helping to encourage good use of the land rather than its exploitation.

I think Ray Lowes — and my dad — would approve.

SELECTED BIBLIOGRAPHY

All About Birds. "Sandhill Crane." https://www.allaboutbirds
.org/guide/Sandhill_Crane.

Bodsworth, Fred. "The Bruce." *Maclean's*, July 3, 1965.

The Bruce Trail Conservancy. *The Bruce Trail Reference
Guide*, 30th edition. 2020.

Bunyan, John. *The Pilgrim's Progress*. New York: G.H.
McKibbin, 1899.

Burcher, Robert. *My Summer of Glorious Freedom.* The Battered
Silicon Dispatch Box, 2020.

Burfoot, Amby. "Running's Most Interesting Recluse:
Bernd Heinrich." *Outside*, January 19, 2022. https://
www.outsideonline.com/running/news/people
/runnings-most-interesting-recluse-bernd-heinrich/.

Cowley, Christine. *Devil's Glen Country Club: The First 50
Years*. Collingwood: Moss Pillow Publishing, 2014.

de Botton, Alain. *The Art of Travel*. London: Hamish
Hamilton, 2014.

Dykman, Sarah. *Bicycling with Butterflies: My 10,201-Mile Journey Following the Monarch Migration*. Portland, OR: Timber Press, 2021.

Flamborough Archives & Heritage Society. "The Smokey Hollow Walk." September 10, 2020. https://flamboroughhistory.com/the-smokey-hollow-walk/.

Fox, William Sherwood. *The Bruce Beckons*. Toronto: University of Toronto Press, 1952.

Gladwell, Malcolm. *Outliers: The Story of Success*. New York: Back Bay Books, 2011.

Heinrich, Bernd. *The Trees in My Forest*. New York: Ecco, 2009.

Johnson, Joe. *The Vascular Plants of the Bruce Peninsula, Ontario*. Self-published, 2016.

Lopez, Barry, and Julia Martin. *Syntax of the River: The Pattern Which Connects*. San Antonio, TX: Trinity University Press, 2023.

Lowes, Ray. *The Bruce Trail News* 1, no. 2 (1963).

McNichol, Phil. "The Saugeen Land Claim and the 'Path of Peace.'" Finding Hope Ness, December 11, 2021. https://findinghopeness.com/2021/12/11/the-saugeen -land-claim-and-the-path-of-peace/.

Pearson, Norman. *The Making of the Bruce Trail 1954–2004*. Port Stanley, ON: Norman Pearson & Associates Limited, 2005.

Ross, Nicola. *Caledon Hikes: Loops & Lattes*. Belfountain, ON: Woodrising Consulting Inc., 2015.

Ross, Nicola, *Waterloo, Wellington & Guelph Hikes: Loops & Lattes*. Belfountain, ON: Woodrising Consulting Inc., 2019.

Ross, Nicola. *Collingwood, the Blue Mountains & Beaver Valley Hikes: Loops & Lattes*. Belfountain, ON: Woodrising Consulting Inc., 2020.

Rubinoff, Joel. "Local Hiking Guide Beats 'Harry Potter' to Become Indie Bestseller." *Waterloo Region Record*, January 29, 2022. https://www.therecord.com/news /waterloo-region/local-hiking-guide-beats-harry-potter -to-become-indie-bestseller/article_d1a100ae-2d68 -5a77-b9f0-973905c07f81.html.

Saul, John Ralston. "On This Day, 175 Years Ago, Canada Became a Democracy. Why Aren't We Celebrating?" *Globe and Mail*. March 11, 2023. https://www .theglobeandmail.com/opinion/article-on-this-day-175 -years-ago-canada-became-a-democracy-why-arent-we/.

Savage, Ron. *Secrets of Sydenham*. Self-published, 2020.

Simard, Suzanne. *Finding the Mother Tree: Discovering the Wisdom of the Forest*. Toronto: Penguin Canada, 2022.

Tovell, Walter, et al. *Guide to the Geology of the Niagara Escarpment*. Niagara Escarpment Commission, 1992.

Trimble, Berniece. *Belfountain Caves, Castles and Quarries in the Caledon Hills*. Belfountain, ON: The Belfountain Rockside Women's Institute, 1975.

Tyson, David E. *Trail to the Bruce: The Story of the Building of the Bruce Trail*. Tellwell Talent, 2017.

Weber, Ken. "The Phenomenon That Was Rock Hill Park." *In The Hills*, June 24, 2022.

Worster, David. *A Passion for Nature: The Life of John Muir*. Oxford: Oxford University Press, 2011.

ACKNOWLEDGEMENTS

I wish my parents were still alive so they could read this book and I could thank them for moving to Caledon, which was a wild place in the 1950s. Between them they instilled in me a love of the landscape that soaked in deep as I explored the hills and valleys on horseback. My siblings and I had a wonderful childhood, and we remain a closely knit family that shares many happy memories of Woodrising, our farm near Belfountain. I thank them too and especially my younger sister, Dori, and next older one, Kate, for accompanying me on parts of my Bruce Trail adventure, walking me joyfully into Tobermory. After reading part of my manuscript, my brother, Oakland, encouraged me to send it to a publisher. And when ECW made me an offer, my eldest sister, Ces, convinced me to accept it.

Many people contributed to the path that has resulted in this book: my editor Signe Ball at *In The Hills* magazine for teaching me how to write, John Denison at the Boston

Mills Press for suggesting loop routes all those years ago and Pati Ruiz Corzo with Grupo Ecológico Sierra Gorda in Mexico for doing so much to protect "her Sierra." CJ Sheldon at Over the Moon Designs taught me to make a bird look like a bird and didn't flinch when I added whimsy to my rustic illustrations. Her Sunday afternoon class is my favourite two hours of the week.

The extraordinary Don Scallen, who lives and breathes syntax, read every word to make sure I didn't make an ecological blunder. Beth Gilhespy, the former executive director of the Bruce Trail Conservancy, loaned her depth of knowledge by reviewing my efforts to describe the Niagara Escarpment's geology. And Lindy Mechefsky, my instructor at the French River Writing Retreat, guided me on the introduction.

I had such fun hiking with friends who braved the heat, bugs and my company: Gill Stead, who is also the designer of my hiking guides; Susan Gesner, who is always up for a hike; Cheryl Mitchell, my tennis partner and longest friend; my sisters Kate and Dori; and of course, Frida, my brindle mutt from Mexico.

My heart goes out to the Bruce Trail's four founders, Ray Lowes, Philip Gosling, Norman Pearson and Robert McLaren, for dreaming up their crazy scheme and making it happen. Along with so many other Bruce Trail supporters, the founders taught me that loving something isn't enough, it's what you do about it that counts. Their philosophy remains the guiding light that has sparked an organization which has turned the Bruce Trail into a provincial treasure and the greatest protector of all for the Niagara Escarpment. Thank you to all the Bruce Trail's volunteers, staff, landowners, members and the Bruce Trail Conservancy itself.

I've recognized the First Nations peoples in a separate acknowledgement, but it never hurts to do it again. Thank you for sharing access to Gchi-Bimadinaa (The Great Cliff That Runs Along), Kastenhraktátye (Along the Cliffs), l'Escarpement du Niagara, the Niagara Escarpment.

I cautiously abandoned my self-publishing ways for this book, trusting "my baby" to ECW Press in Toronto. To be honest, I sent them the manuscript for the sole purpose of determining if it was worth my while to publish it myself. When ECW made me an offer, I was so impressed with my editor Jen Knoch's enthusiasm for the project and her heart-felt interest in the topic that I was won over. Since then, Jen's careful overseeing of the project has proven again and again that I made the right decision.

Working with ECW has been a rewarding experience in large part because *40/40*, as Jen nicknamed *40 Days & 40 Hikes*, has become "our" book. Writing and solo hiking are lonely pursuits, so I relish being part of a team. My thanks go to Jessica Albert for digging up the gorgeous artwork that graces *40/40*'s cover. Lisa Frenette and Jen Albert did the eye-crunching job of copy editing and proofreading. Having Claire Pokorchak as my publicist makes me feel like a star. Claire has graciously worked with my inclination to self-promote — the result of having produced six self-published books. I'm grateful to Emily Ferko for introducing *40/40* into markets that I had neither the time nor the skills to penetrate when working on my own. And lest you think a font is a font is a font, Jennifer Gallinger did a bang-up job of typesetting the book.

Finally, a big hug to Alex for being my biggest — and most persistent — supporter. You made me prove that when I say "Just wait," it's amazing what I accomplish.

For every book sold, 1% of the cover price will be donated to the Bruce Trail Conservancy, which conserves, restores and manages land along the Niagara Escarpment to protect its ecosystems for the benefit of all.